Prince Tenyou's Brothers and Their Beast-Servants

Kougai

The third prince. Two-faced and ambitious.

Reiun

The second prince. Intelligent and bored by his own idleness.

Oushin

The first prince. Sickly and passive.

Boku

Prince Kougai's beast-servant.

Youbi

Prince Reiun's beast-servant.

Teiga

Prince Oushin's beast-servant.

The Assassination of Sogetsu

Rangetsu's twin was brought to the imperial palace to serve Prince Tenyou as his beast-servan, but he was brutally killed soon after.

Ririn

An imperial princess.

CONTENTS

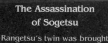

In a world where humans rule the half-beast *yjin*, Rangetsu disguises herself as a man to become Fourth Prince Tenyou's beast-servant. Although initially believing the prince to be responsible for her brother's death, Rangetsu soon sees his true nature and vows to help him rule with virtue. As Rangetsu's impossible feelings for her prince grow stronger, she catches the eye of the mercurial third prince Kougai...

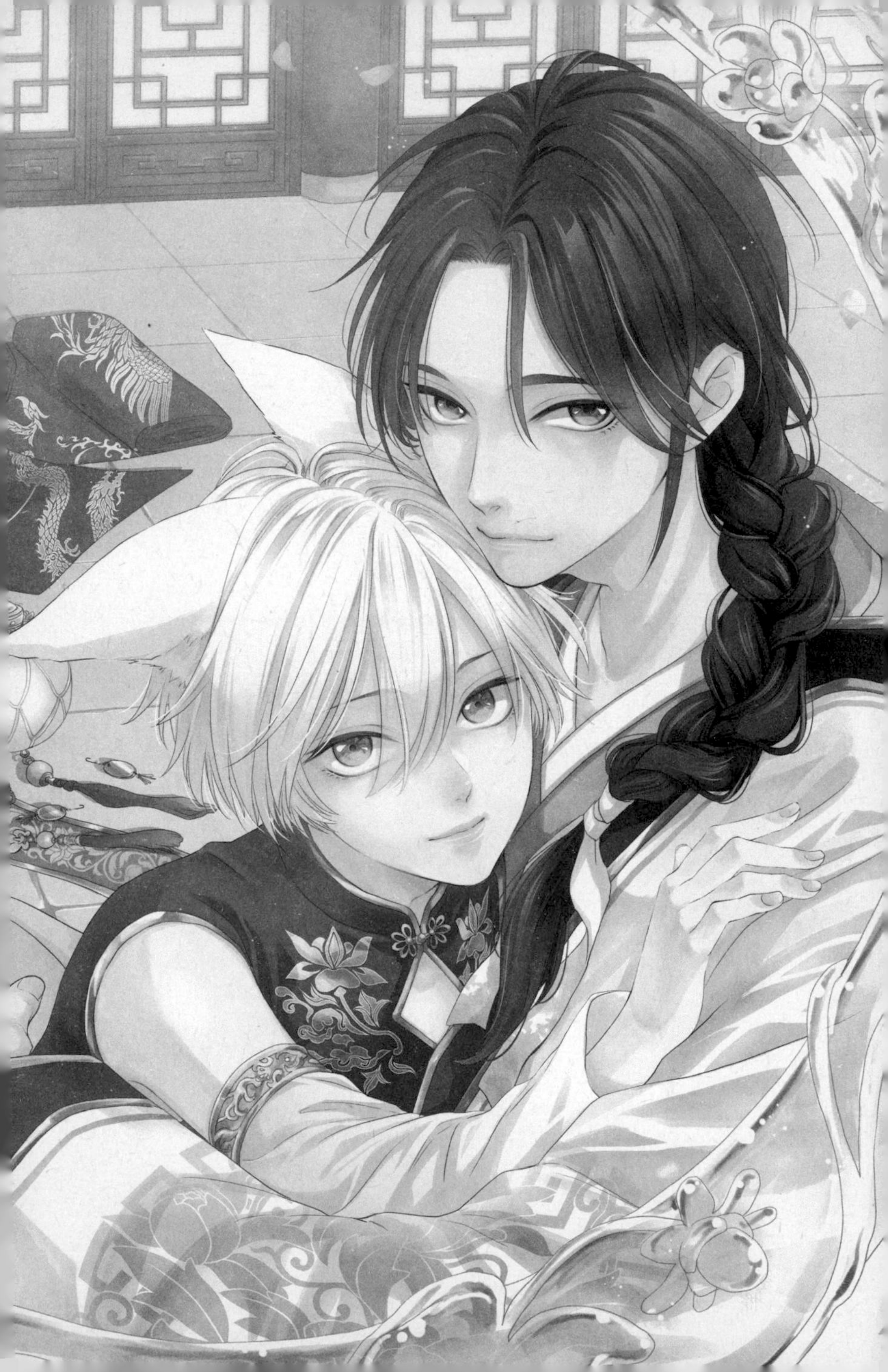

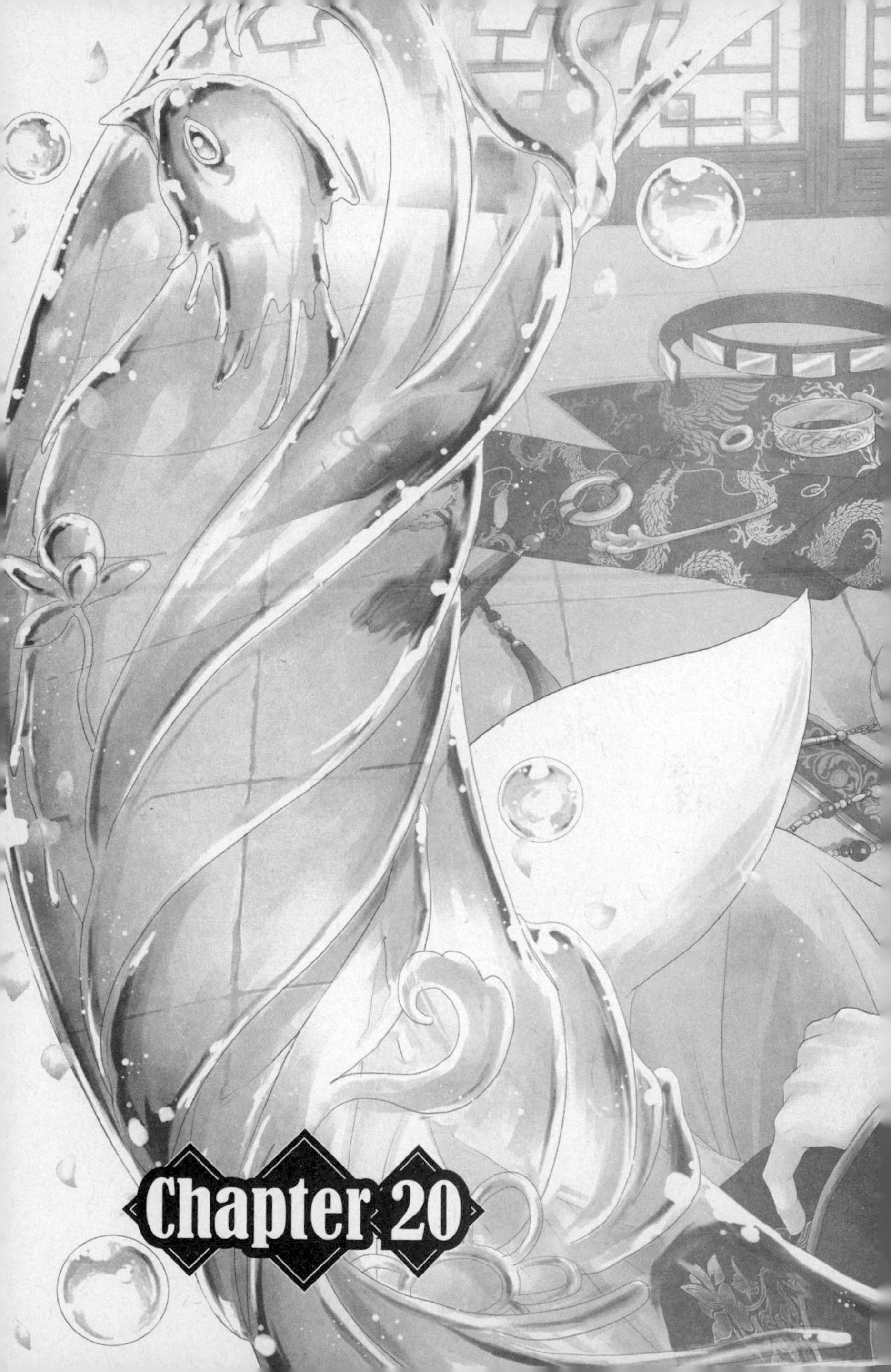
Chapter 20

THE
KING'S
Beast

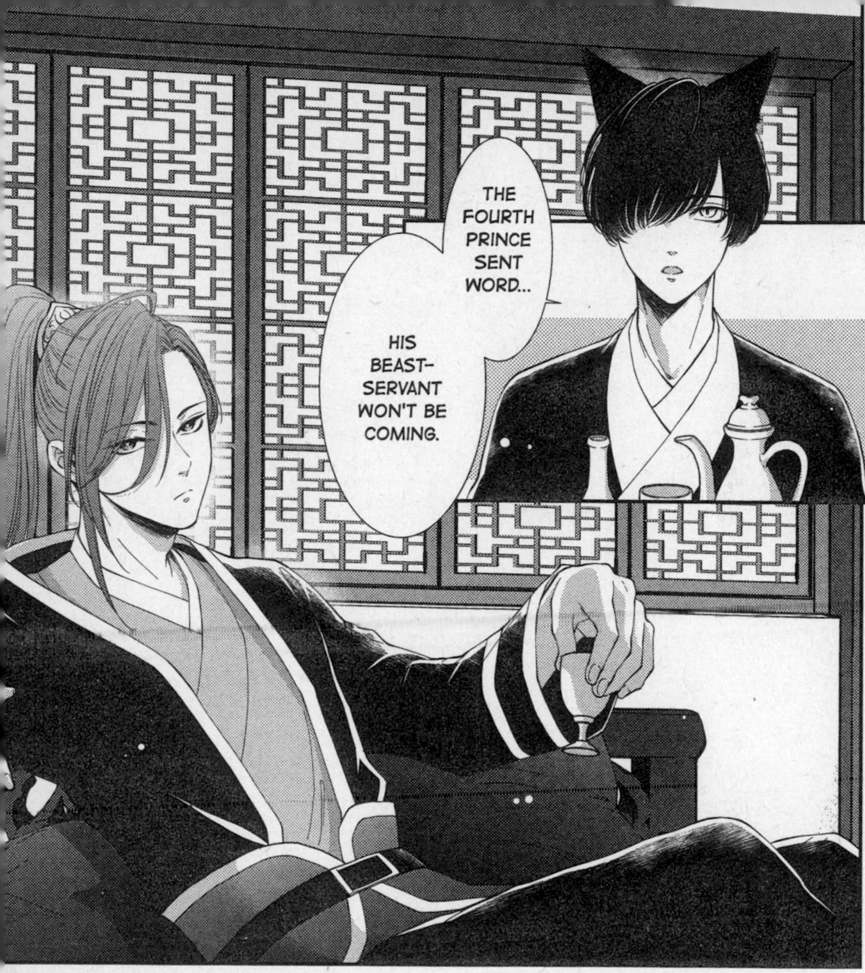
THE FOURTH PRINCE SENT WORD...
HIS BEAST-SERVANT WON'T BE COMING.

THE KING'S Beast

麗

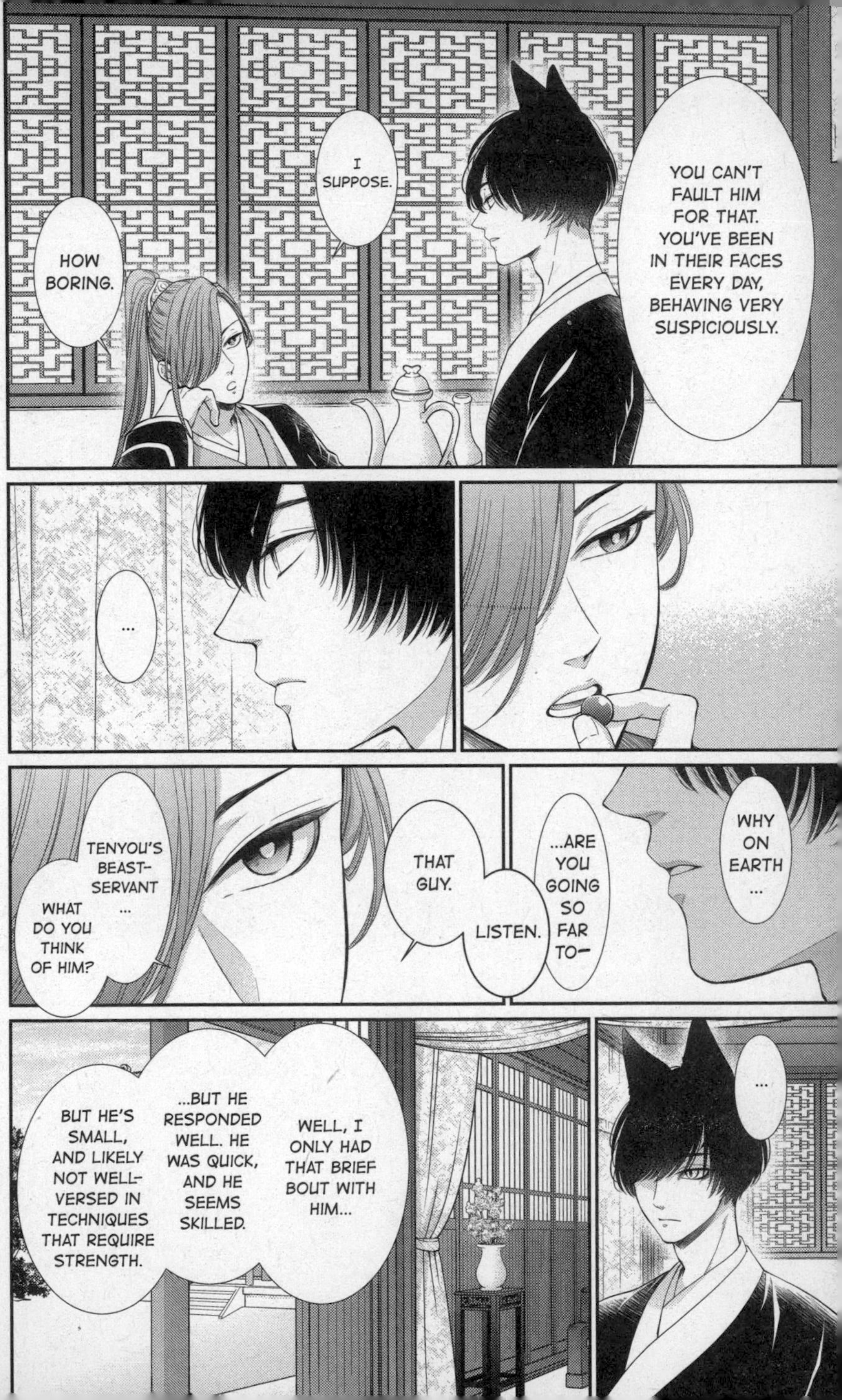
YOU CAN'T FAULT HIM FOR THAT. YOU'VE BEEN IN THEIR FACES EVERY DAY, BEHAVING VERY SUSPICIOUSLY.
I SUPPOSE.
HOW BORING.
...
WHY ON EARTH ...
...ARE YOU GOING SO FAR TO—
LISTEN.
THAT GUY.
TENYOU'S BEAST-SERVANT ...
WHAT DO YOU THINK OF HIM?
...
WELL, I ONLY HAD THAT BRIEF BOUT WITH HIM...
...BUT HE RESPONDED WELL. HE WAS QUICK, AND HE SEEMS SKILLED.
BUT HE'S SMALL, AND LIKELY NOT WELL-VERSED IN TECHNIQUES THAT REQUIRE STRENGTH.

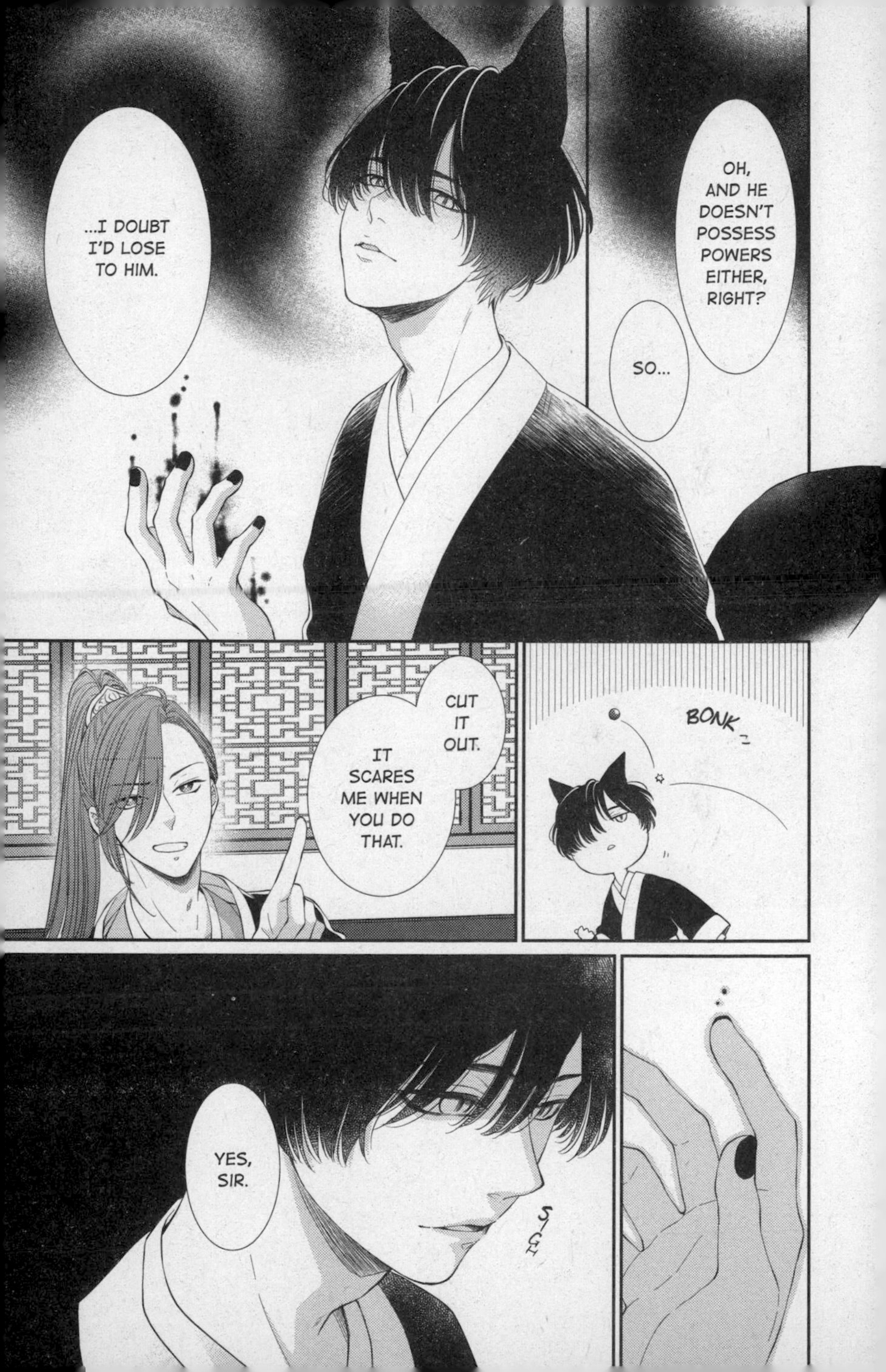
OH, AND HE DOESN'T POSSESS POWERS EITHER, RIGHT?
SO...
...I DOUBT I'D LOSE TO HIM.
BONK
CUT IT OUT.
IT SCARES ME WHEN YOU DO THAT.
YES, SIR.
SIGH

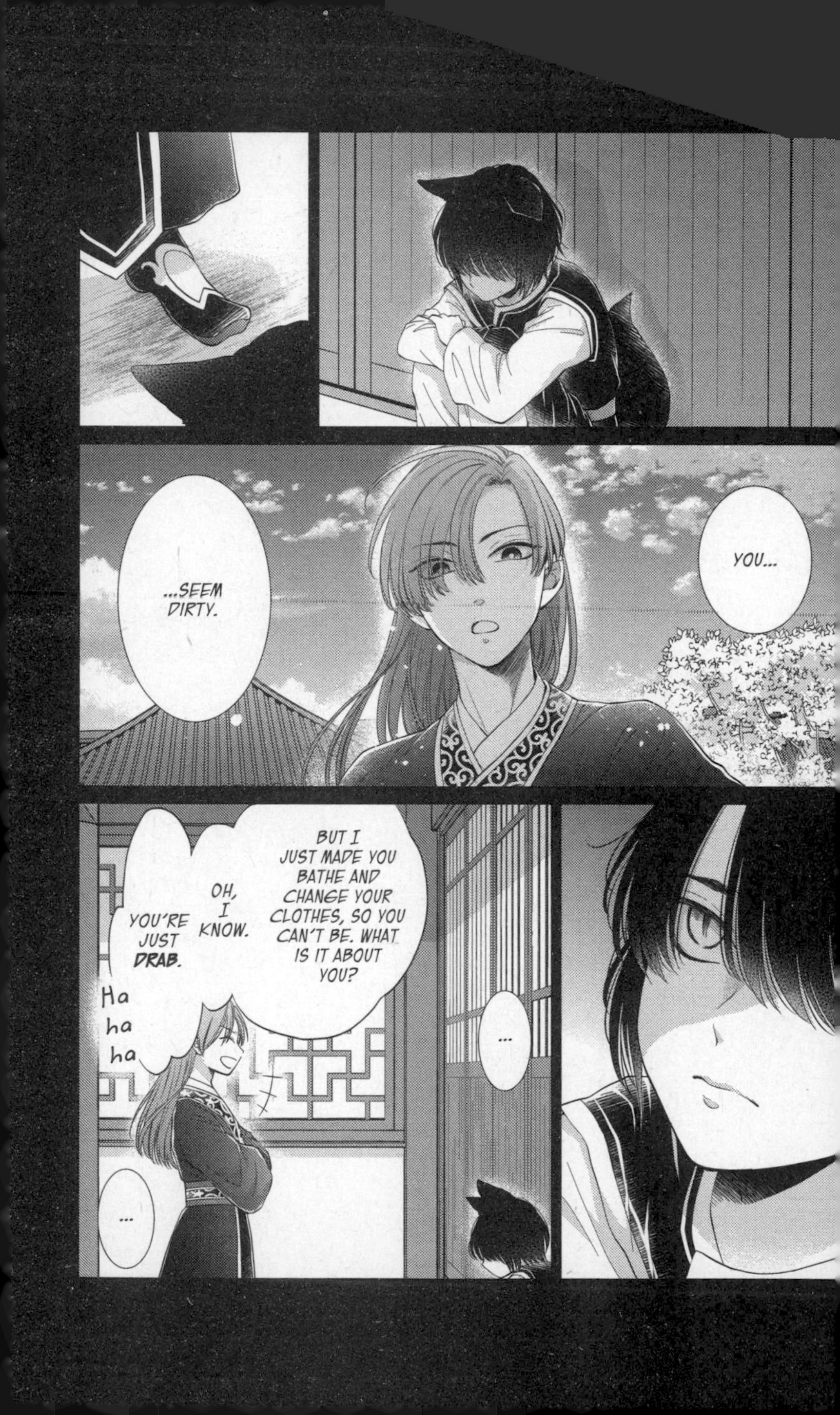
YOU...
...SEEM DIRTY.
BUT I JUST MADE YOU BATHE AND CHANGE YOUR CLOTHES, SO YOU CAN'T BE. WHAT IS IT ABOUT YOU?
OH, I KNOW.
YOU'RE JUST **DRAB.**
...
Ha ha ha
...

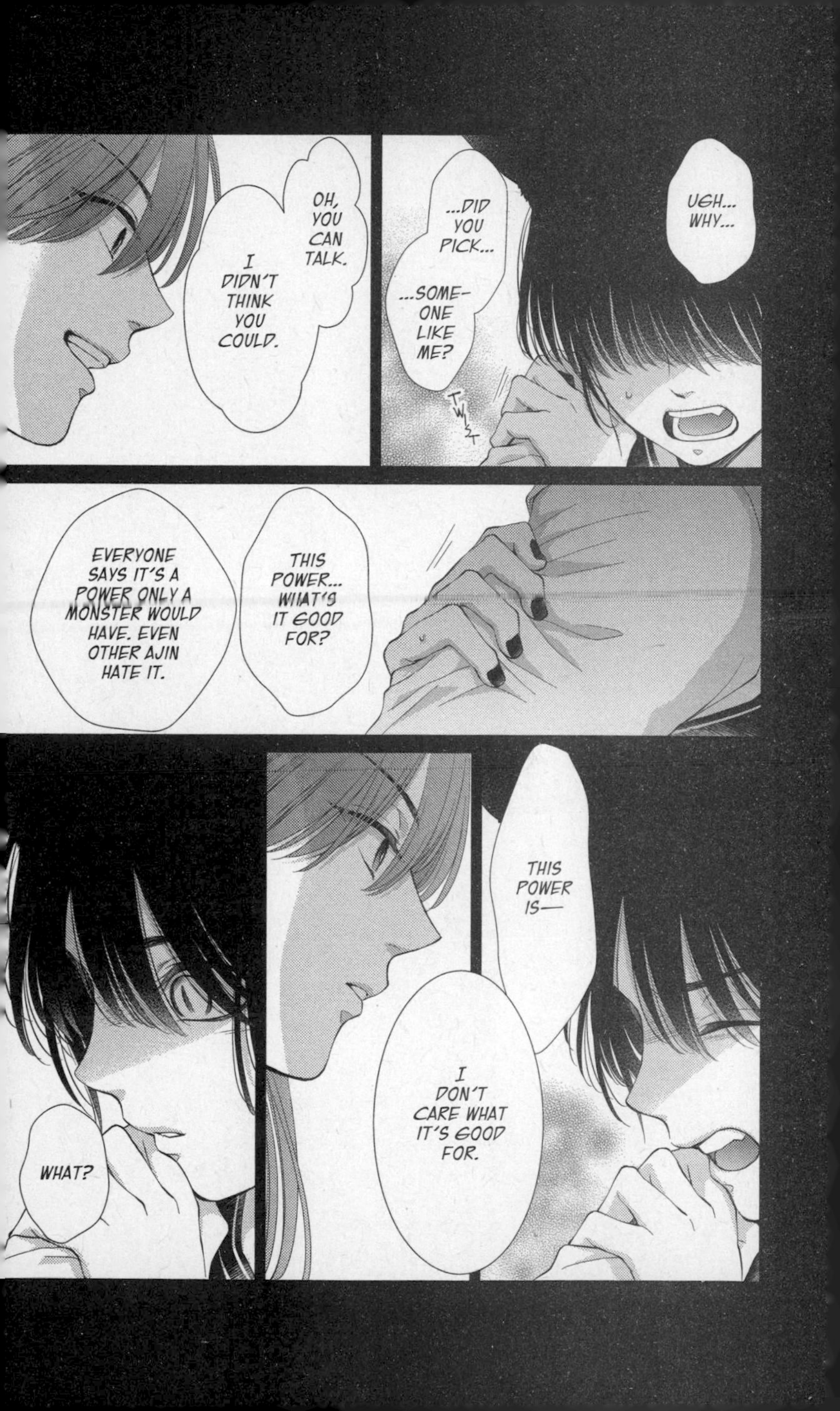
UGH... WHY...
...DID YOU PICK...
...SOME-ONE LIKE ME?
TWIST
OH, YOU CAN TALK.
I DIDN'T THINK YOU COULD.
THIS POWER... WHAT'S IT GOOD FOR?
EVERYONE SAYS IT'S A POWER ONLY A MONSTER WOULD HAVE. EVEN OTHER AJIN HATE IT.
THIS POWER IS—
I DON'T CARE WHAT IT'S GOOD FOR.
WHAT?

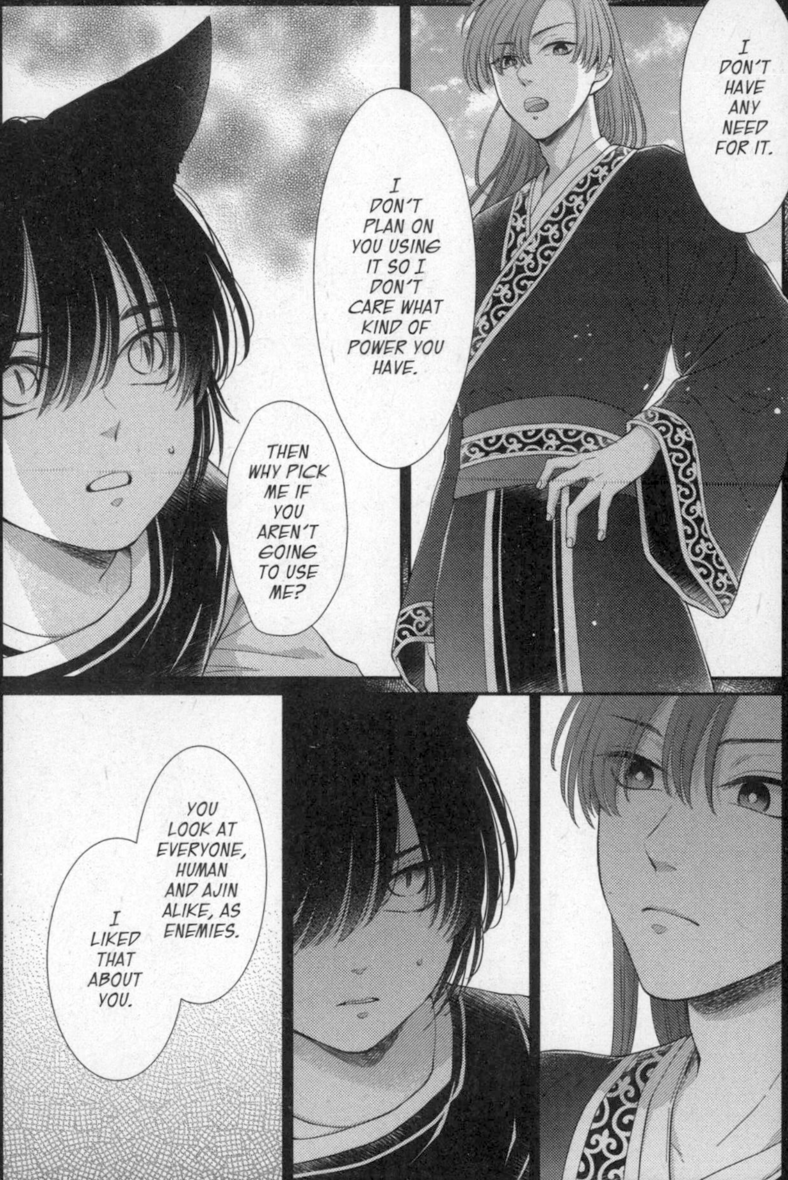
I DON'T HAVE ANY NEED FOR IT.
I DON'T PLAN ON YOU USING IT SO I DON'T CARE WHAT KIND OF POWER YOU HAVE.
THEN WHY PICK ME IF YOU AREN'T GOING TO USE ME?
YOU LOOK AT EVERYONE, HUMAN AND AJIN ALIKE, AS ENEMIES.
I LIKED THAT ABOUT YOU.

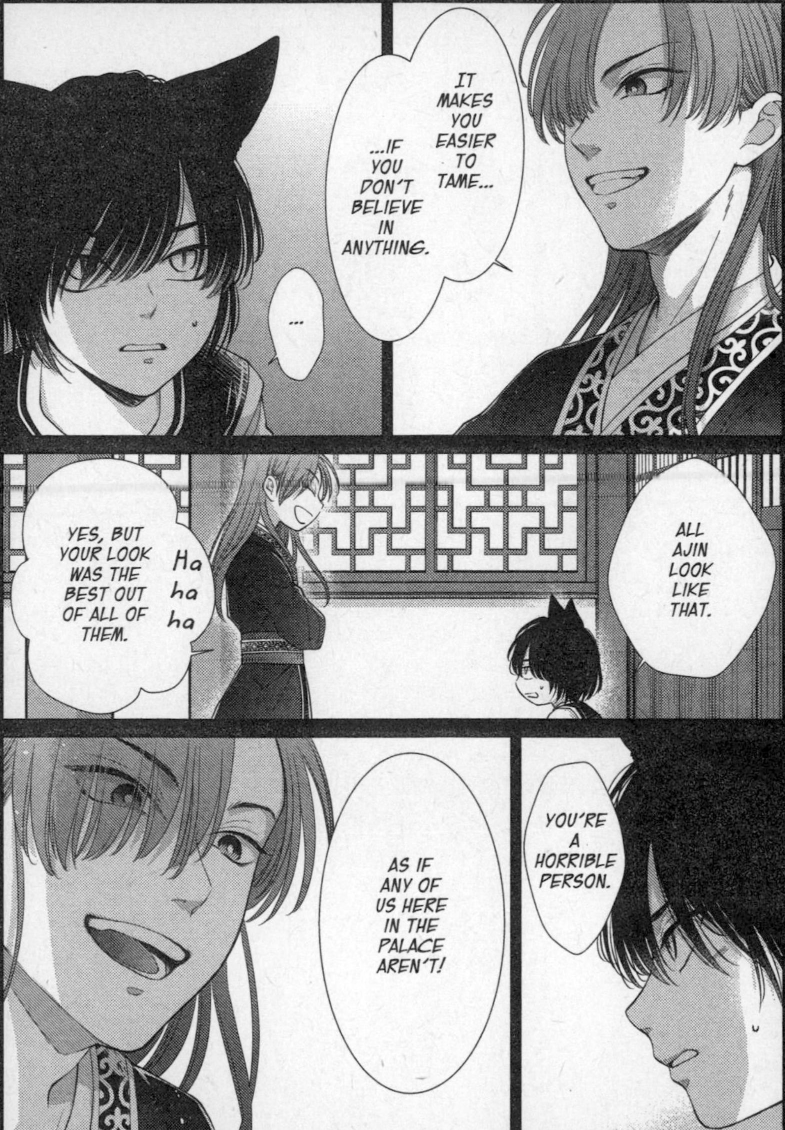
IT MAKES YOU EASIER TO TAME...
...IF YOU DON'T BELIEVE IN ANYTHING.
...
ALL AJIN LOOK LIKE THAT.
YES, BUT YOUR LOOK WAS THE BEST OUT OF ALL OF THEM.
Ha ha ha
YOU'RE A HORRIBLE PERSON.
AS IF ANY OF US HERE IN THE PALACE AREN'T!

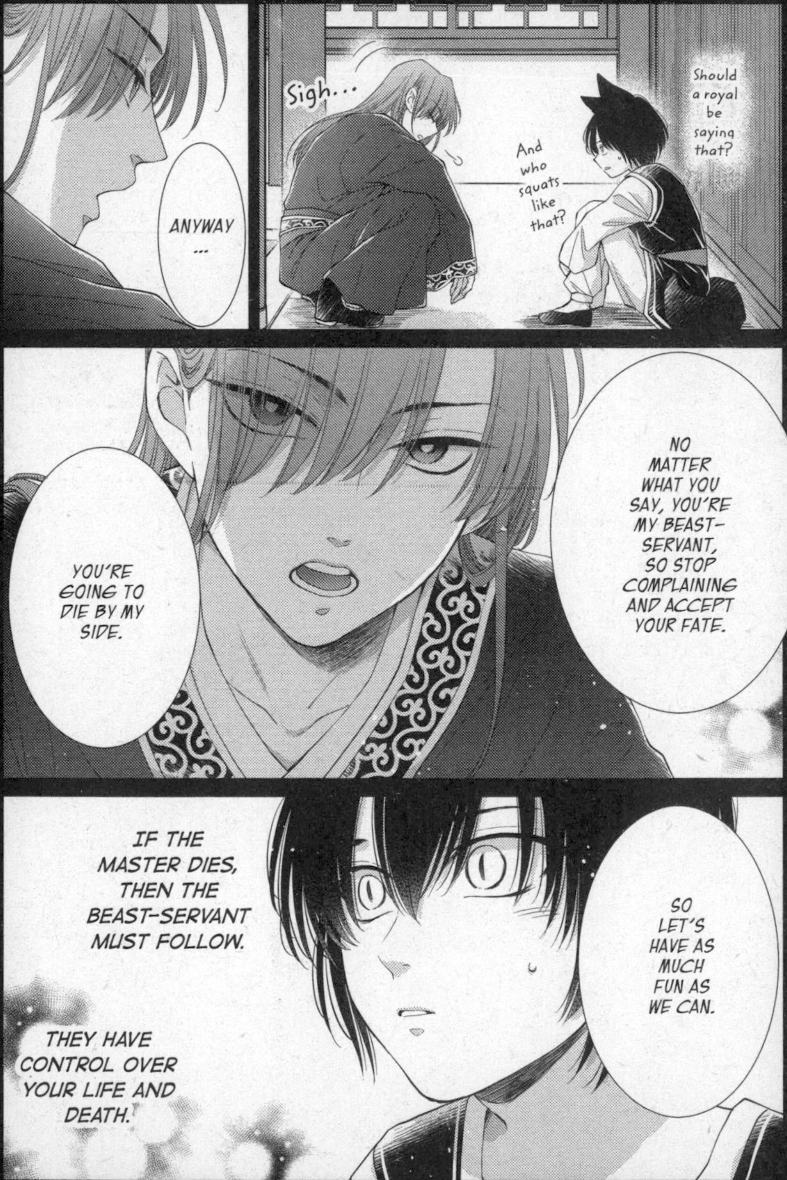
Should a royal be saying that?
And who squats like that?
Sigh...
ANYWAY ...
NO MATTER WHAT YOU SAY, YOU'RE MY BEAST-SERVANT, SO STOP COMPLAINING AND ACCEPT YOUR FATE.
YOU'RE GOING TO DIE BY MY SIDE.
SO LET'S HAVE AS MUCH FUN AS WE CAN.
IF THE MASTER DIES, THEN THE BEAST-SERVANT MUST FOLLOW.
THEY HAVE CONTROL OVER YOUR LIFE AND DEATH.

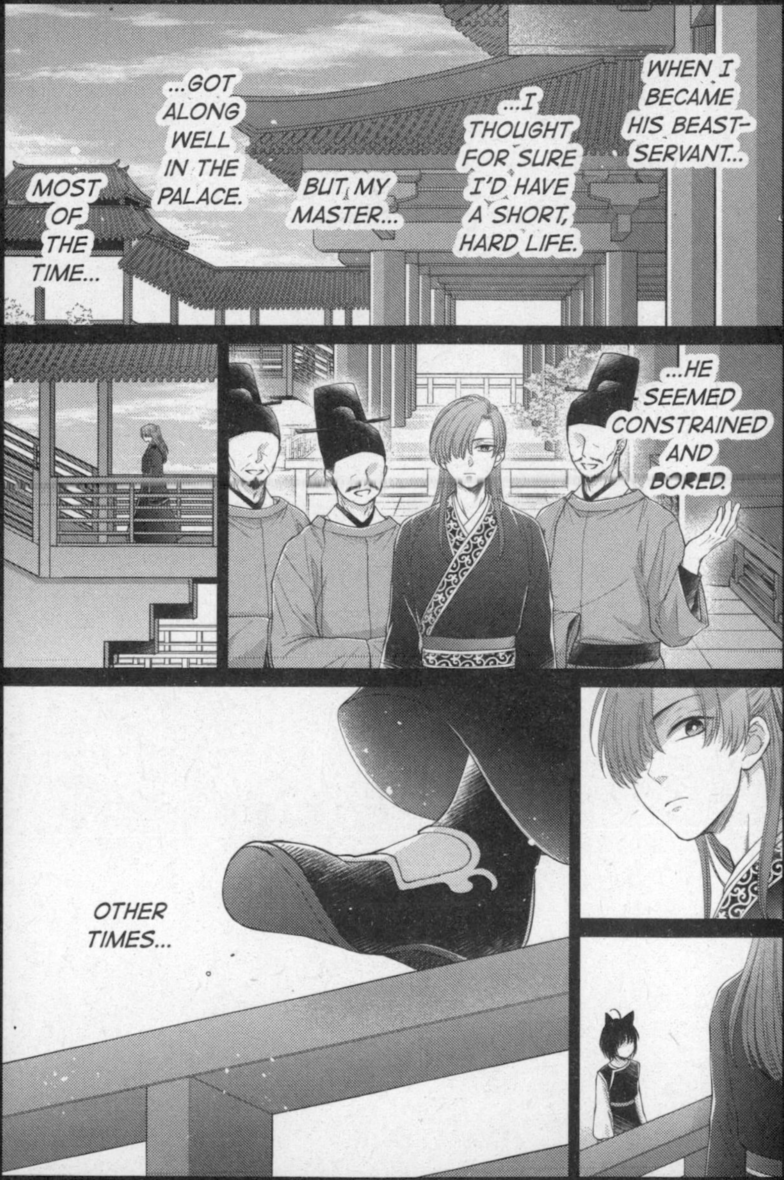
WHEN I BECAME HIS BEAST-SERVANT...
...I THOUGHT FOR SURE I'D HAVE A SHORT, HARD LIFE.
BUT MY MASTER...
...GOT ALONG WELL IN THE PALACE.
MOST OF THE TIME...
...HE SEEMED CONSTRAINED AND BORED.
OTHER TIMES...

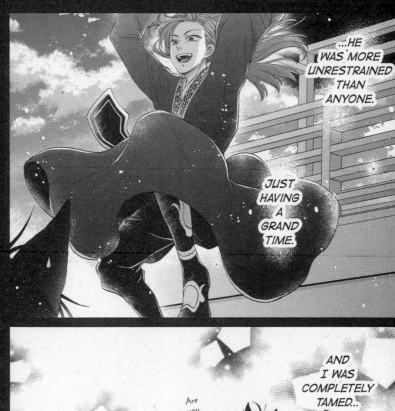

...HE WAS MORE UNRESTRAINED THAN ANYONE.
JUST HAVING A GRAND TIME.
AND I WAS COMPLETELY TAMED...
Are you stupid?
Ha ha ha!
Crap, that was so high. I could've died.
...BY THIS SORT OF PRINCE.

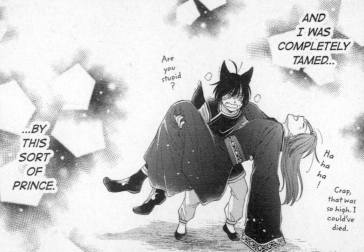

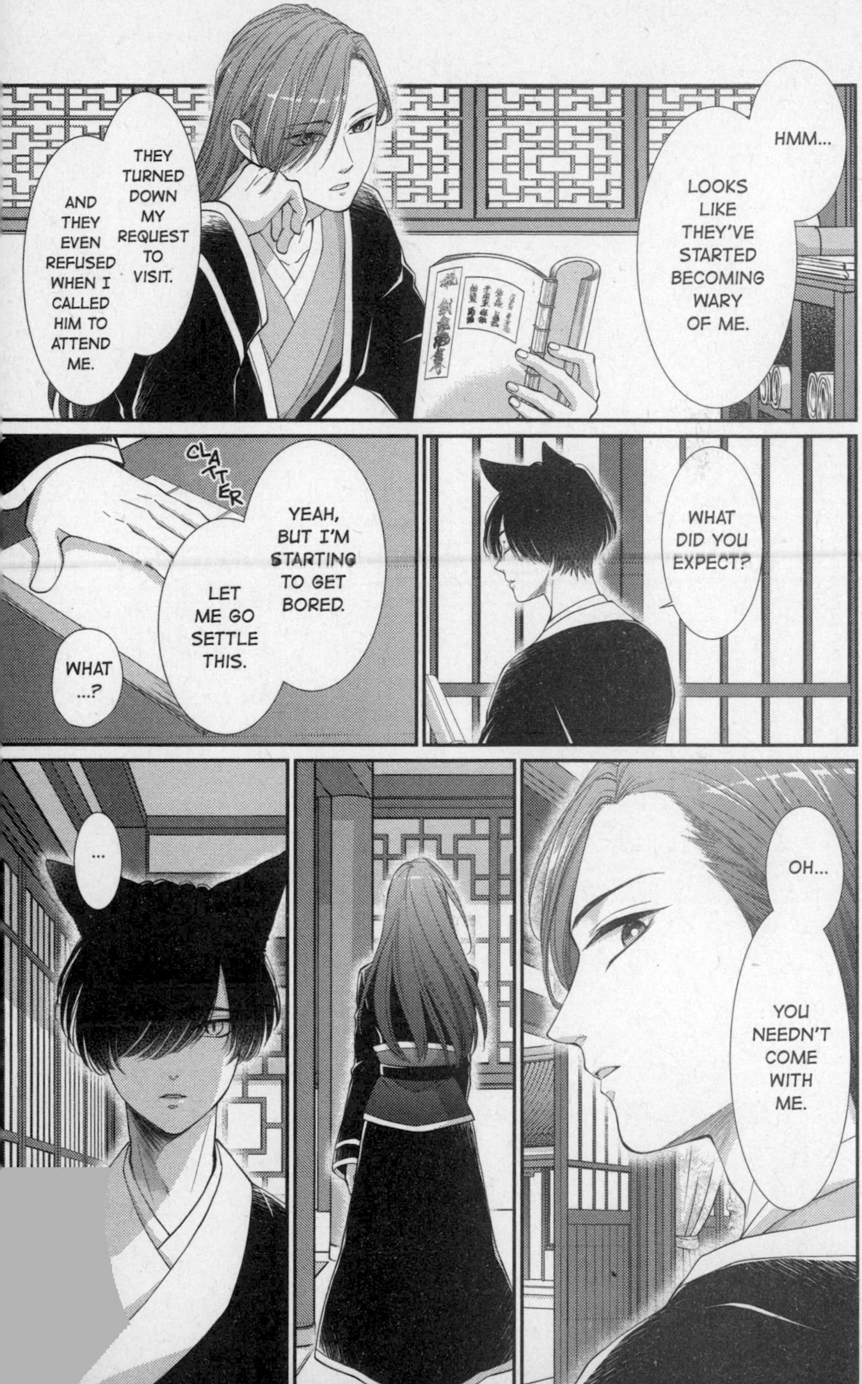
HMM...
LOOKS LIKE THEY'VE STARTED BECOMING WARY OF ME.
THEY TURNED DOWN MY REQUEST TO VISIT.
AND THEY EVEN REFUSED WHEN I CALLED HIM TO ATTEND ME.
WHAT DID YOU EXPECT?
CLATTER
YEAH, BUT I'M STARTING TO GET BORED.
LET ME GO SETTLE THIS.
WHAT ...?
OH...
YOU NEEDN'T COME WITH ME.
...

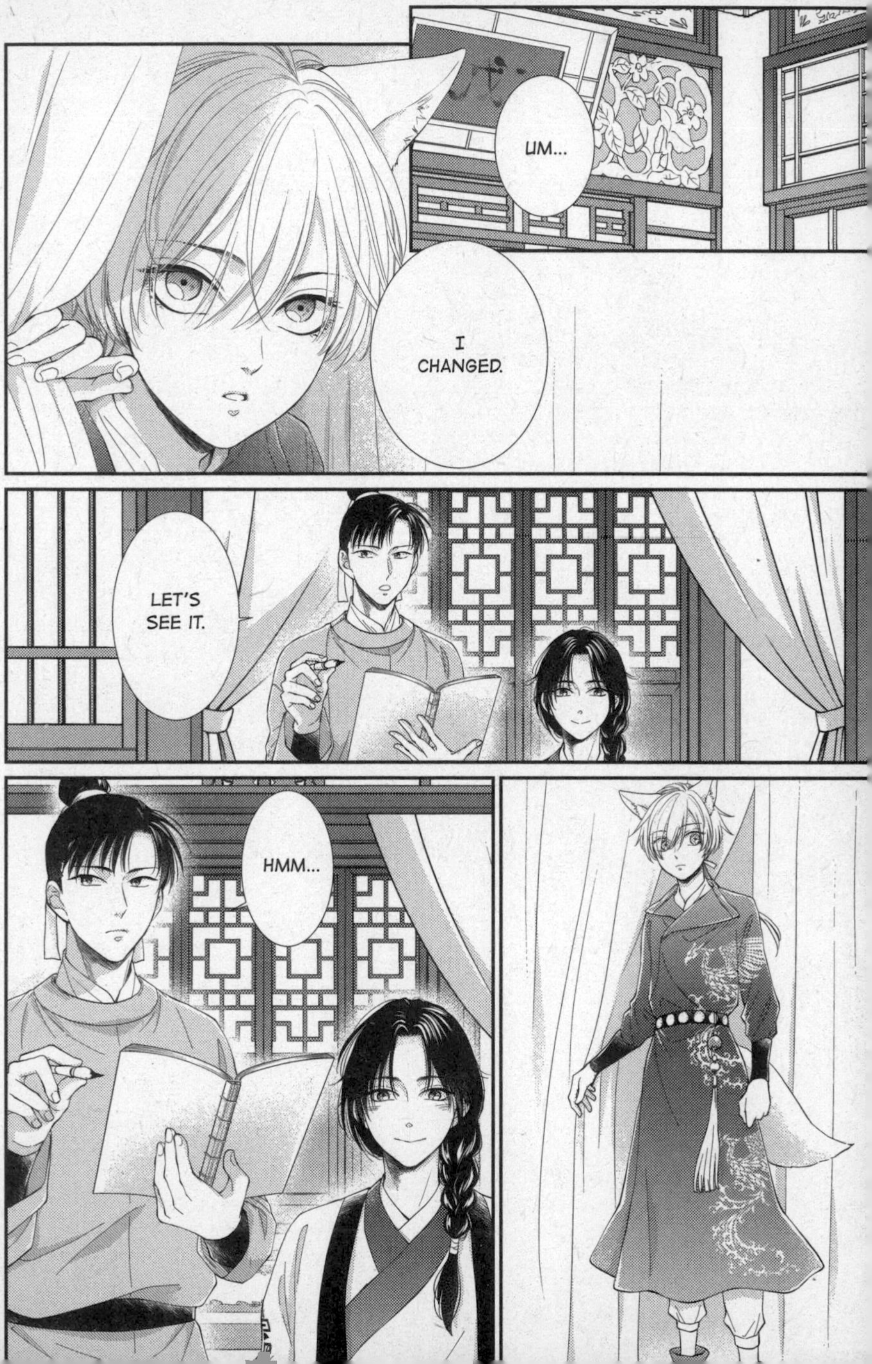
UM...
I CHANGED.
LET'S SEE IT.
HMM...

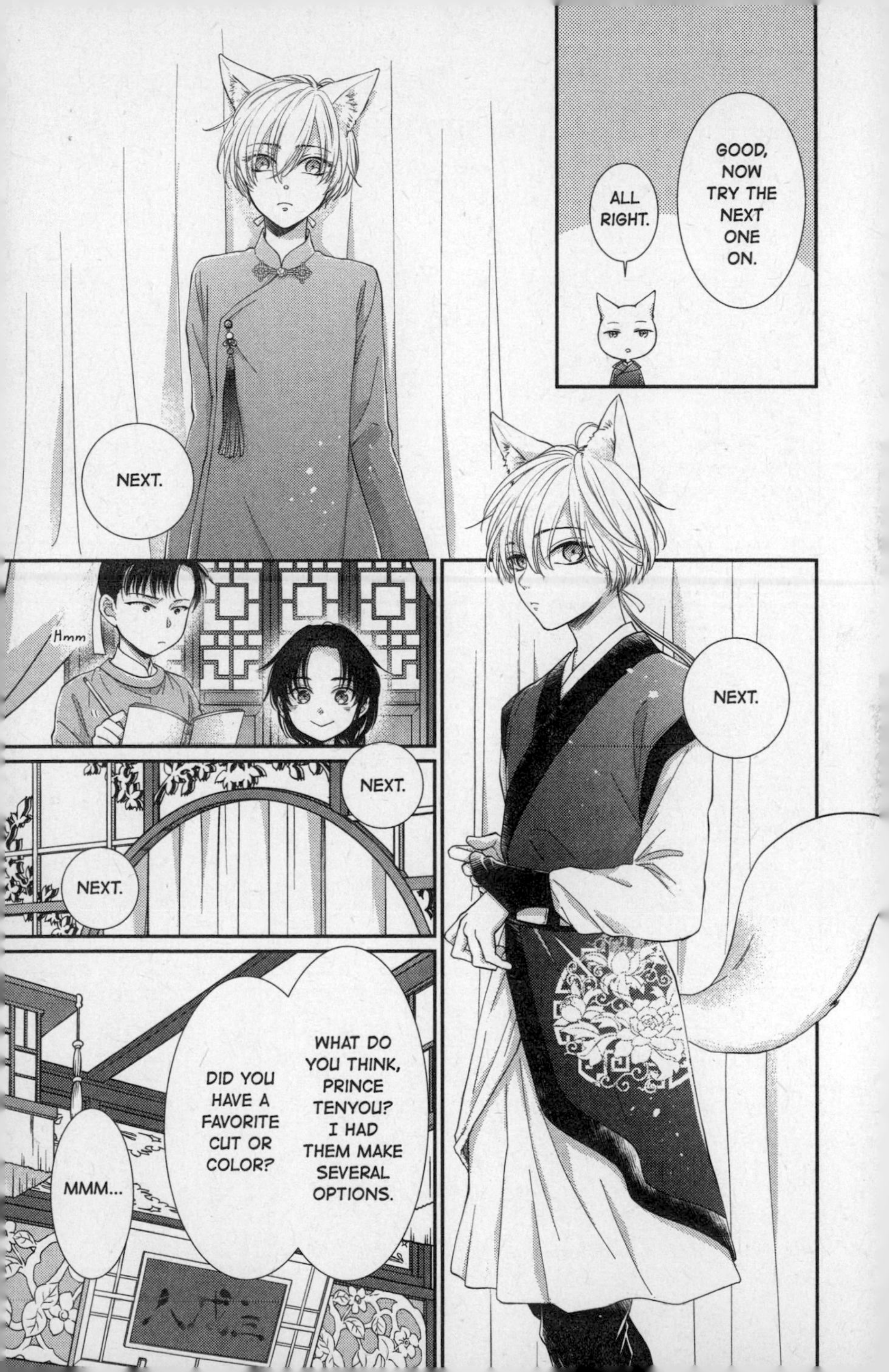
GOOD, NOW TRY THE NEXT ONE ON.
ALL RIGHT.
NEXT.
NEXT.
Hmm
NEXT.
NEXT.
WHAT DO YOU THINK, PRINCE TENYOU? I HAD THEM MAKE SEVERAL OPTIONS.
DID YOU HAVE A FAVORITE CUT OR COLOR?
MMM...

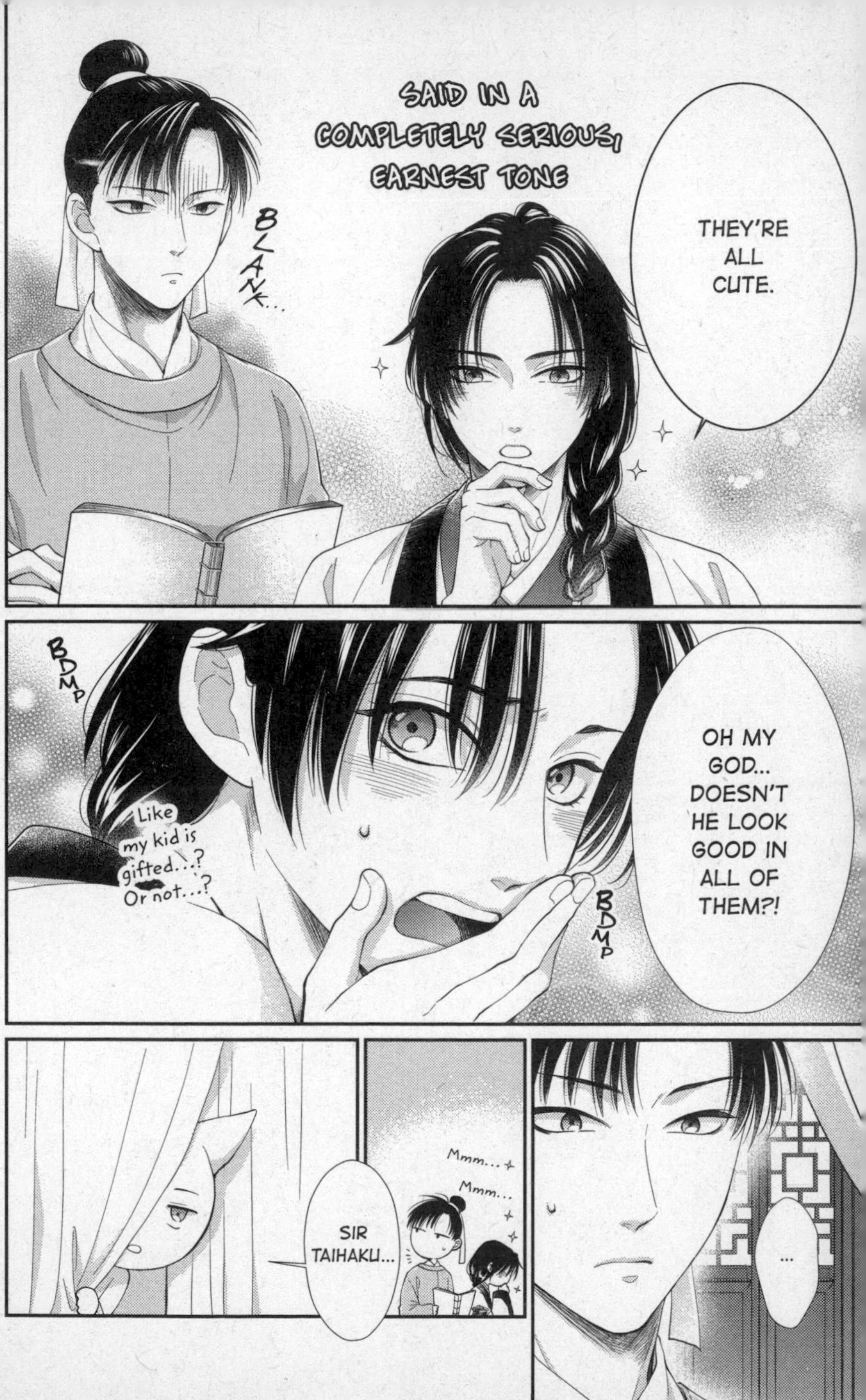
THEY'RE ALL CUTE.
SAID IN A COMPLETELY SERIOUS, EARNEST TONE
BLANK...
OH MY GOD... DOESN'T HE LOOK GOOD IN ALL OF THEM?!
BDMP
BDMP
Like my kid is gifted...? Or not...?
...
Mmm...
Mmm...
SIR TAIHAKU...

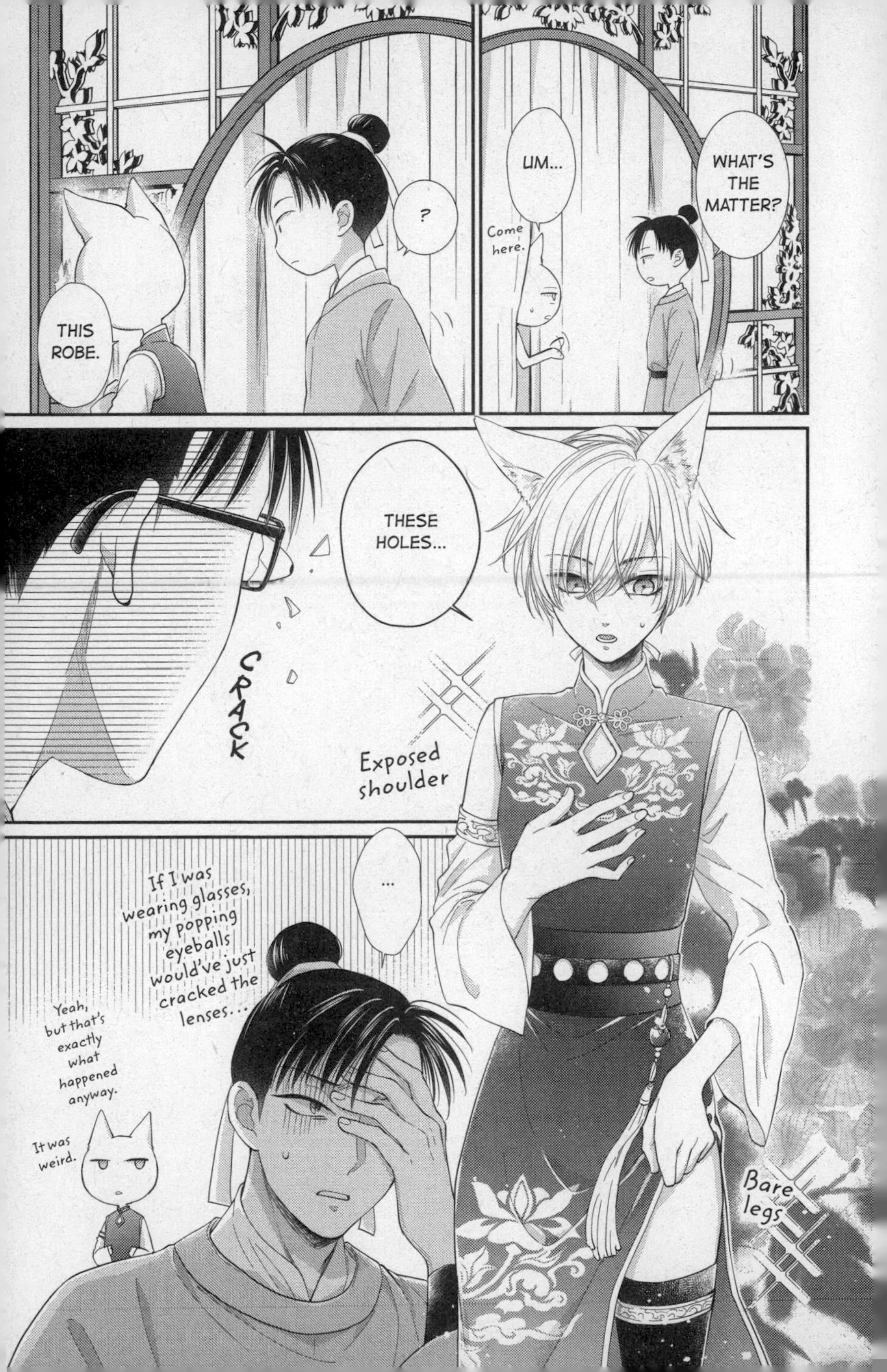
WHAT'S THE MATTER?
UM...
Come here.
?
THIS ROBE.
THESE HOLES...
CRACK
Exposed shoulder
Bare legs
...
If I was wearing glasses, my popping eyeballs would've just cracked the lenses...
Yeah, but that's exactly what happened anyway.
It was weird.

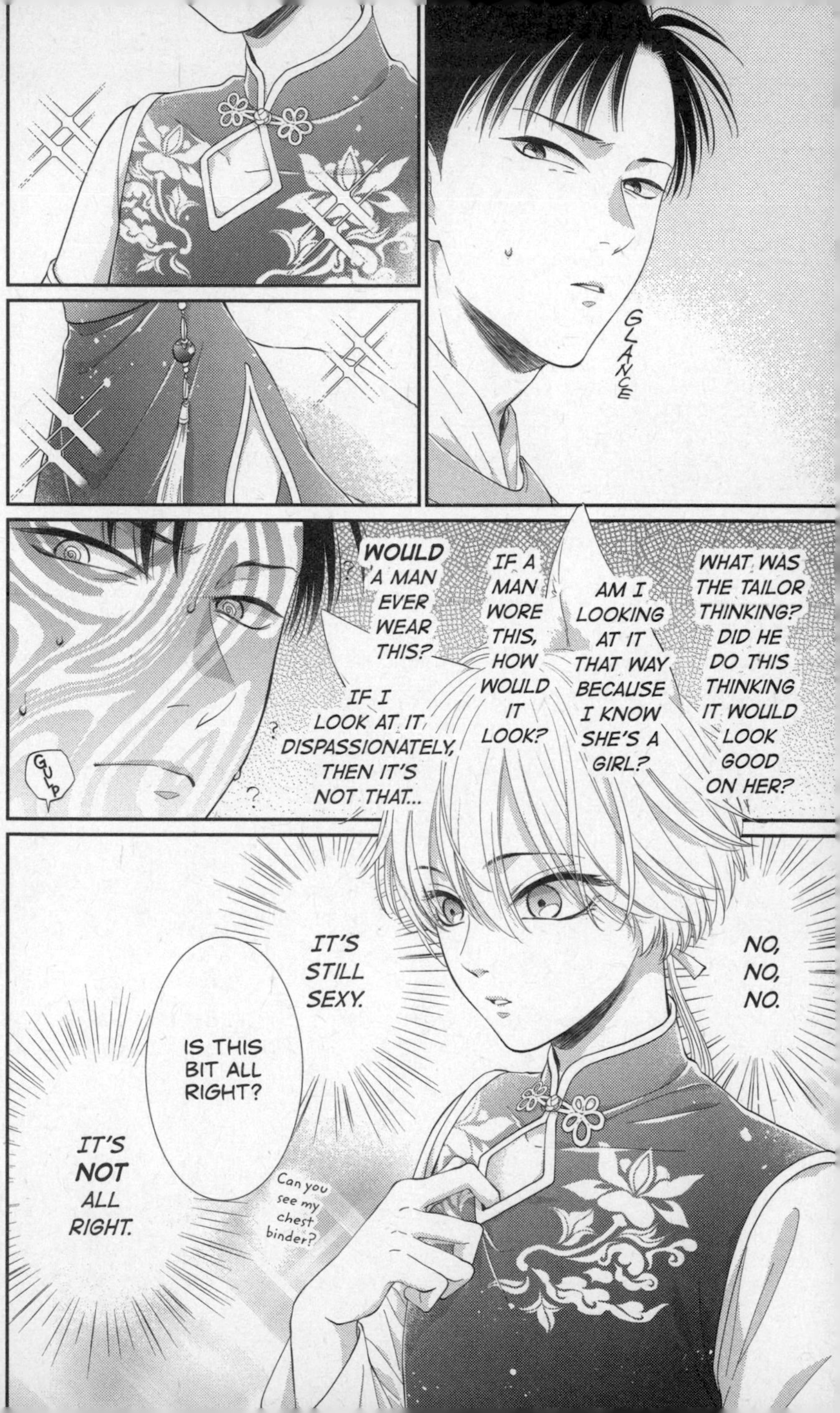
GLANCE
WHAT WAS THE TAILOR THINKING? DID HE DO THIS THINKING IT WOULD LOOK GOOD ON HER?
AM I LOOKING AT IT THAT WAY BECAUSE I KNOW SHE'S A GIRL?
IF A MAN WORE THIS, HOW WOULD IT LOOK?
WOULD A MAN EVER WEAR THIS?
IF I LOOK AT IT DISPASSIONATELY, THEN IT'S NOT THAT...
GULP
NO, NO, NO.
IT'S STILL SEXY.
IS THIS BIT ALL RIGHT?
Can you see my chest binder?
IT'S NOT ALL RIGHT.

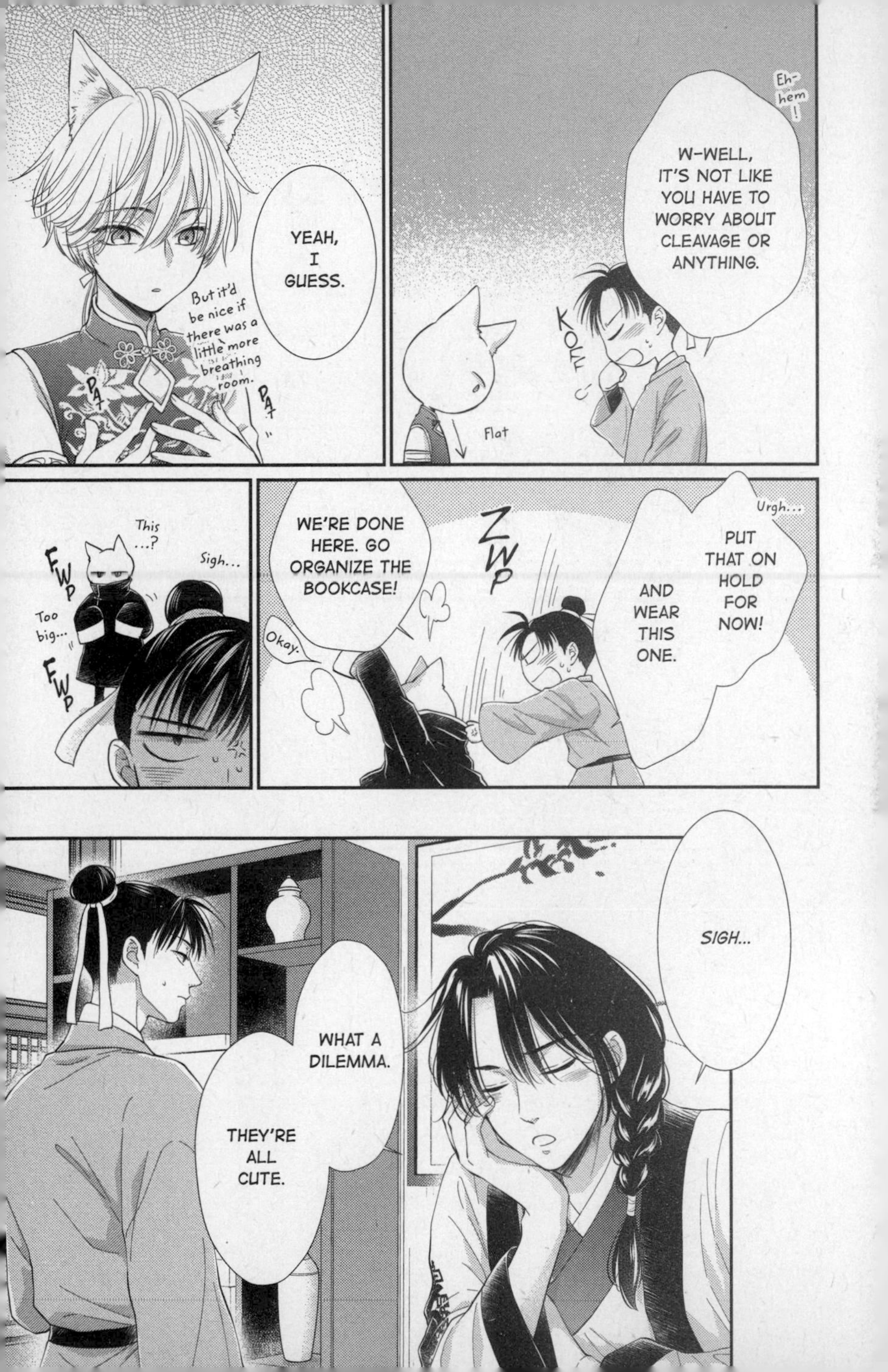
Eh-hem!
W-WELL, IT'S NOT LIKE YOU HAVE TO WORRY ABOUT CLEAVAGE OR ANYTHING.
KOFF
Flat
YEAH, I GUESS.
But it'd be nice if there was a little more breathing room.
PAT
PAT
Urgh...
PUT THAT ON HOLD FOR NOW!
AND WEAR THIS ONE.
ZWP
WE'RE DONE HERE. GO ORGANIZE THE BOOKCASE!
Okay.
This ...?
Sigh...
FWP
Too big...
FWP
SIGH...
WHAT A DILEMMA.
THEY'RE ALL CUTE.

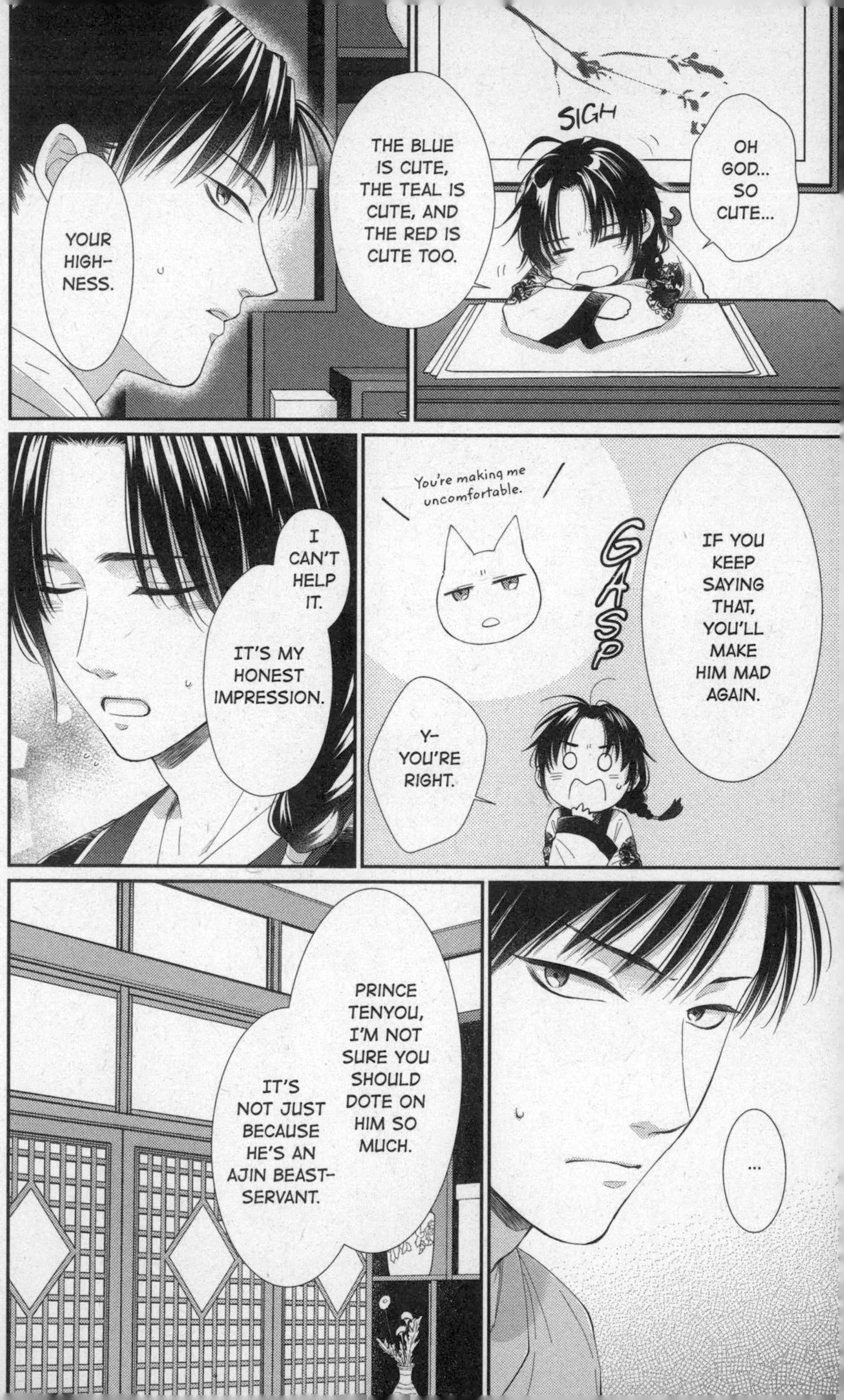
SIGH
OH GOD... SO CUTE...
THE BLUE IS CUTE, THE TEAL IS CUTE, AND THE RED IS CUTE TOO.
YOUR HIGHNESS.
IF YOU KEEP SAYING THAT, YOU'LL MAKE HIM MAD AGAIN.
GASP
You're making me uncomfortable.
Y- YOU'RE RIGHT.
I CAN'T HELP IT.
IT'S MY HONEST IMPRESSION.
...
PRINCE TENYOU, I'M NOT SURE YOU SHOULD DOTE ON HIM SO MUCH.
IT'S NOT JUST BECAUSE HE'S AN AJIN BEAST-SERVANT.

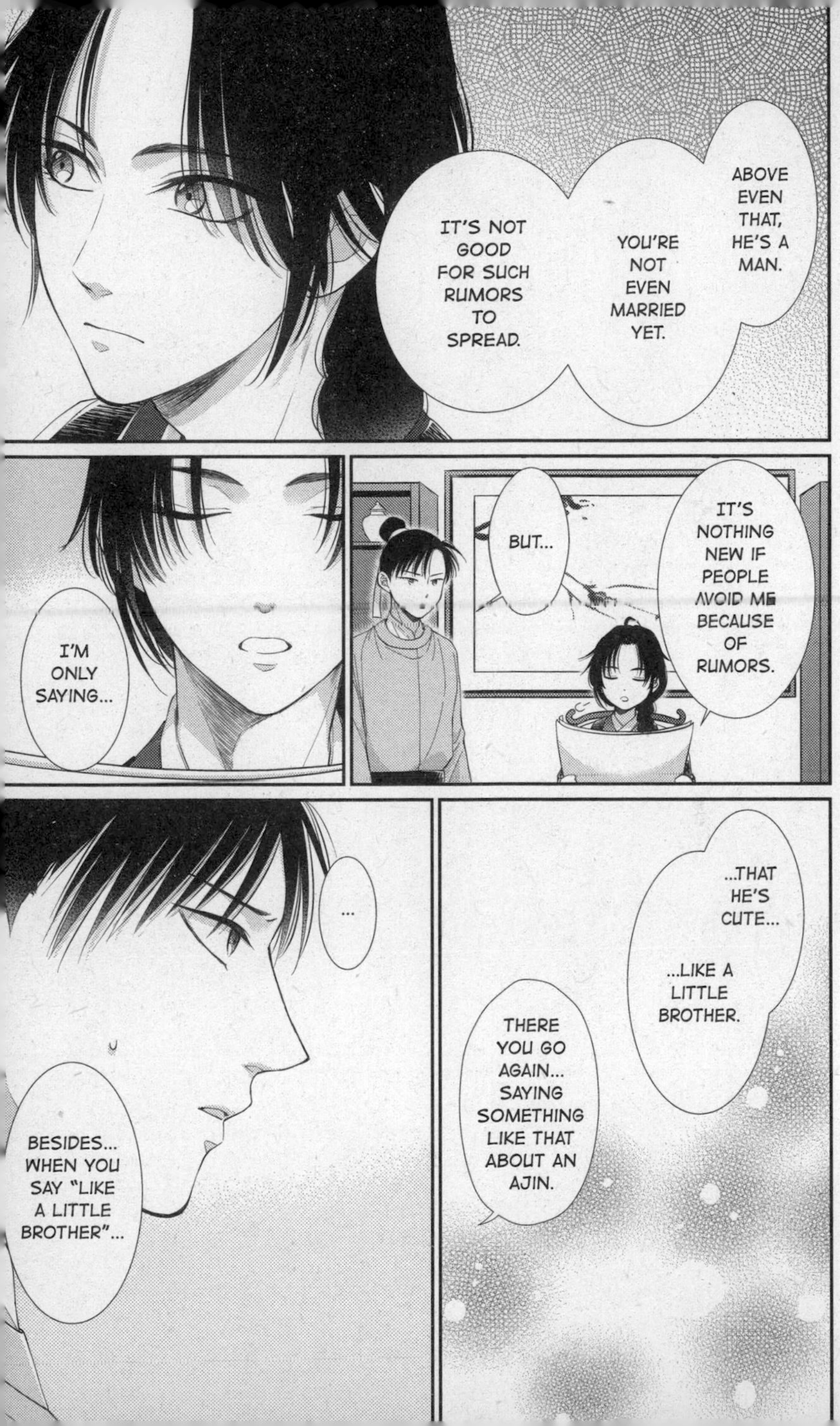
IT'S NOT GOOD FOR SUCH RUMORS TO SPREAD. YOU'RE NOT EVEN MARRIED YET. ABOVE EVEN THAT, HE'S A MAN.
IT'S NOTHING NEW IF PEOPLE AVOID ME BECAUSE OF RUMORS.
BUT...
I'M ONLY SAYING...
...THAT HE'S CUTE... ...LIKE A LITTLE BROTHER.
THERE YOU GO AGAIN... SAYING SOMETHING LIKE THAT ABOUT AN AJIN.
...
BESIDES... WHEN YOU SAY "LIKE A LITTLE BROTHER"...

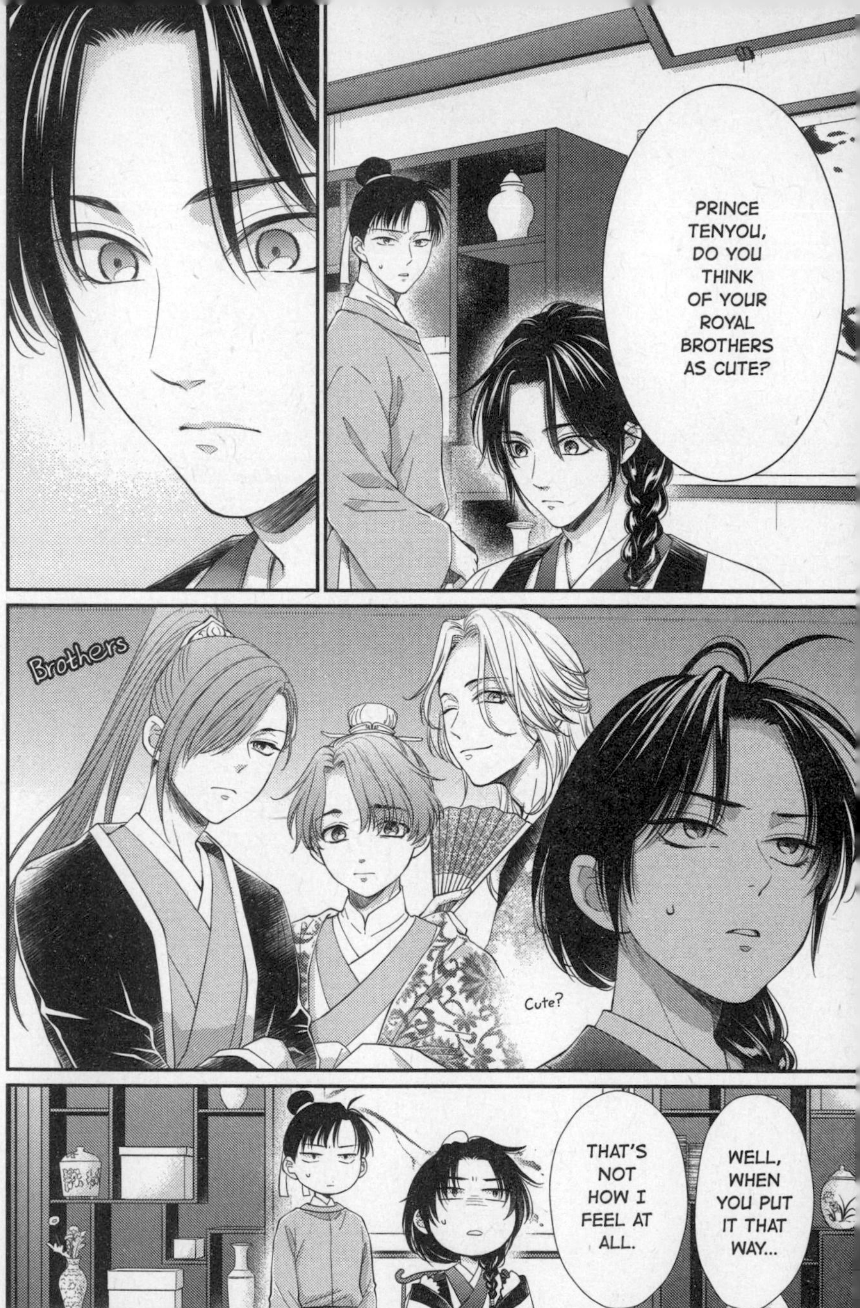
PRINCE TENYOU, DO YOU THINK OF YOUR ROYAL BROTHERS AS CUTE?
Brothers
Cute?
WELL, WHEN YOU PUT IT THAT WAY...
THAT'S NOT HOW I FEEL AT ALL.

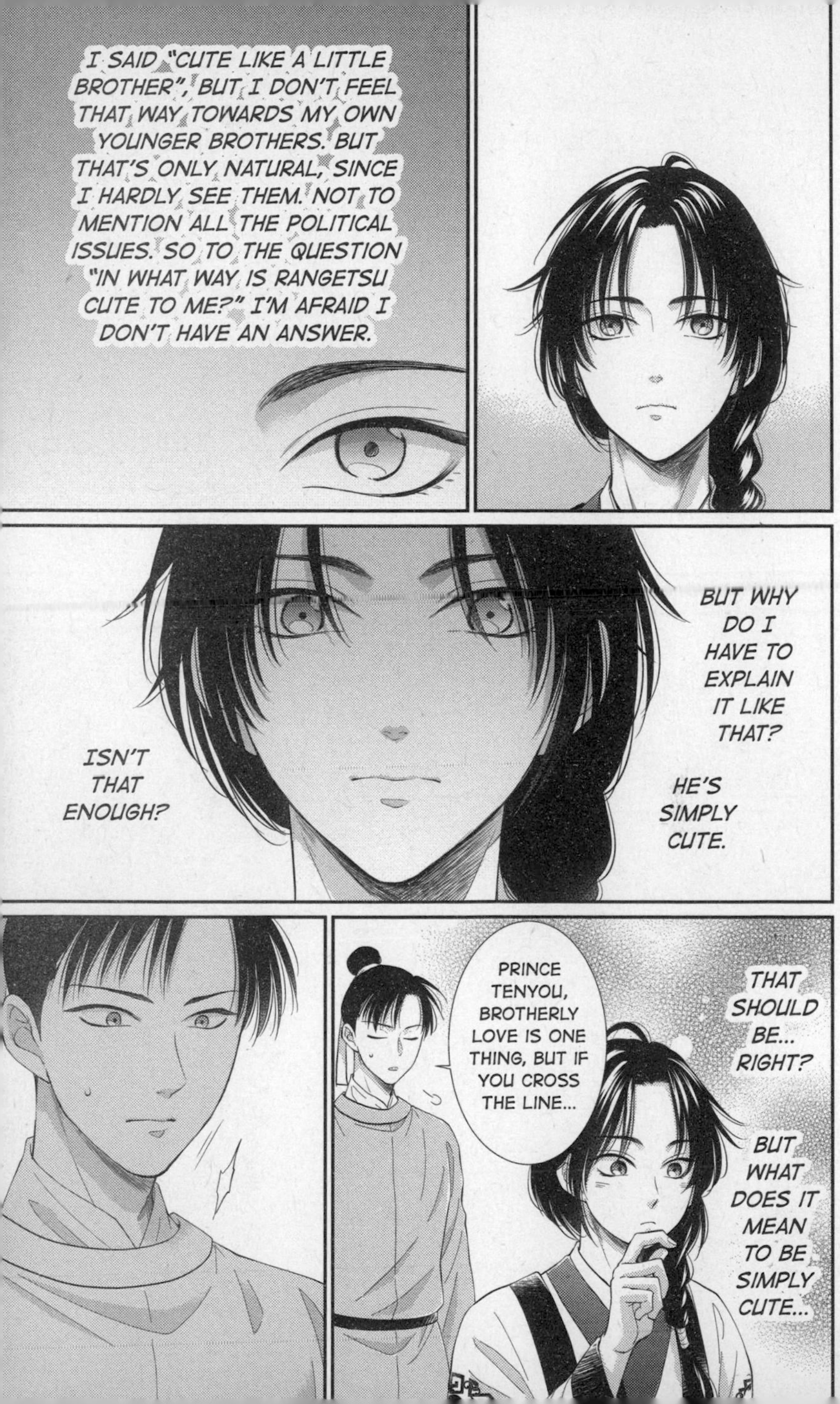
I SAID "CUTE LIKE A LITTLE BROTHER", BUT I DON'T FEEL THAT WAY TOWARDS MY OWN YOUNGER BROTHERS. BUT THAT'S ONLY NATURAL, SINCE I HARDLY SEE THEM. NOT TO MENTION ALL THE POLITICAL ISSUES. SO TO THE QUESTION "IN WHAT WAY IS RANGETSU CUTE TO ME?" I'M AFRAID I DON'T HAVE AN ANSWER.
BUT WHY DO I HAVE TO EXPLAIN IT LIKE THAT?
HE'S SIMPLY CUTE.
ISN'T THAT ENOUGH?
THAT SHOULD BE... RIGHT?
PRINCE TENYOU, BROTHERLY LOVE IS ONE THING, BUT IF YOU CROSS THE LINE...
BUT WHAT DOES IT MEAN TO BE SIMPLY CUTE...

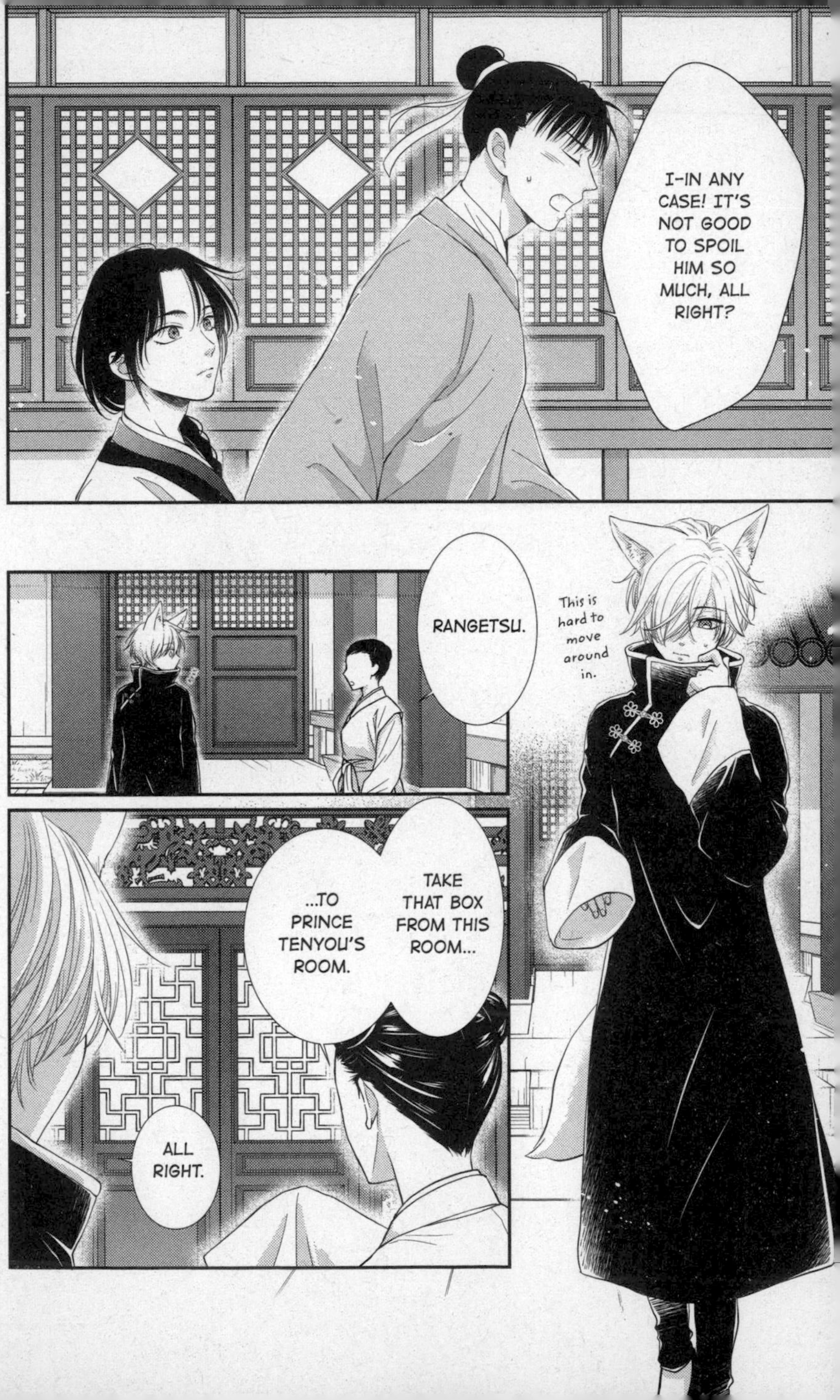
I-IN ANY CASE! IT'S NOT GOOD TO SPOIL HIM SO MUCH, ALL RIGHT?
This is hard to move around in.
RANGETSU.
TAKE THAT BOX FROM THIS ROOM...
...TO PRINCE TENYOU'S ROOM.
ALL RIGHT.

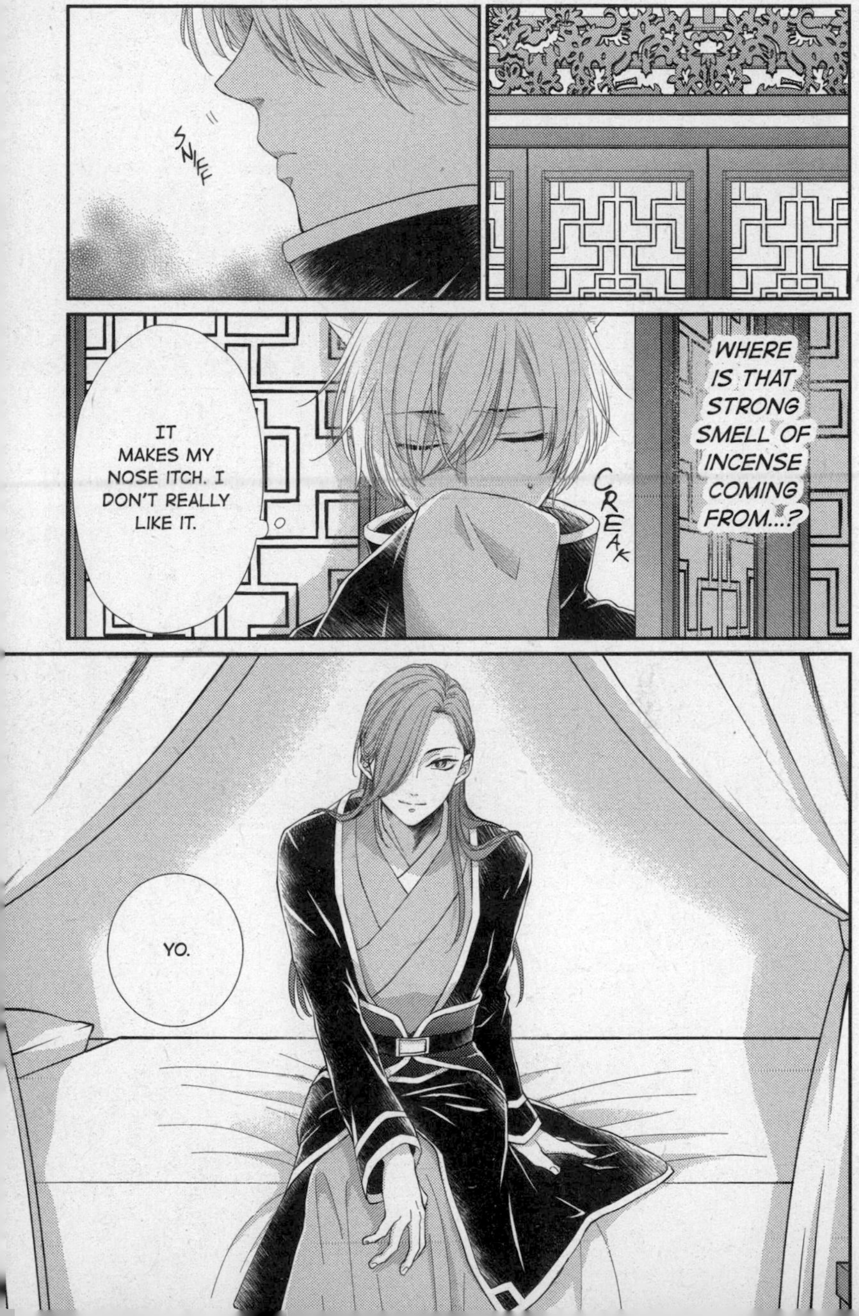
SNIFF
WHERE IS THAT STRONG SMELL OF INCENSE COMING FROM...?
CREAK
IT MAKES MY NOSE ITCH. I DON'T REALLY LIKE IT.
YO.

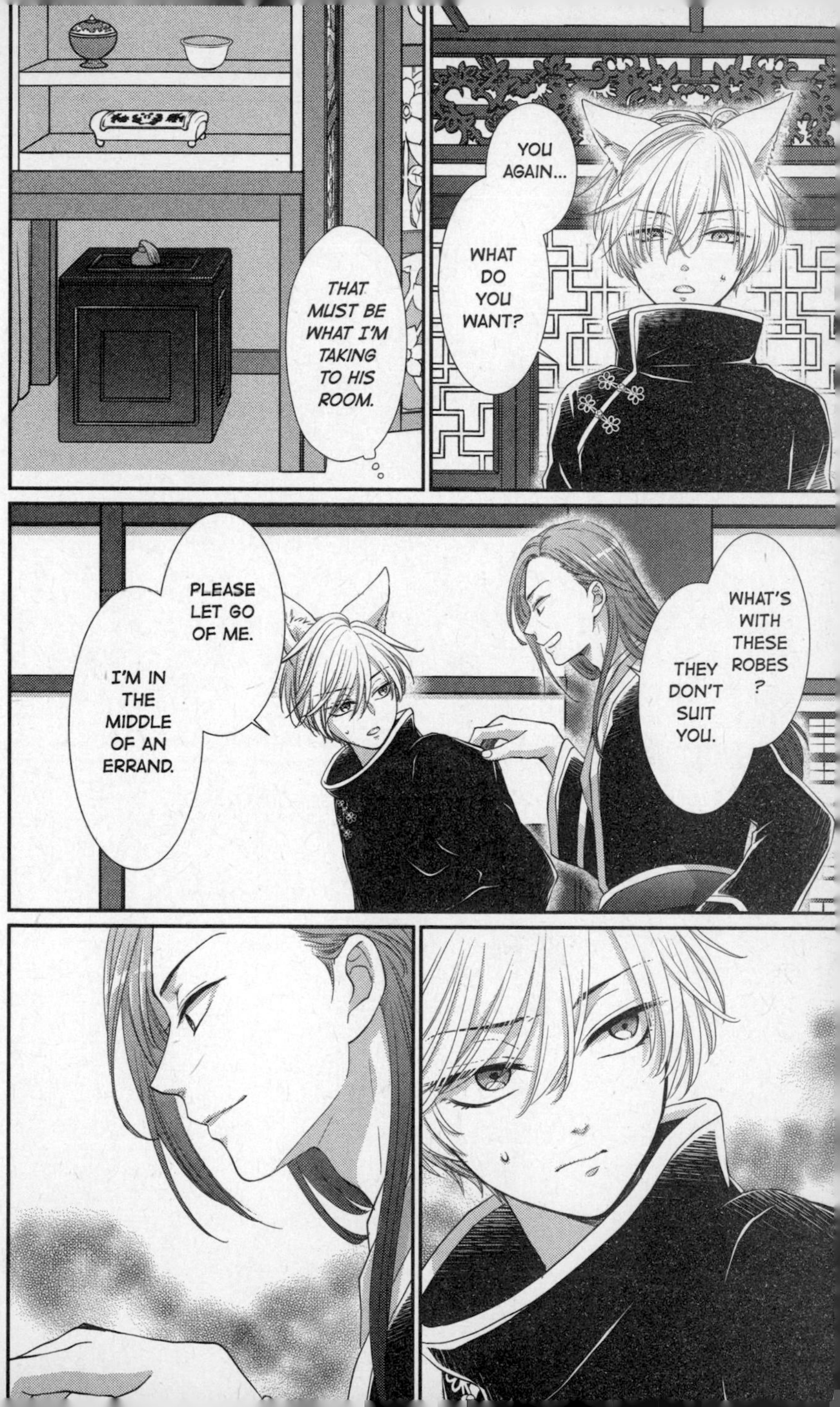
YOU AGAIN...
WHAT DO YOU WANT?
THAT MUST BE WHAT I'M TAKING TO HIS ROOM.
WHAT'S WITH THESE ROBES?
THEY DON'T SUIT YOU.
PLEASE LET GO OF ME.
I'M IN THE MIDDLE OF AN ERRAND.

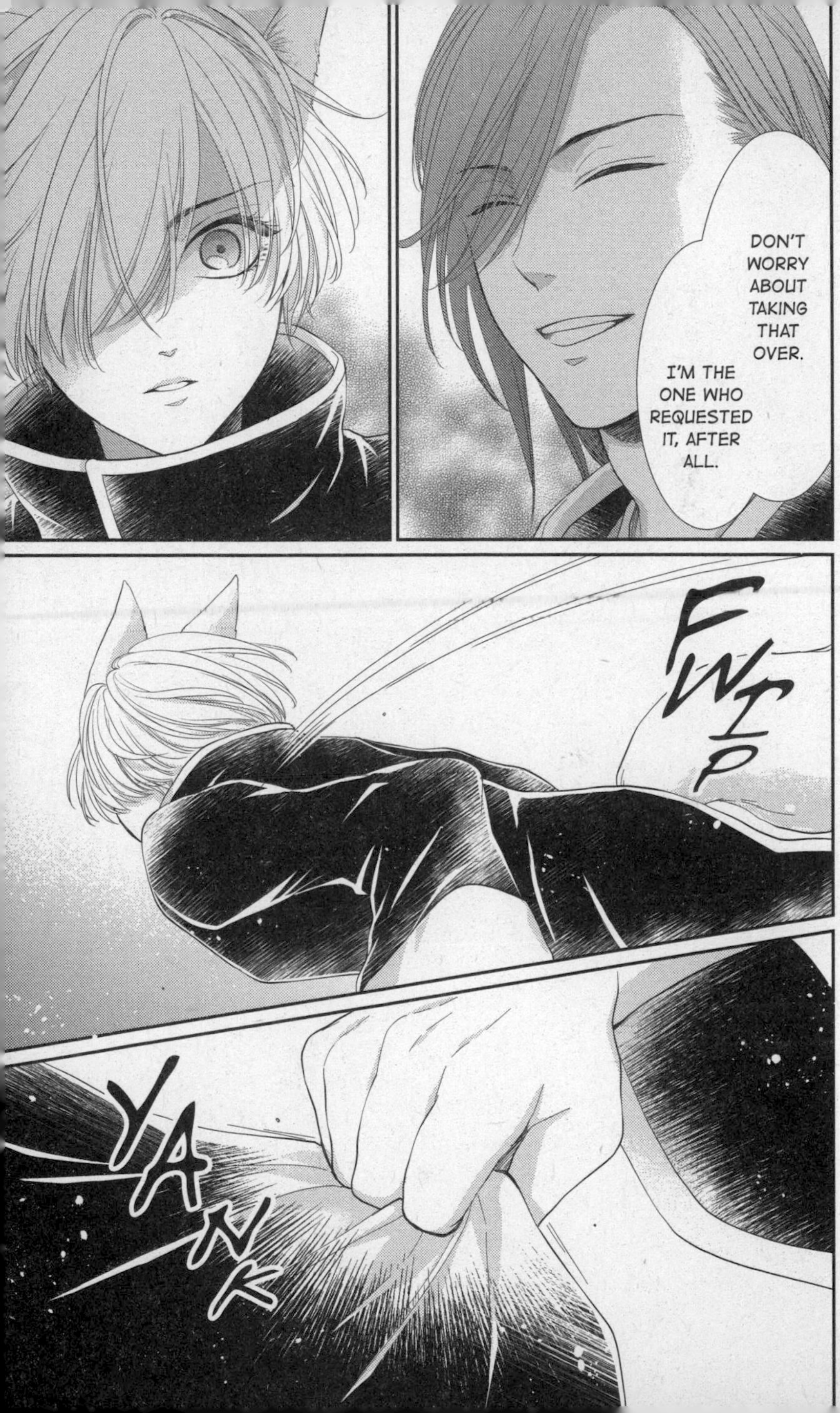
DON'T WORRY ABOUT TAKING THAT OVER.
I'M THE ONE WHO REQUESTED IT, AFTER ALL.
FWIP
YANK

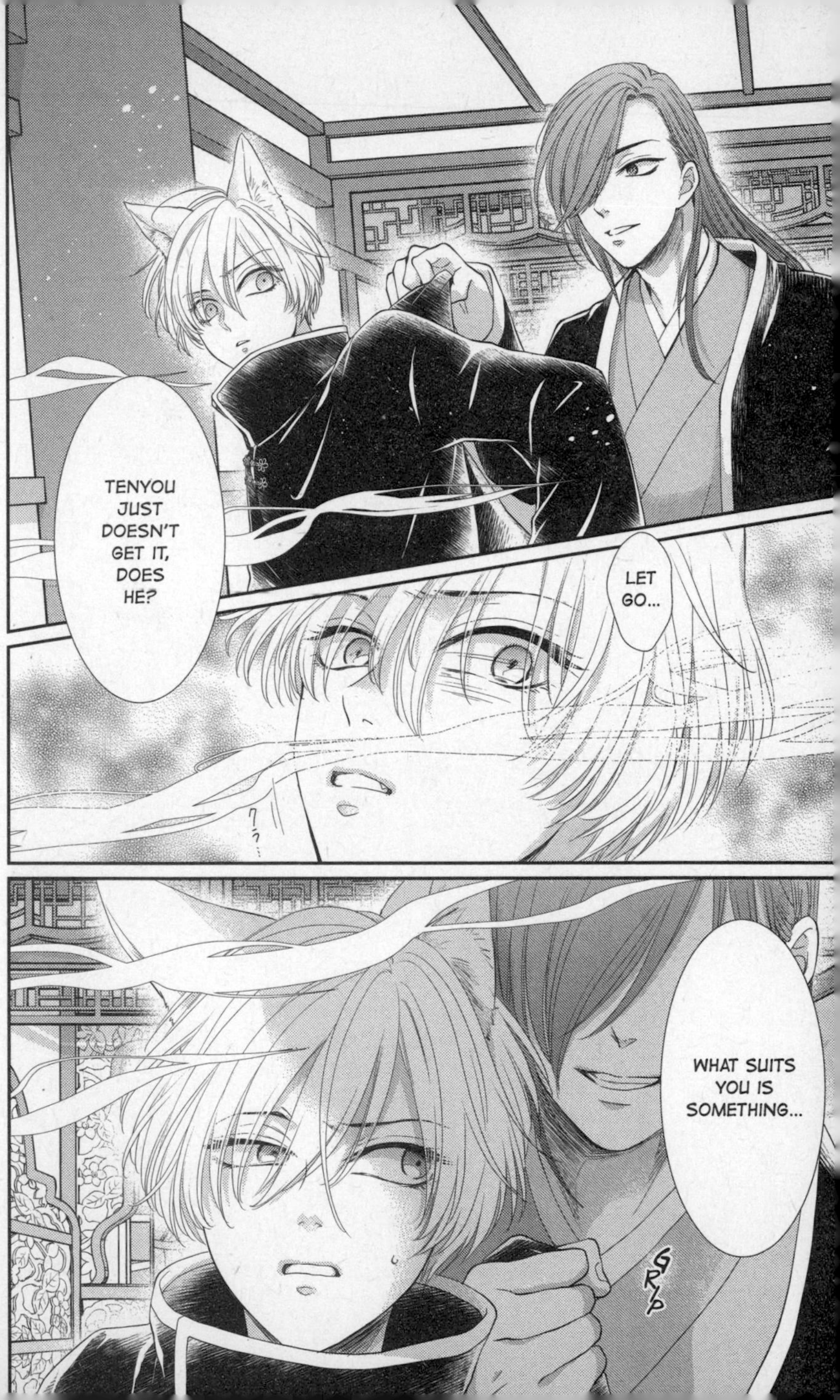
TENYOU JUST DOESN'T GET IT, DOES HE?
LET GO...
WHAT SUITS YOU IS SOMETHING...
GRIP

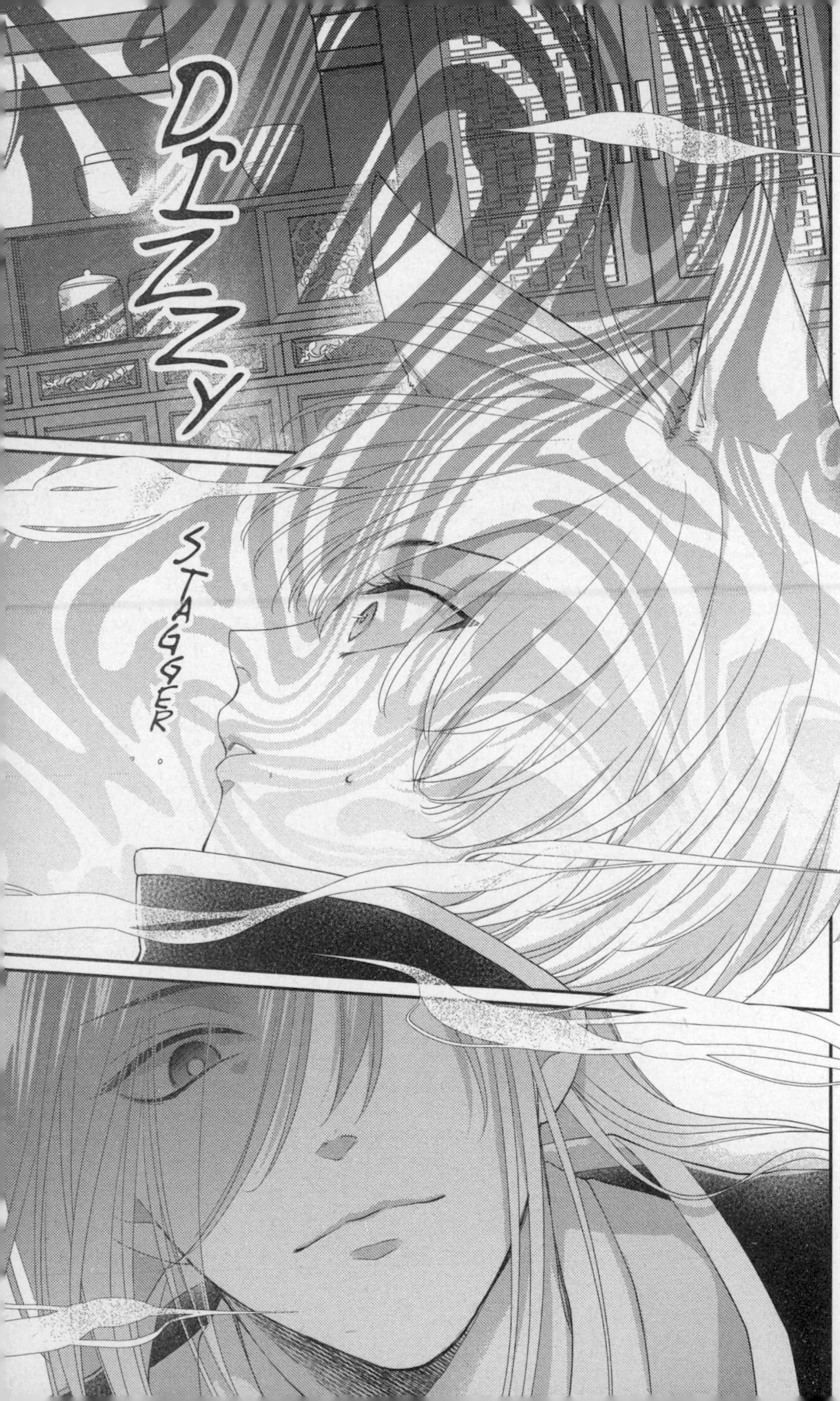
DIZZY
STAGGER

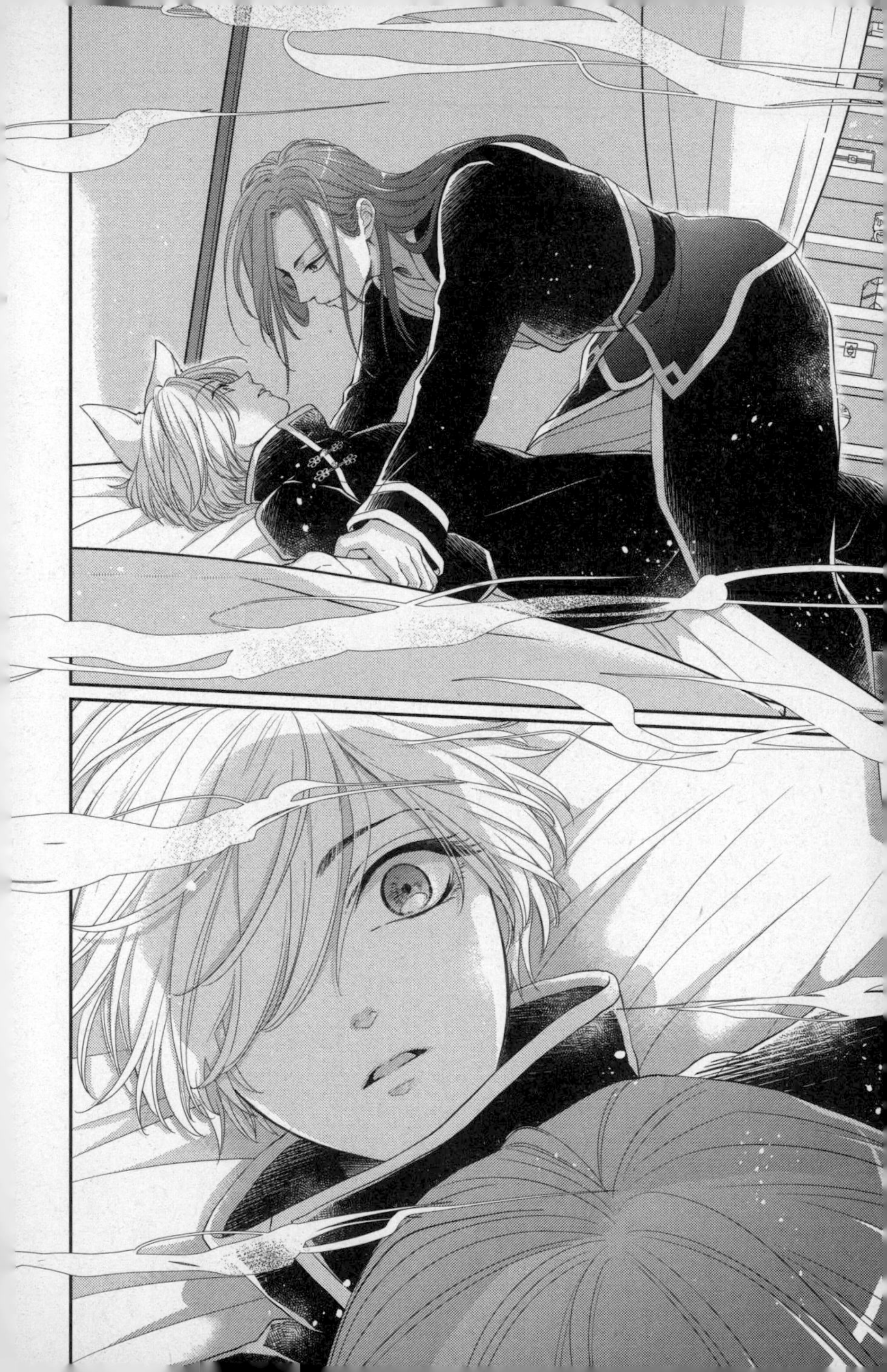

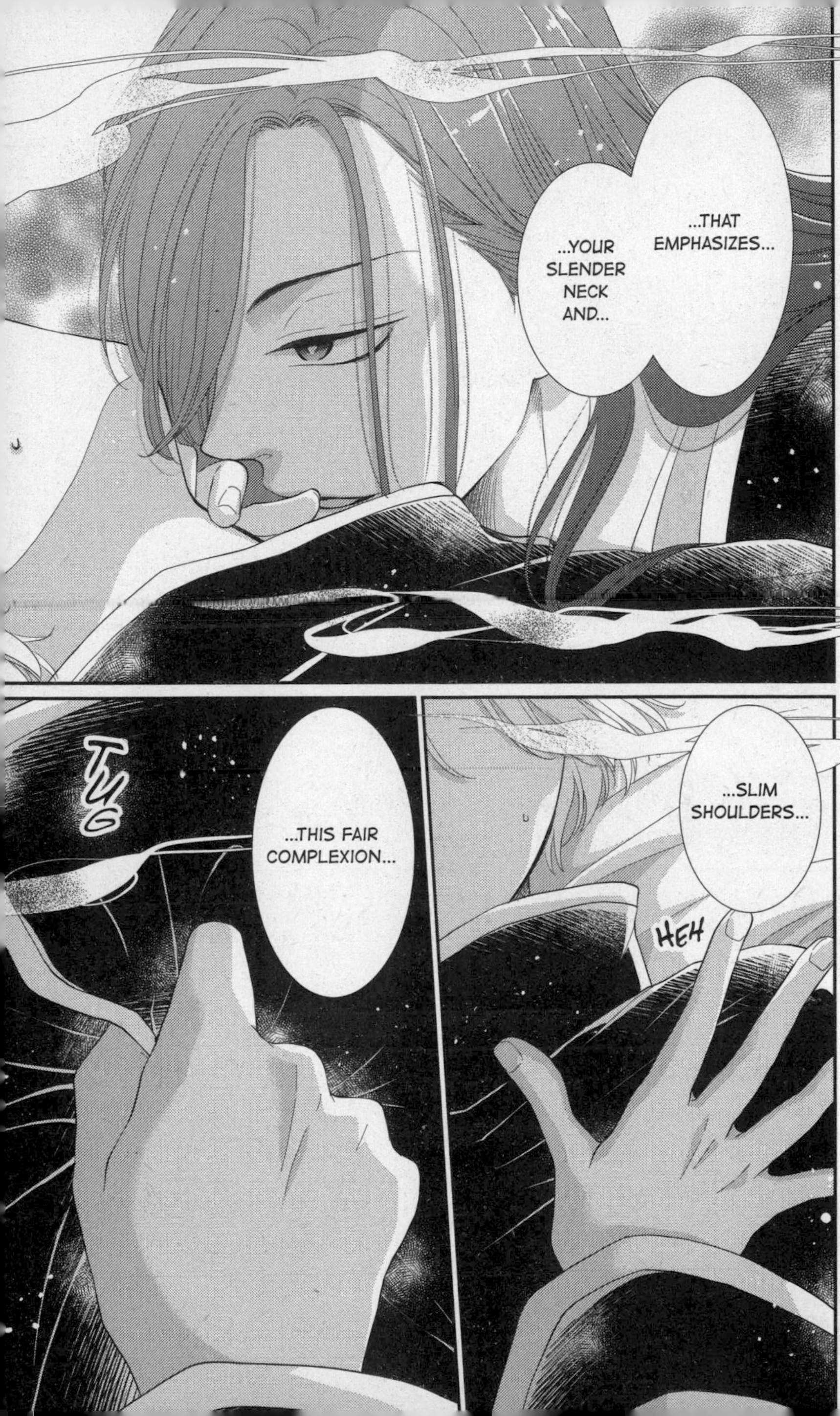
...THAT EMPHASIZES...
...YOUR SLENDER NECK AND...
...SLIM SHOULDERS...
HEH
...THIS FAIR COMPLEXION...
TUG

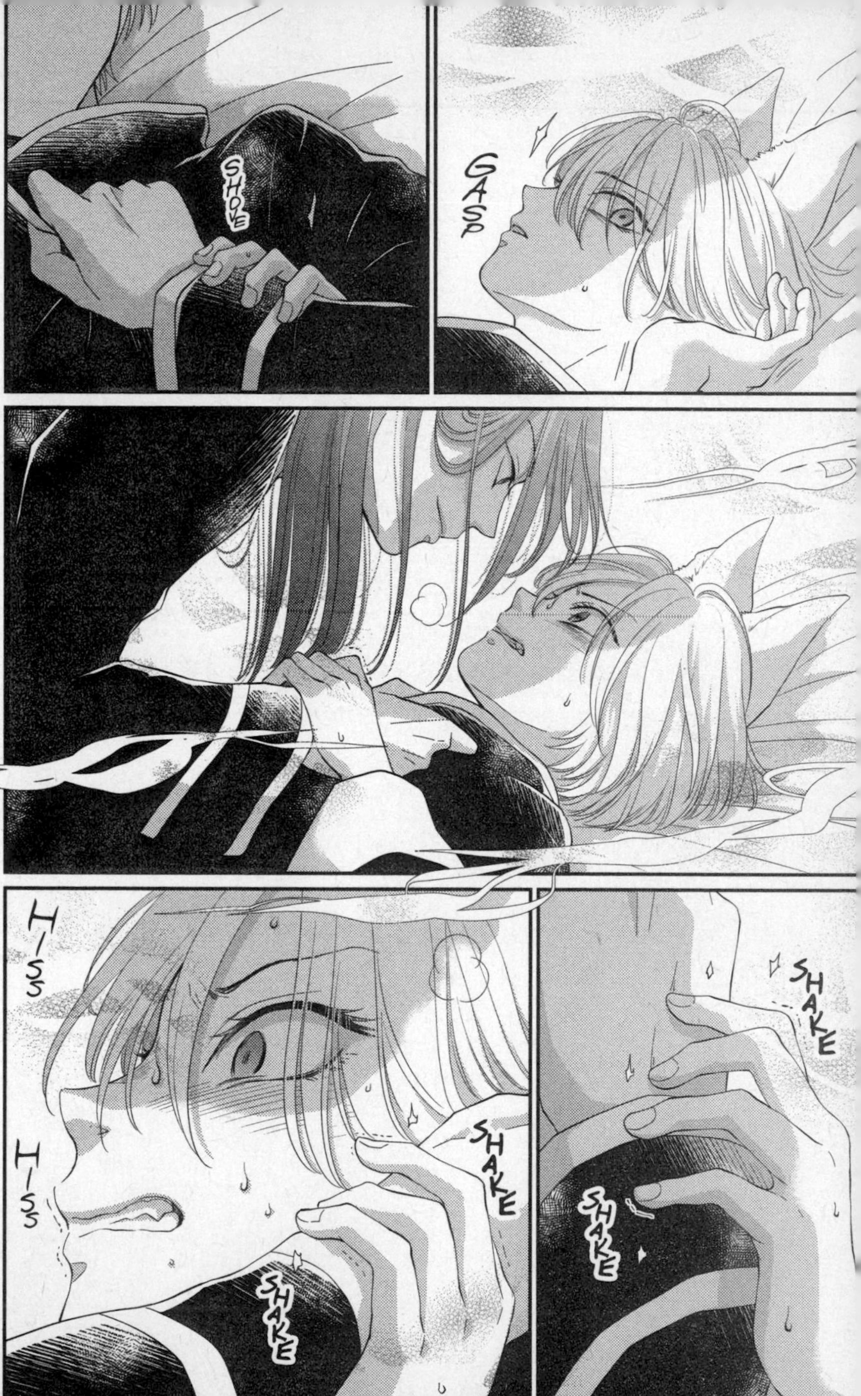
GASP
SHOVE
SHAKE
SHAKE
HISS
HISS
SHAKE
SHAKE

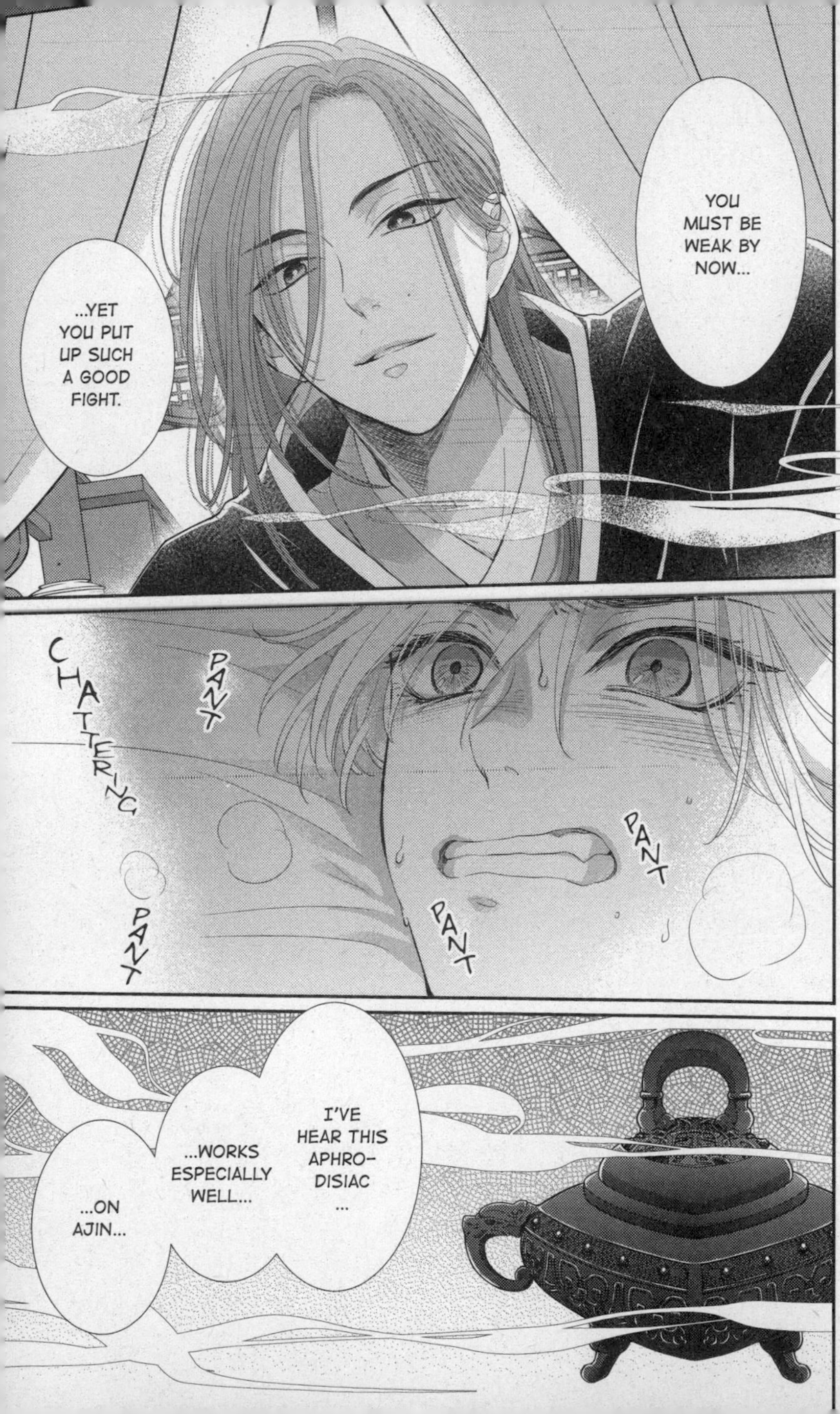
YOU MUST BE WEAK BY NOW...
...YET YOU PUT UP SUCH A GOOD FIGHT.
PANT
PANT
PANT
CHATTERING
PANT
I'VE HEAR THIS APHRO-DISIAC ...
...WORKS ESPECIALLY WELL...
...ON AJIN...

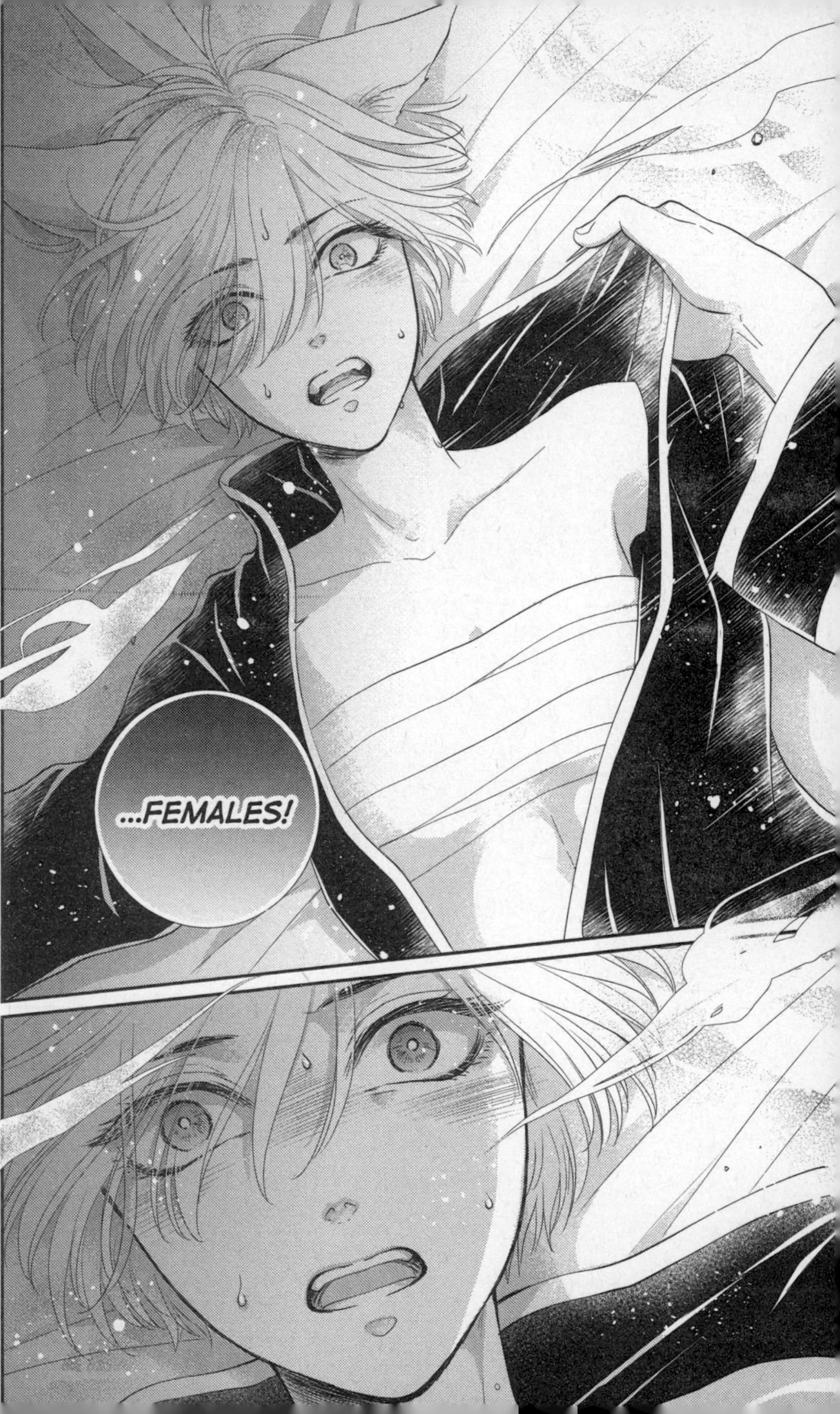
...FEMALES!

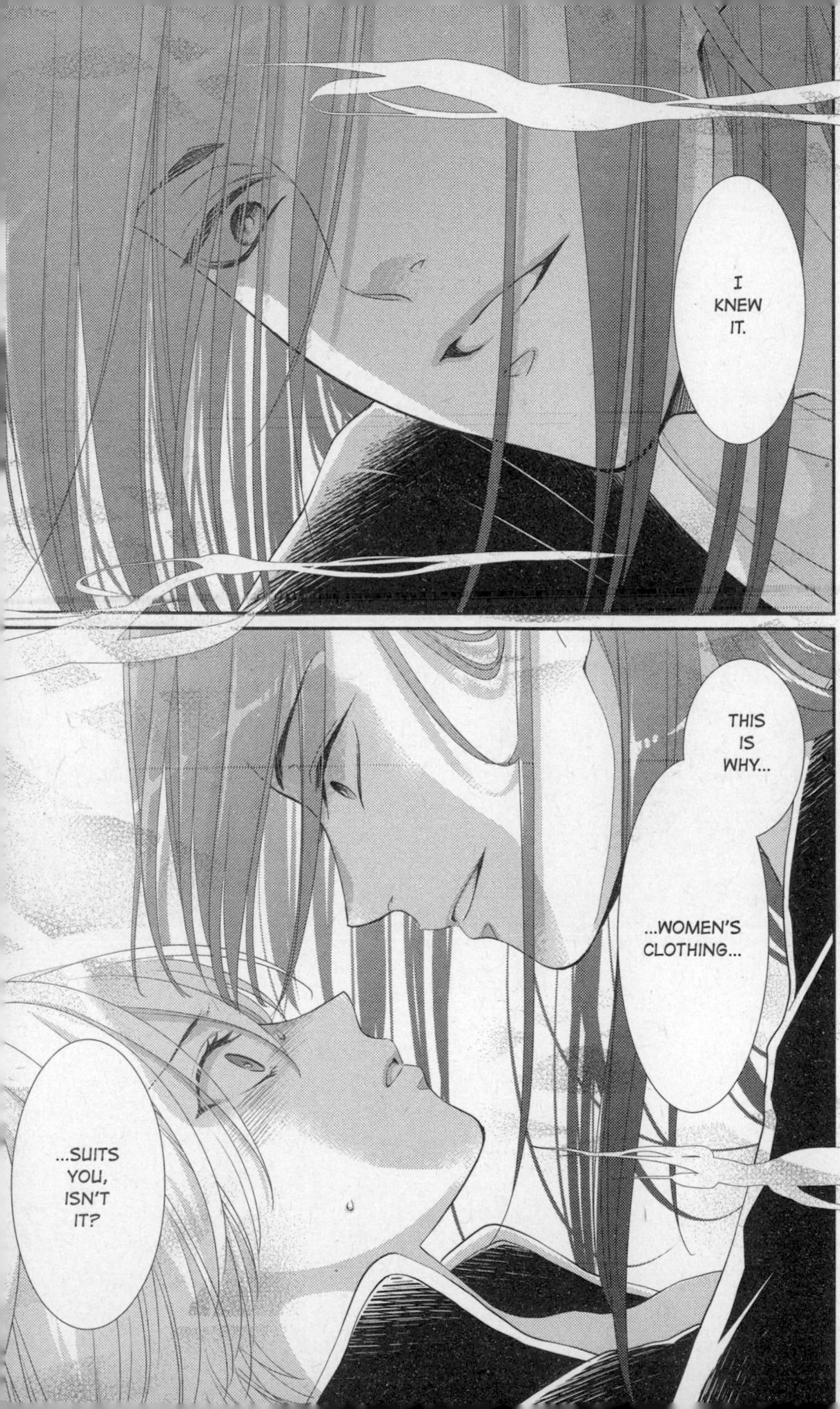
I KNEW IT.
THIS IS WHY...
...WOMEN'S CLOTHING...
...SUITS YOU, ISN'T IT?

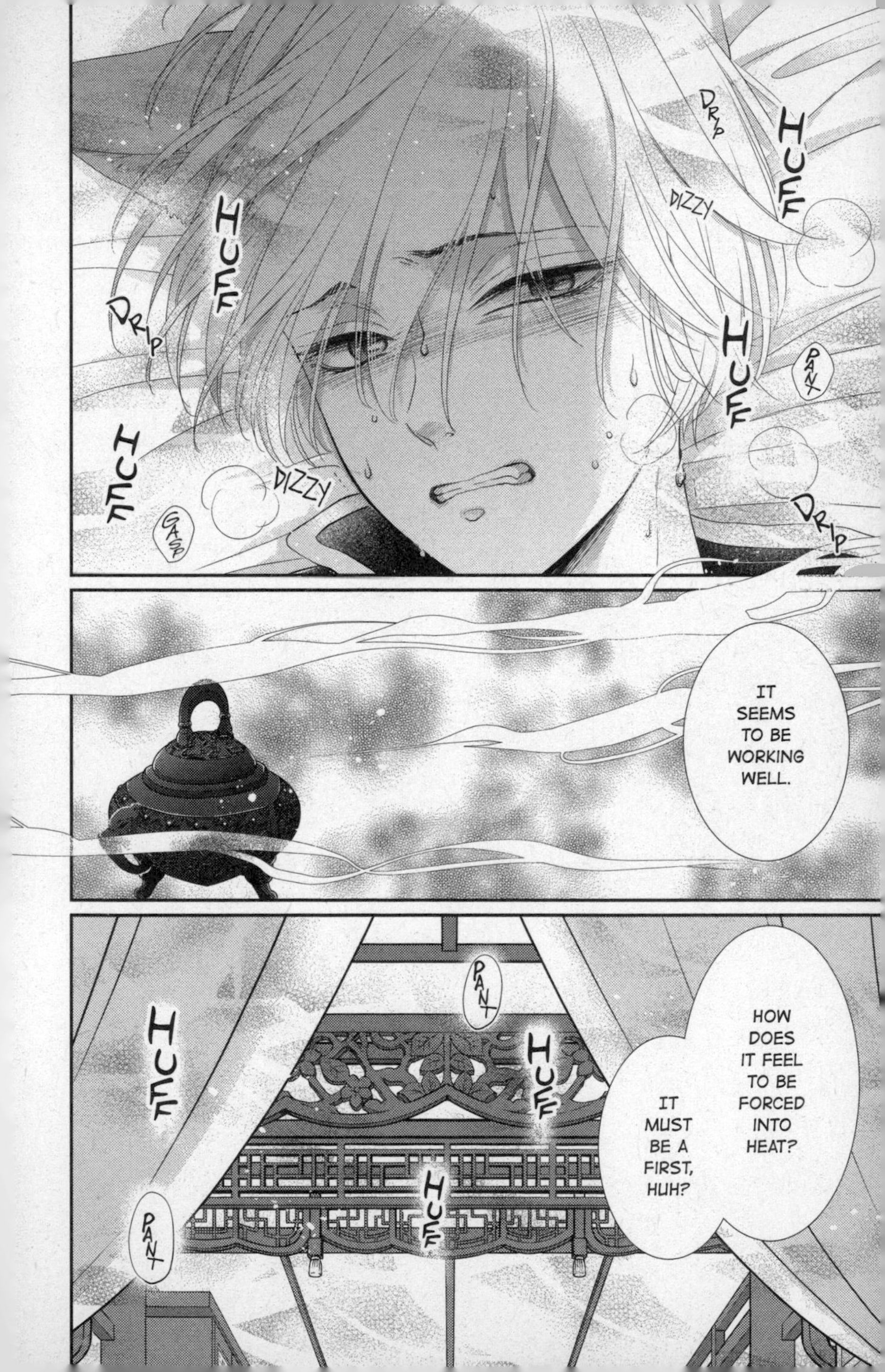
HUFF
DRIP
DIZZY
HUFF
PANT
DRIP
HUFF
DRIP
HUFF
DIZZY
GASP
IT SEEMS TO BE WORKING WELL.
HOW DOES IT FEEL TO BE FORCED INTO HEAT?
IT MUST BE A FIRST, HUH?
PANT
HUFF
HUFF
HUFF
PANT

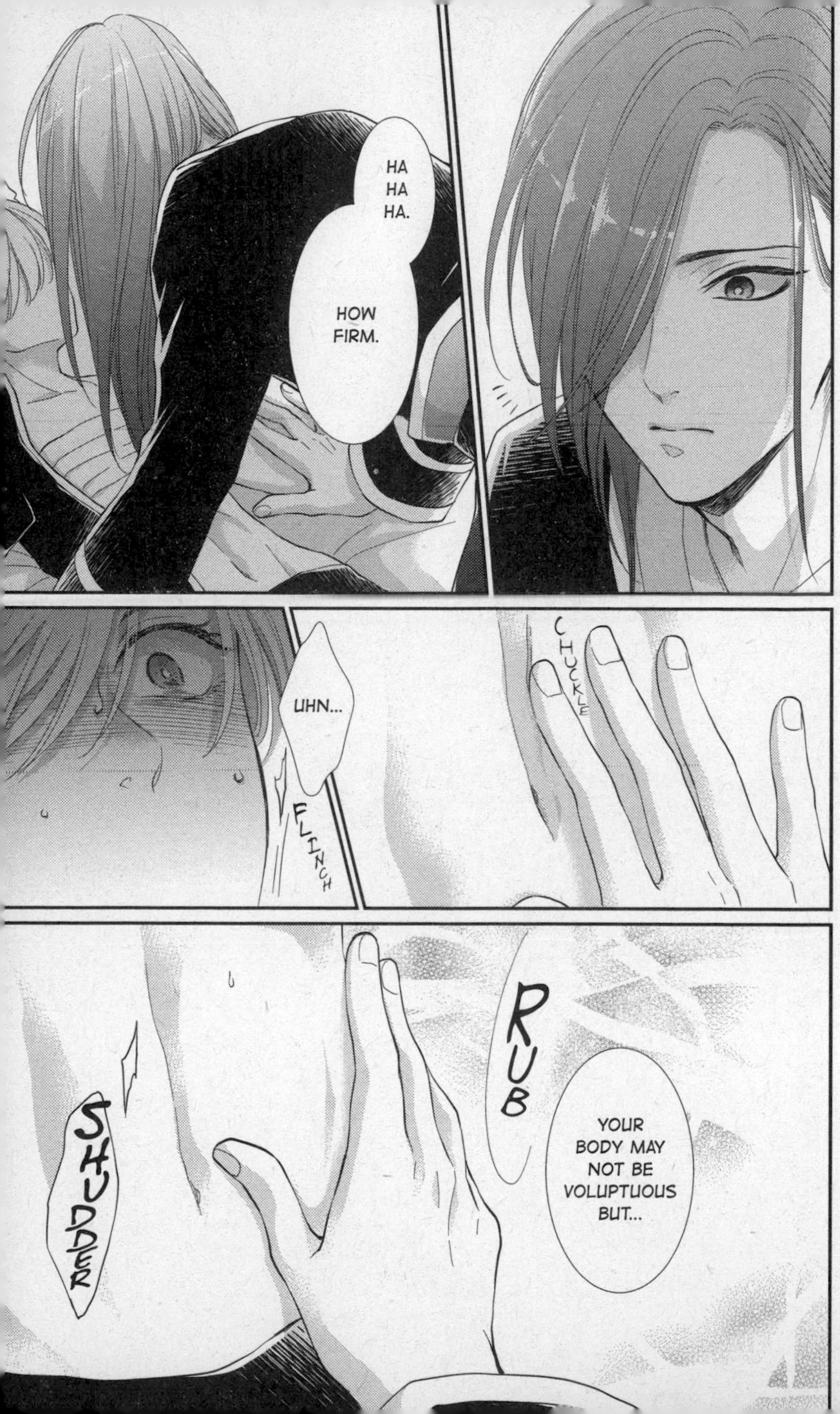
HA HA HA.
HOW FIRM.
CHUCKLE
UHN...
FLINCH
RUB
YOUR BODY MAY NOT BE VOLUPTUOUS BUT...
SHUDDER

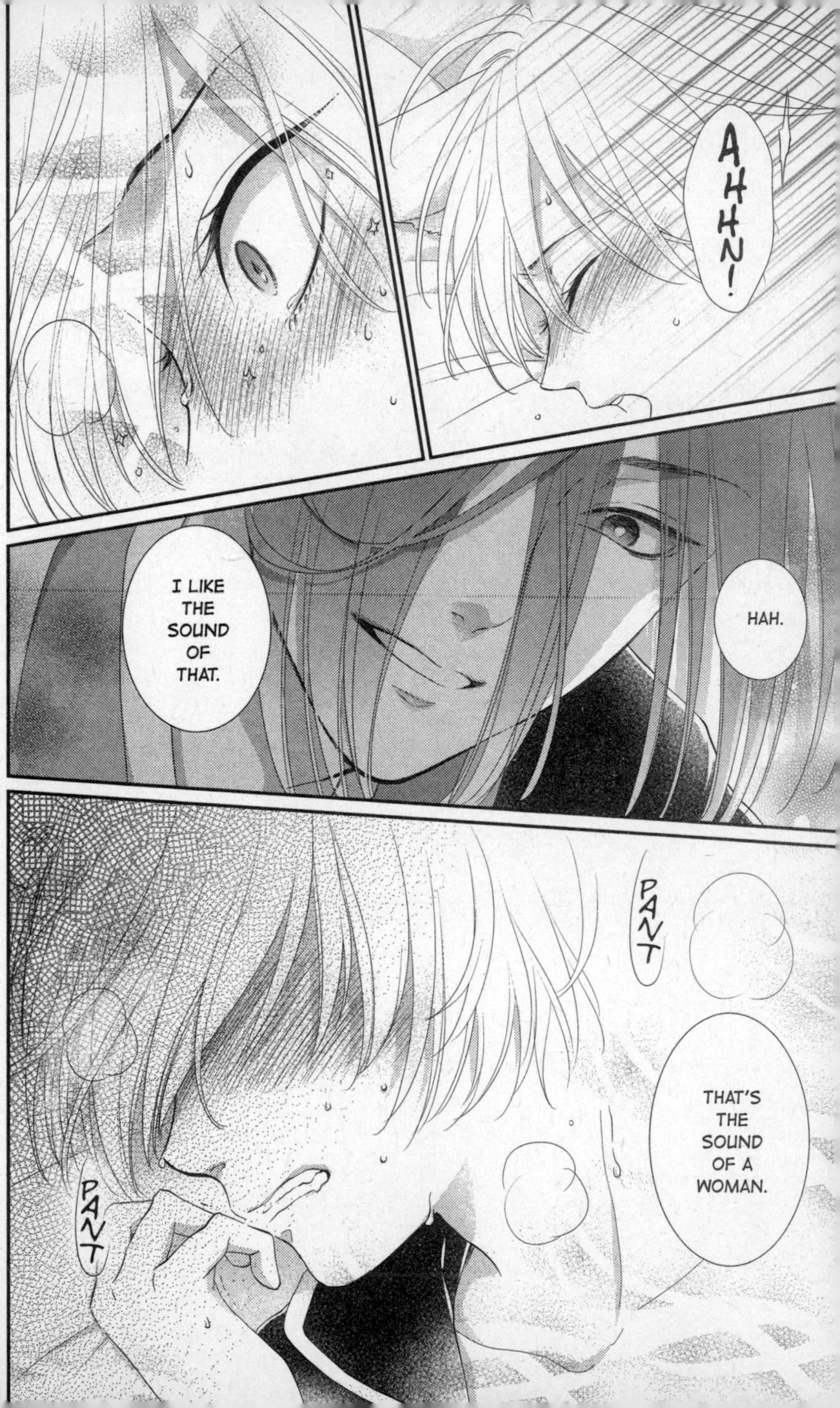
AHHN!
HAH.
I LIKE THE SOUND OF THAT.
PANT PANT
THAT'S THE SOUND OF A WOMAN.
PANT PANT

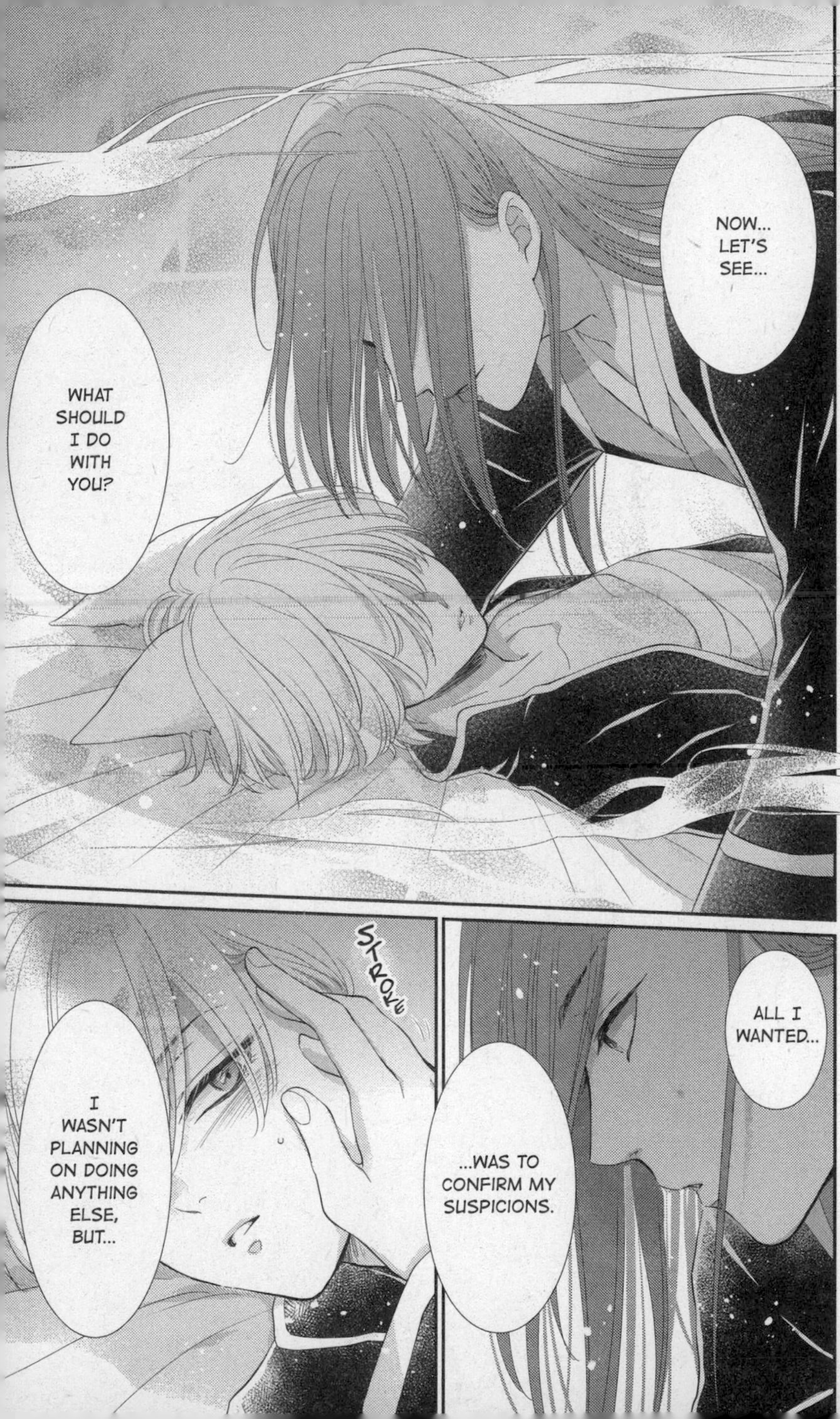
NOW... LET'S SEE...
WHAT SHOULD I DO WITH YOU?
ALL I WANTED...
...WAS TO CONFIRM MY SUSPICIONS.
STROKE
I WASN'T PLANNING ON DOING ANYTHING ELSE, BUT...

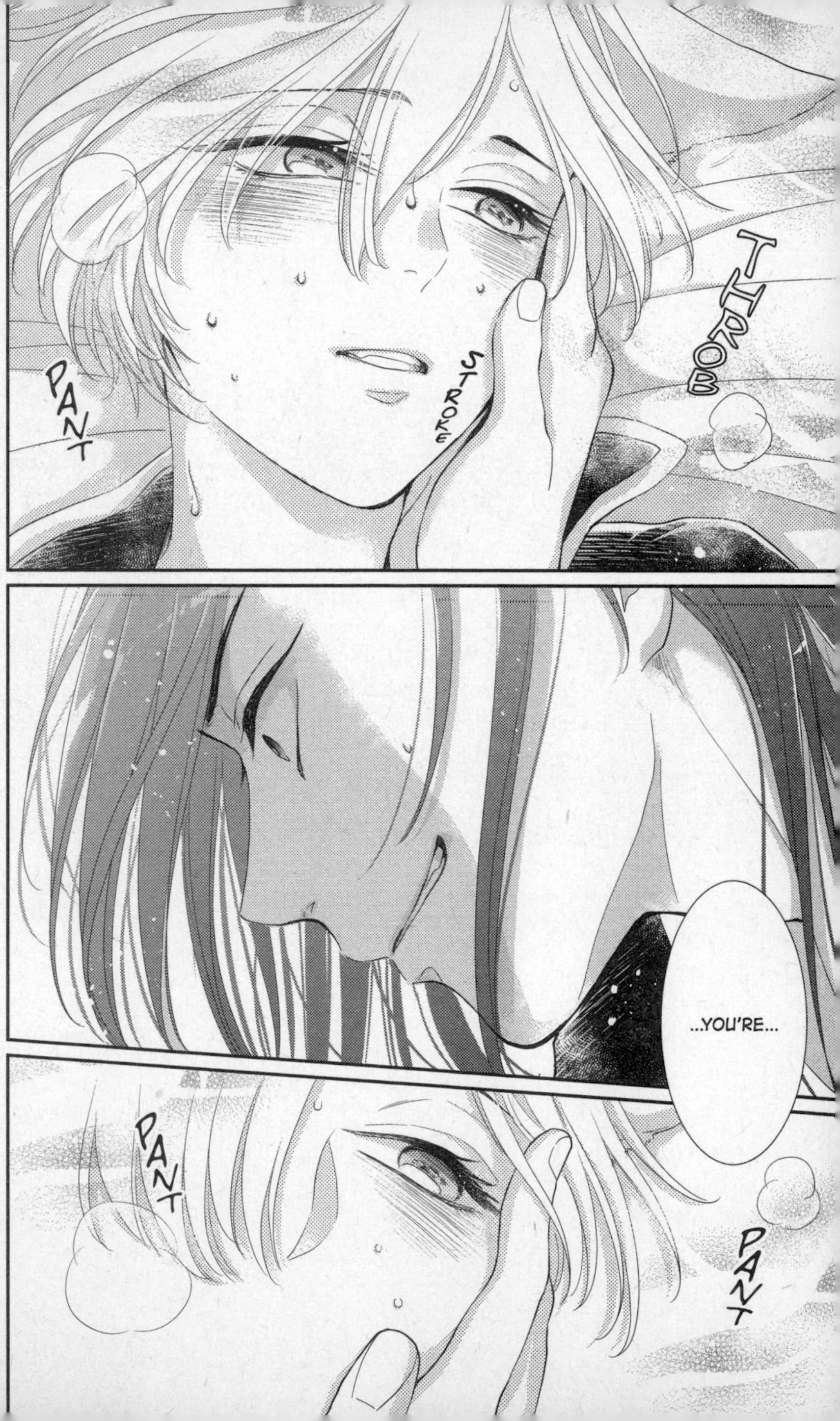
THROB
STROKE
PANT
...YOU'RE...
PANT
PANT

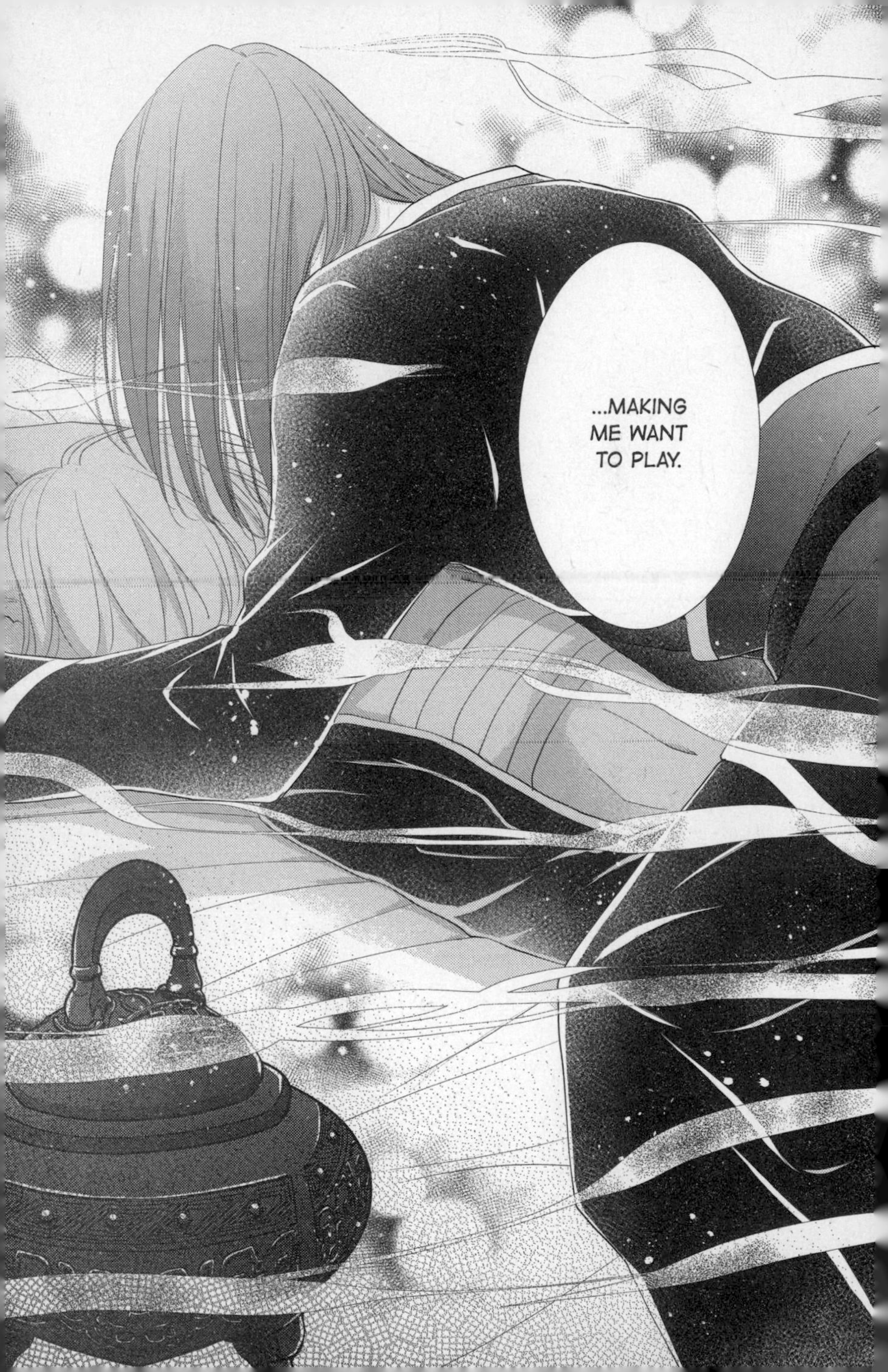
...MAKING ME WANT TO PLAY.

THE KING'S *Beast*

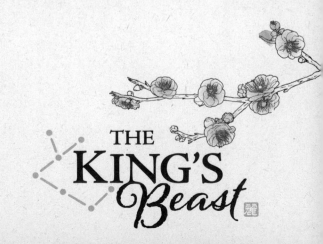

Chapter 21

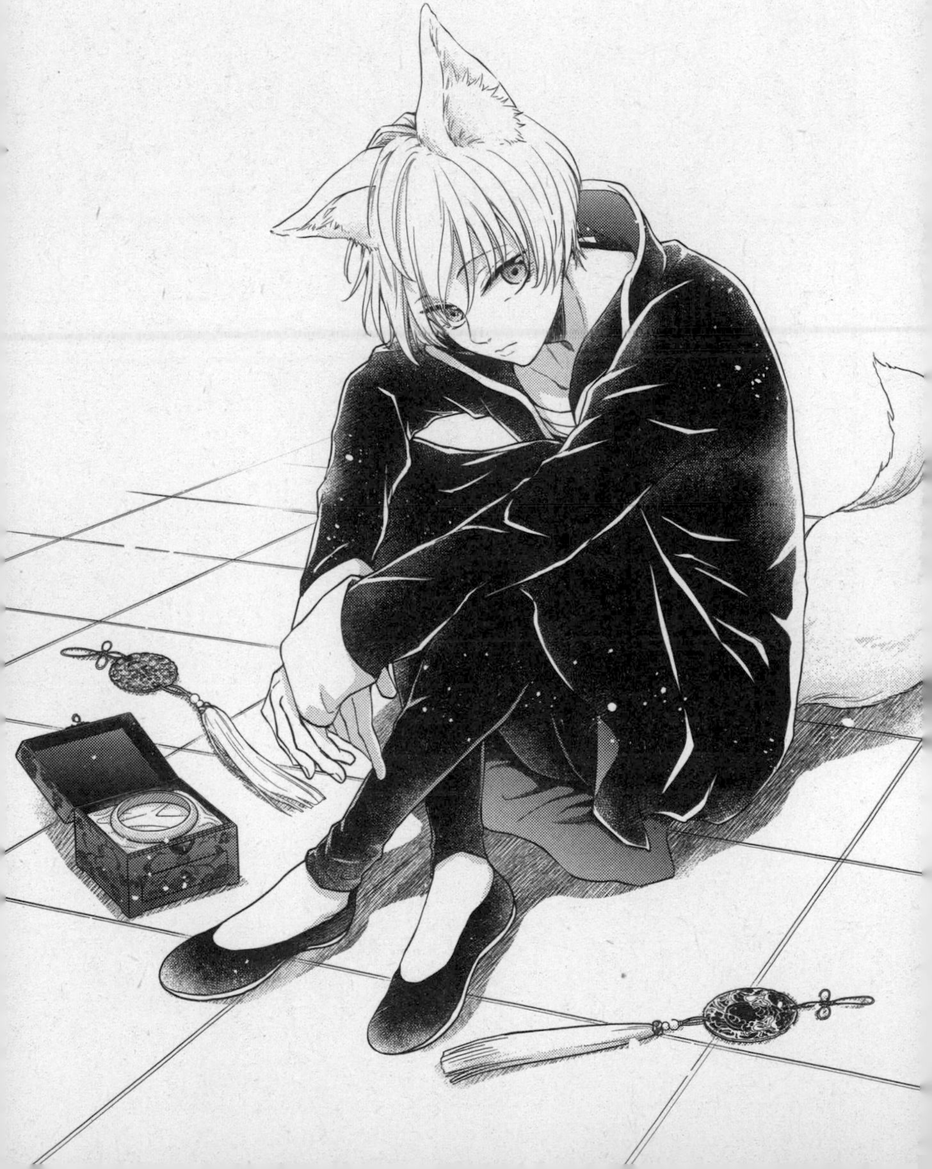

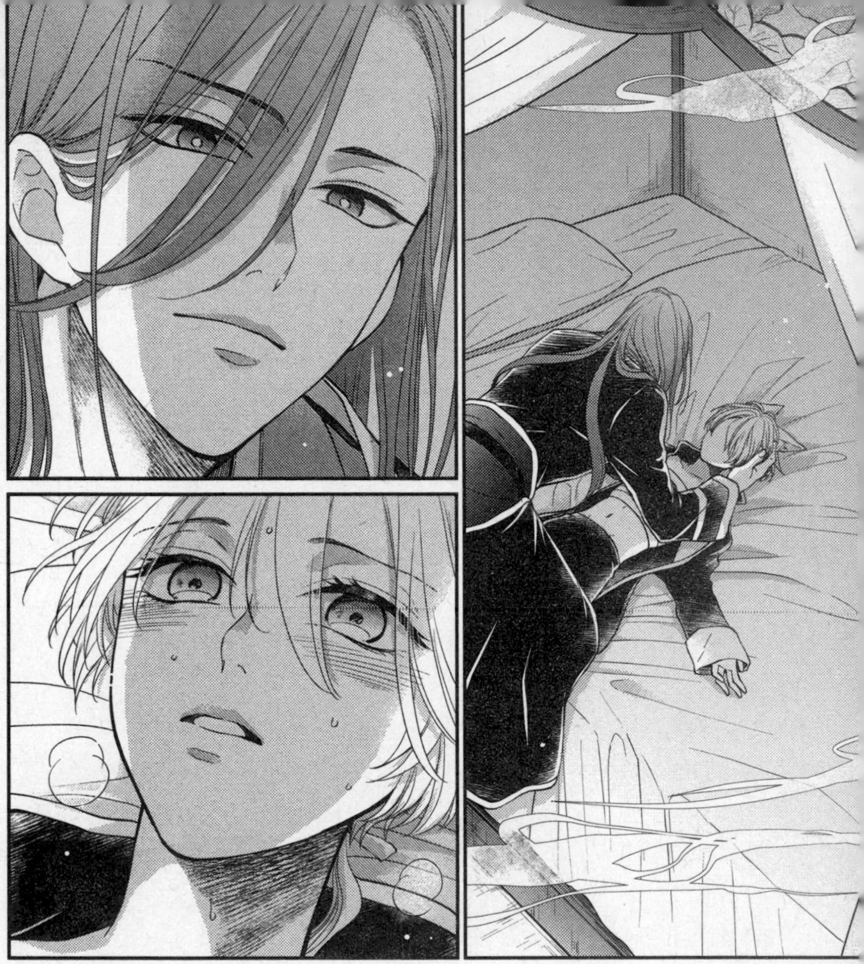

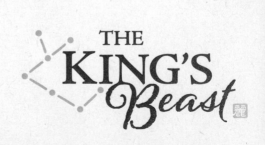

THE KING'S Beast

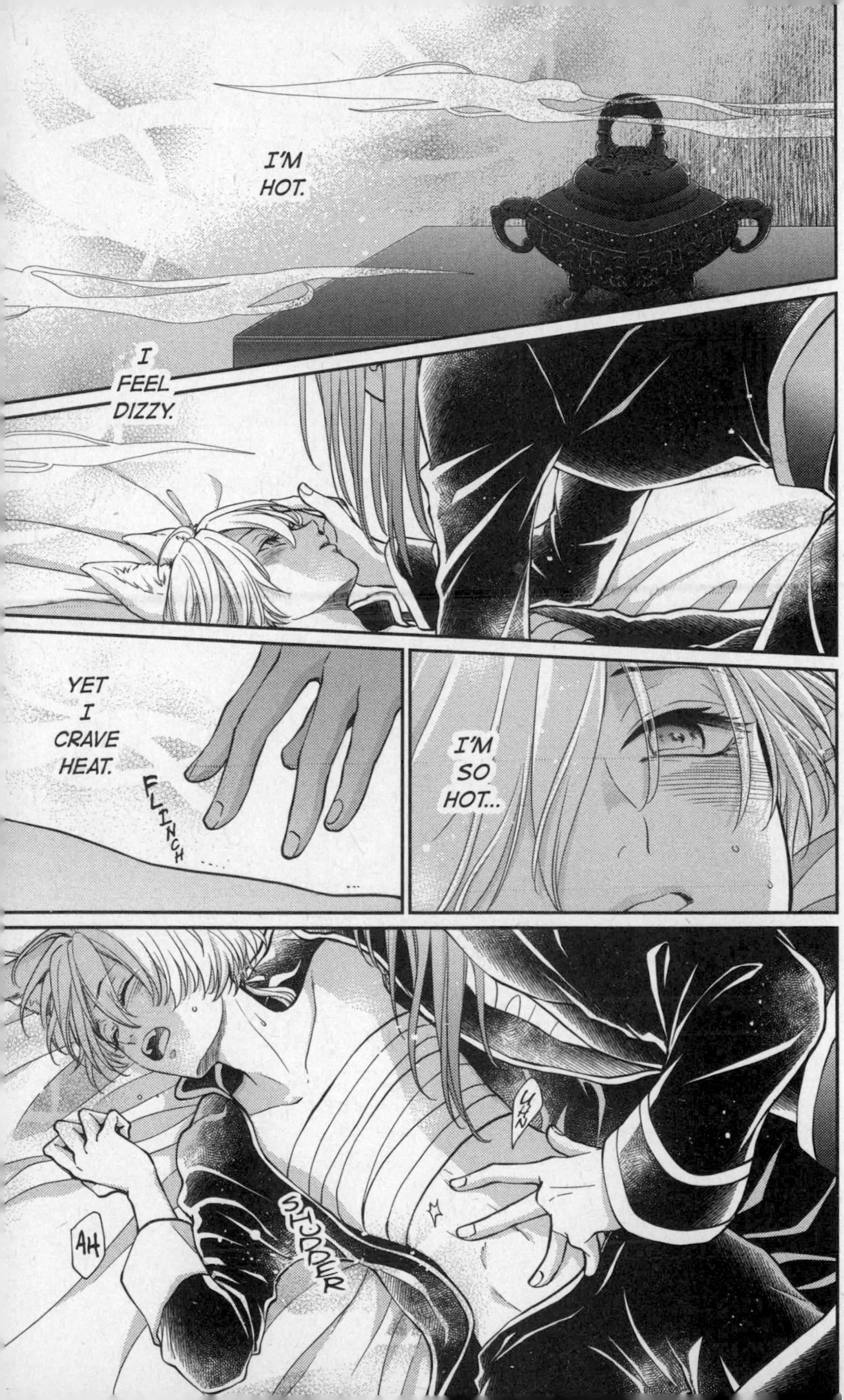
I'M HOT.
I FEEL DIZZY.
I'M SO HOT...
YET I CRAVE HEAT.
FLINCH
UHN
SHUDDER
AH

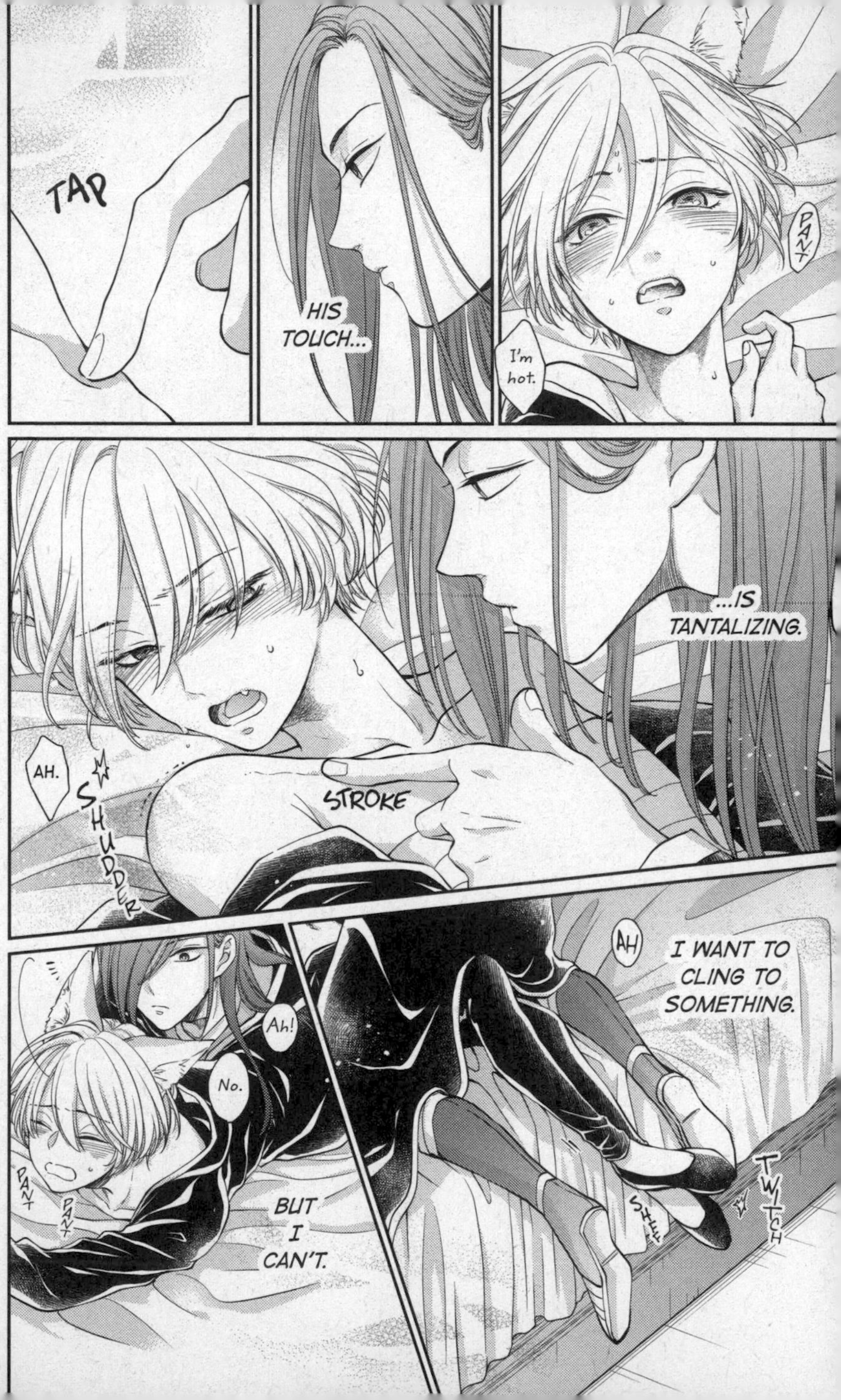
PANT
I'm hot.
HIS TOUCH...
TAP
...IS TANTALIZING.
STROKE
AH.
SHUDDER
I WANT TO CLING TO SOMETHING.
AH
TWITCH
SHFF
Ah!
No.
BUT I CAN'T.
PANT
PANT

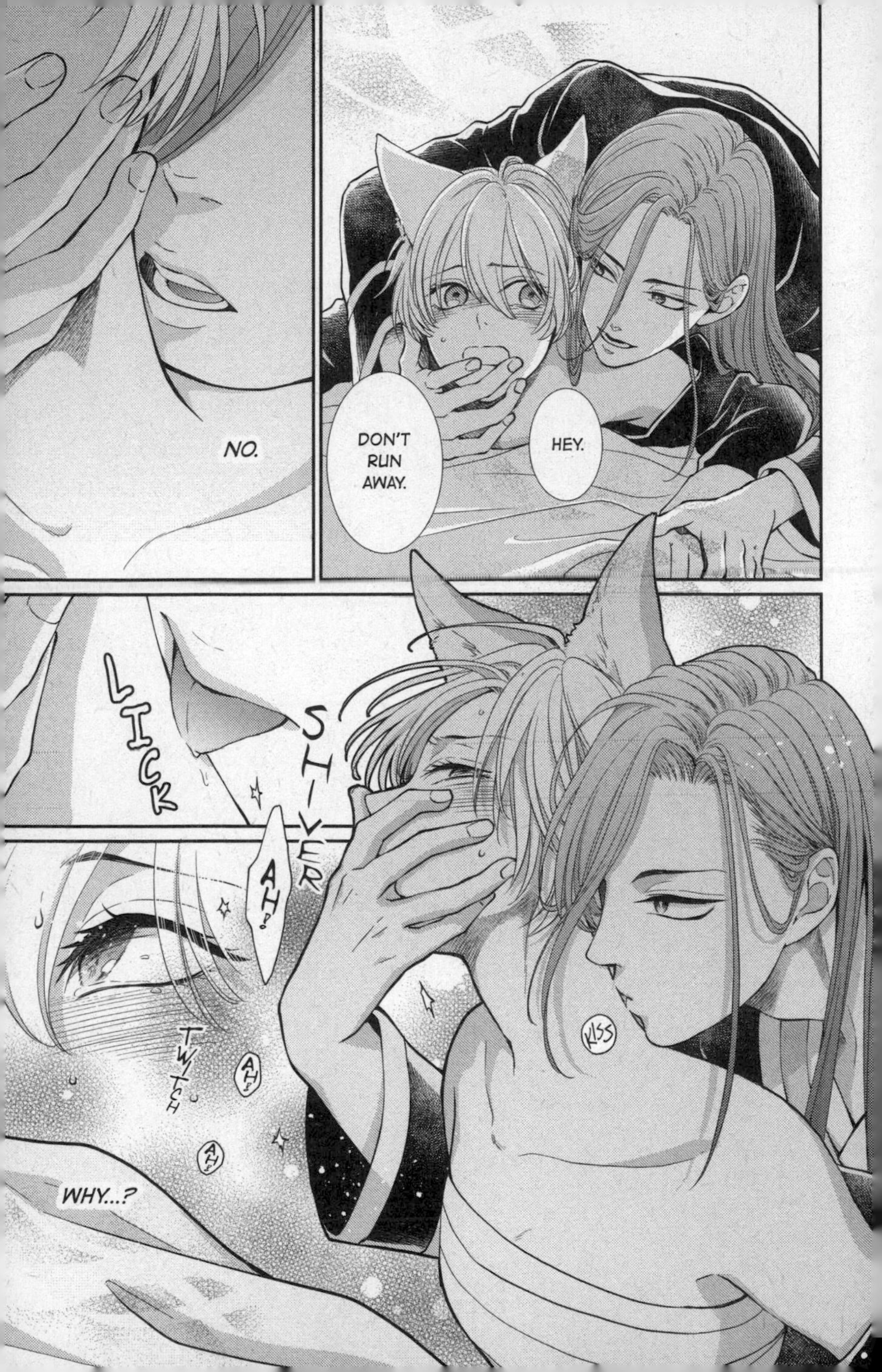
HEY.
DON'T RUN AWAY.
NO.
KISS
SHIVER
LICK
AH!
TWITCH
AH
AH
WHY...?

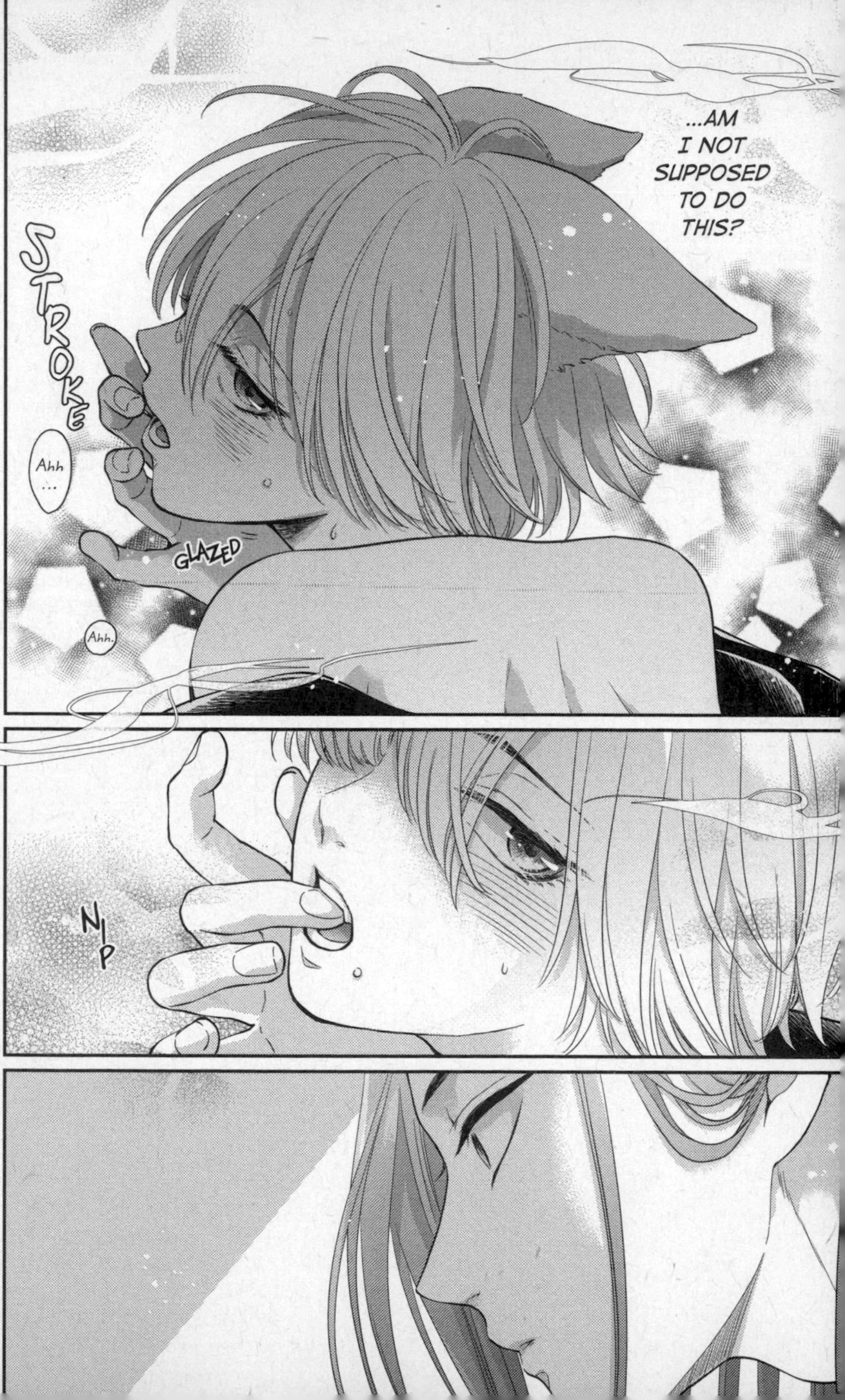

...AM I NOT SUPPOSED TO DO THIS?
STROKE
Ahh...
GLAZED
Ahh.
NIP

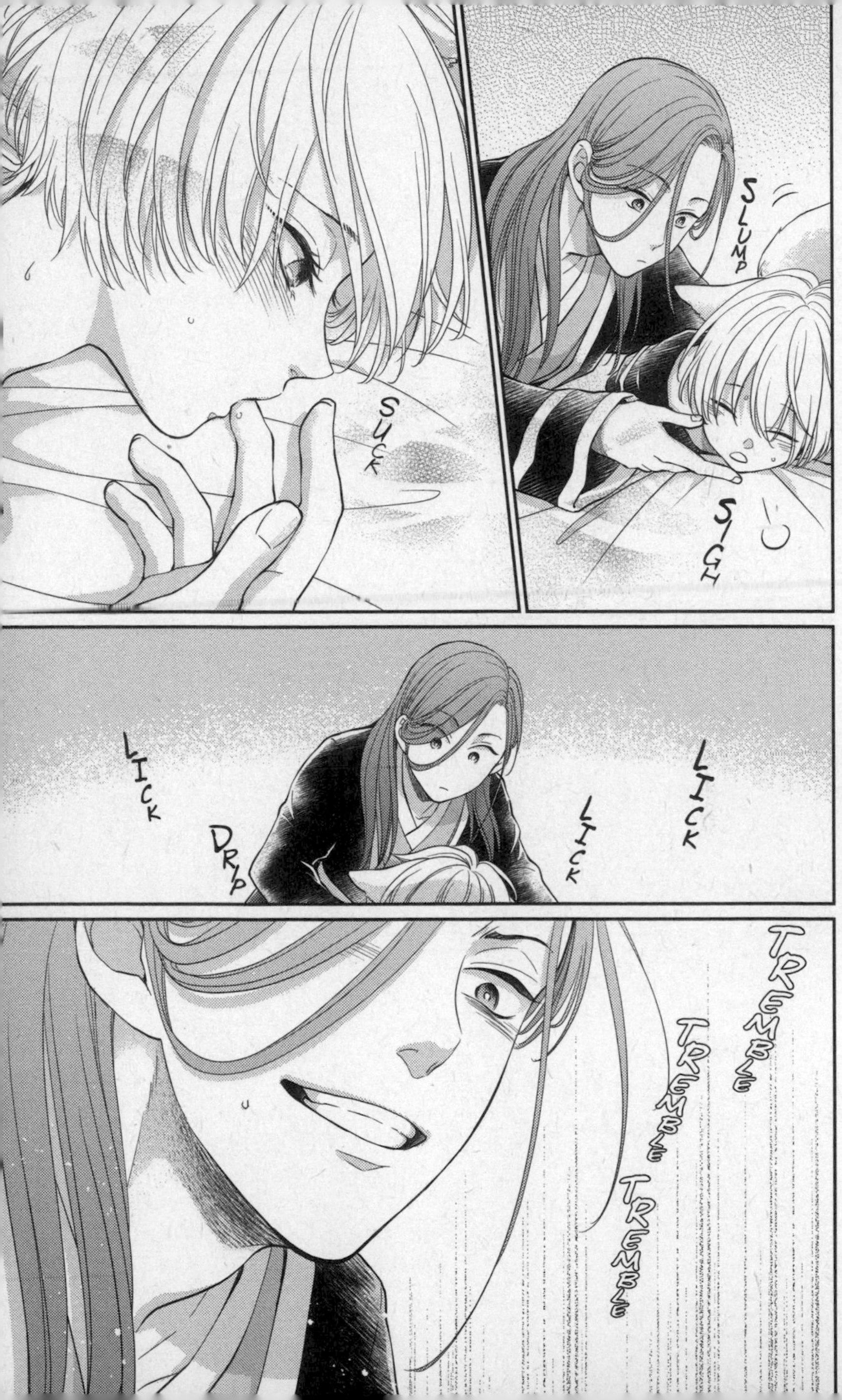
SLUMP
SIGH
SUCK
LICK
LICK
LICK
DRIP
TREMBLE
TREMBLE
TREMBLE

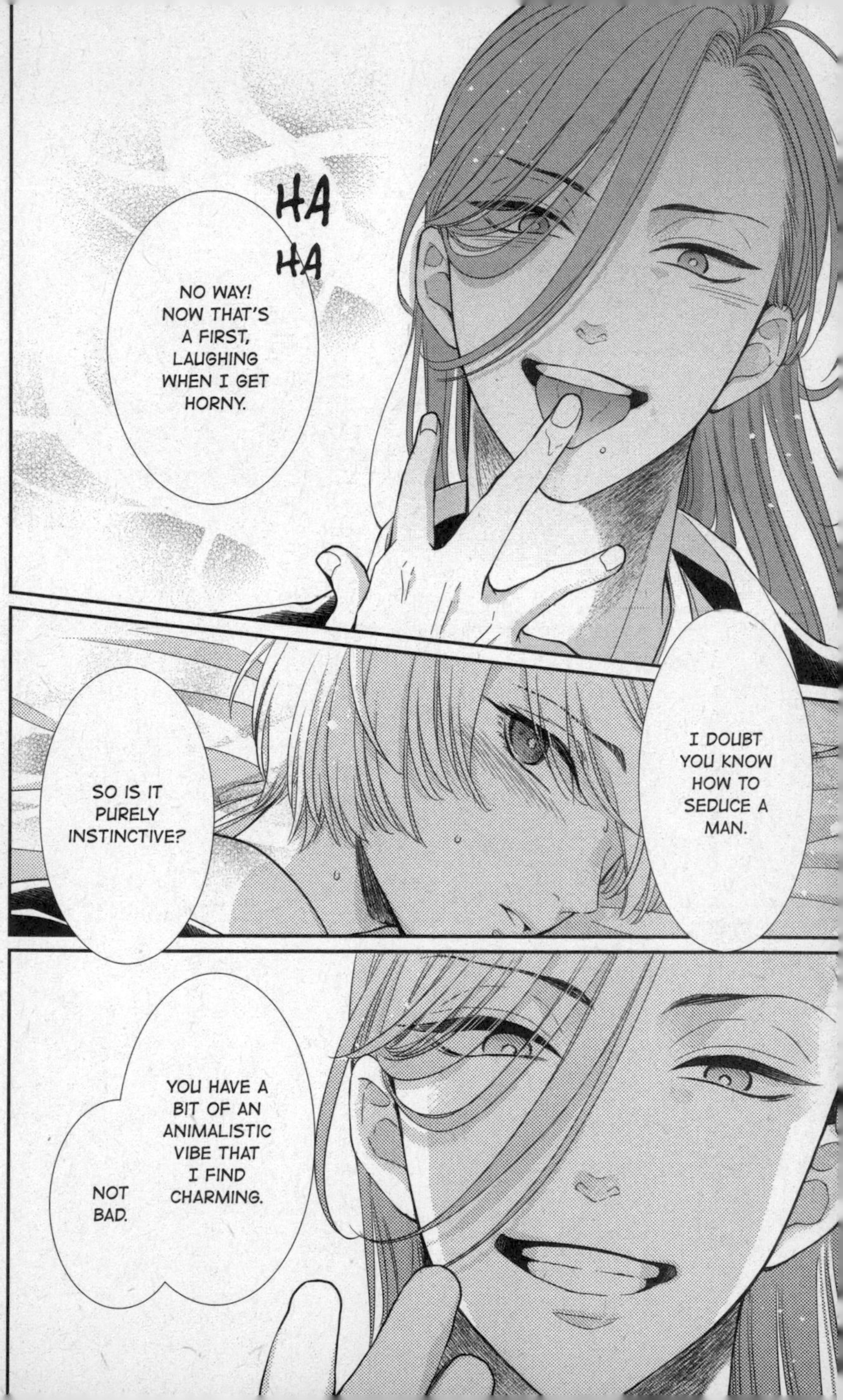
HA HA
NO WAY! NOW THAT'S A FIRST, LAUGHING WHEN I GET HORNY.
I DOUBT YOU KNOW HOW TO SEDUCE A MAN.
SO IS IT PURELY INSTINCTIVE?
YOU HAVE A BIT OF AN ANIMALISTIC VIBE THAT I FIND CHARMING.
NOT BAD.

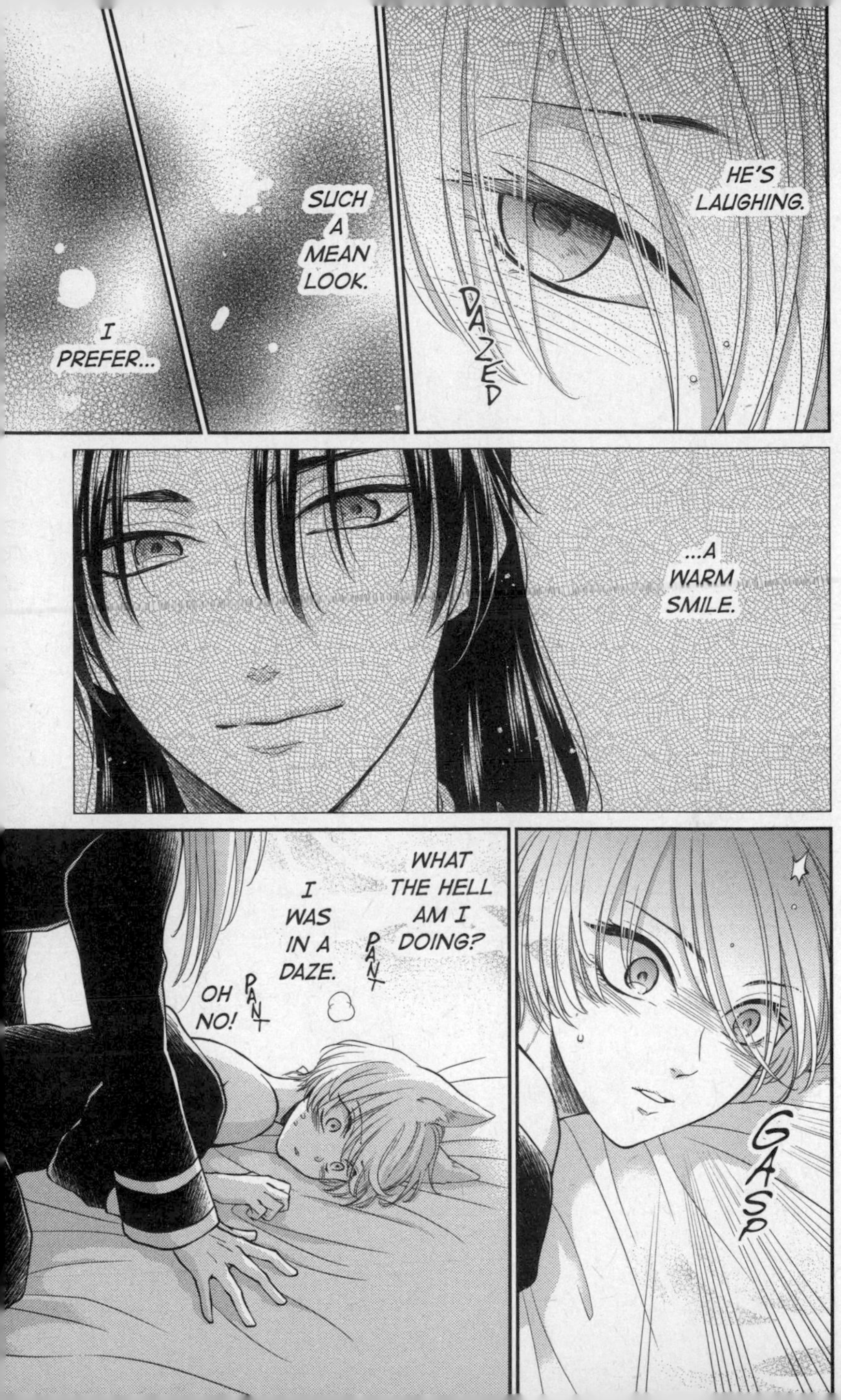
HE'S LAUGHING.
DAZED
SUCH A MEAN LOOK.
I PREFER...
...A WARM SMILE.
GASP
WHAT THE HELL AM I DOING?
I WAS IN A DAZE.
PANT
PANT
OH NO!

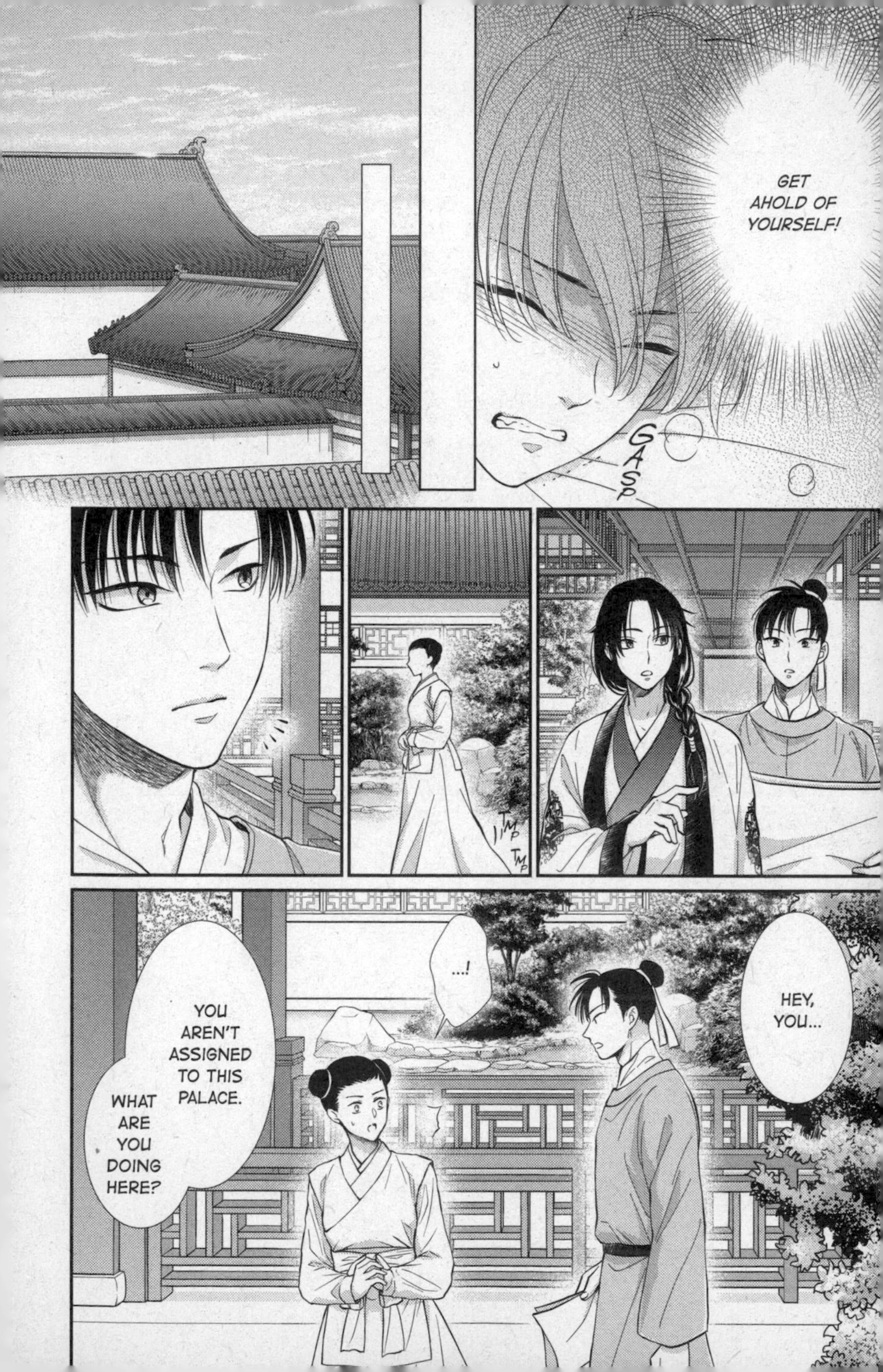
GET AHOLD OF YOURSELF!
GASP
TMP TMP
HEY, YOU...
...!
YOU AREN'T ASSIGNED TO THIS PALACE.
WHAT ARE YOU DOING HERE?

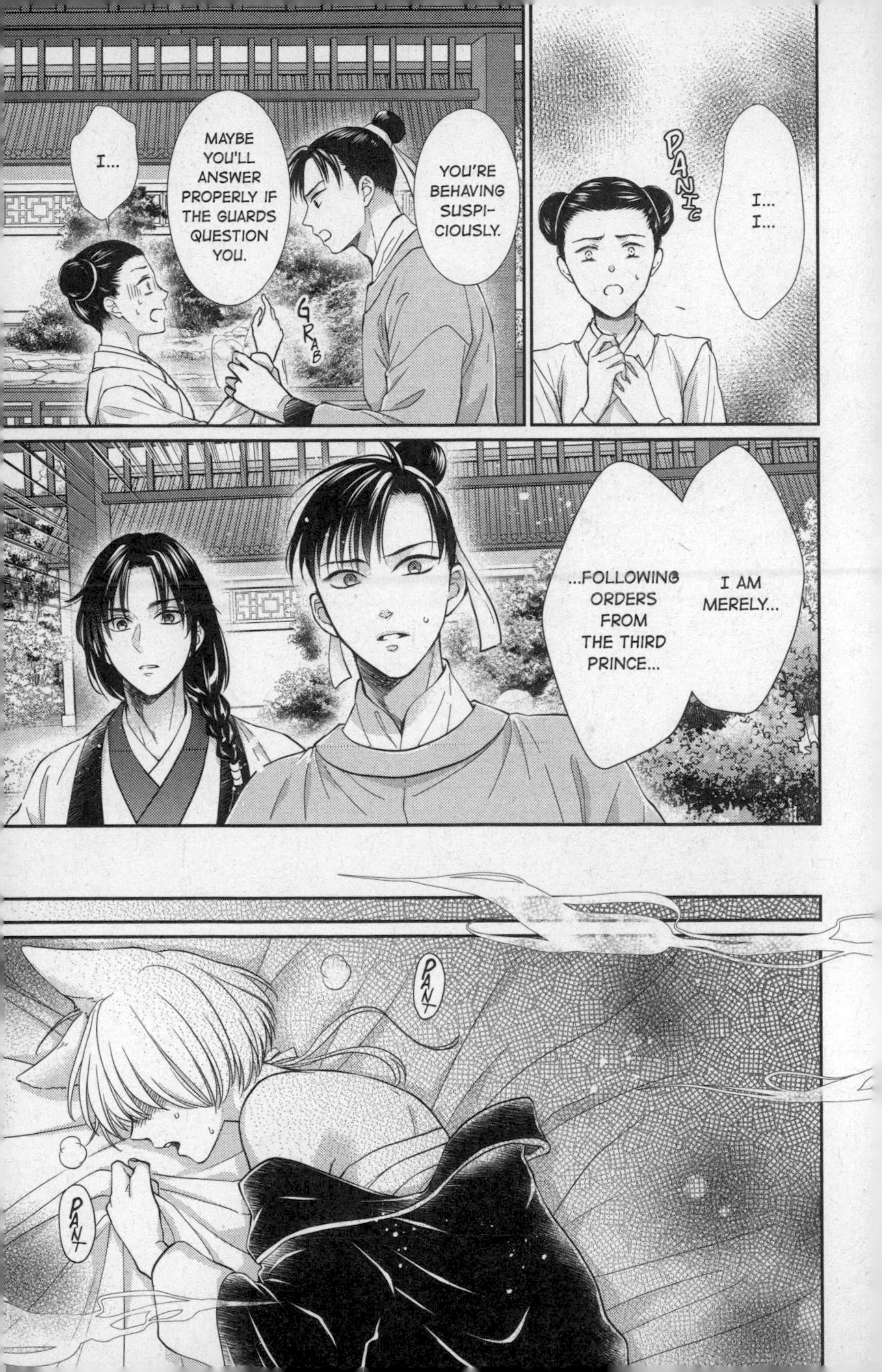
PANIC
I... I...
YOU'RE BEHAVING SUSPICIOUSLY.
MAYBE YOU'LL ANSWER PROPERLY IF THE GUARDS QUESTION YOU.
GRAB
I...
I AM MERELY...
...FOLLOWING ORDERS FROM THE THIRD PRINCE...
PANT
PANT

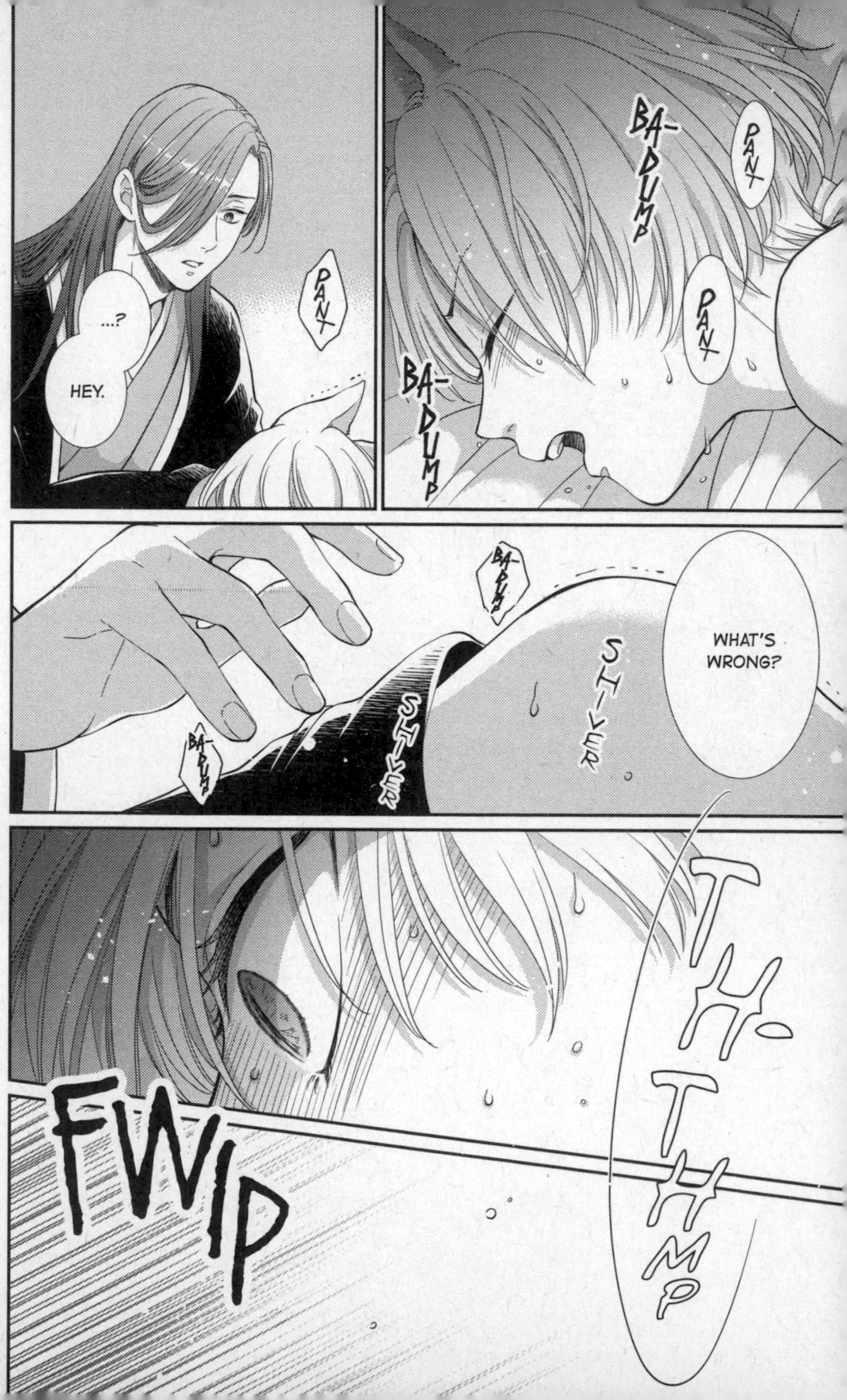
PANT
BA-DUMP
PANT
BA-DUMP
PANT
...?
HEY.
WHAT'S WRONG?
BA-DUMP
SHIVER
SHIVER
BA-DUMP
THUMP
THUMP
FWIP

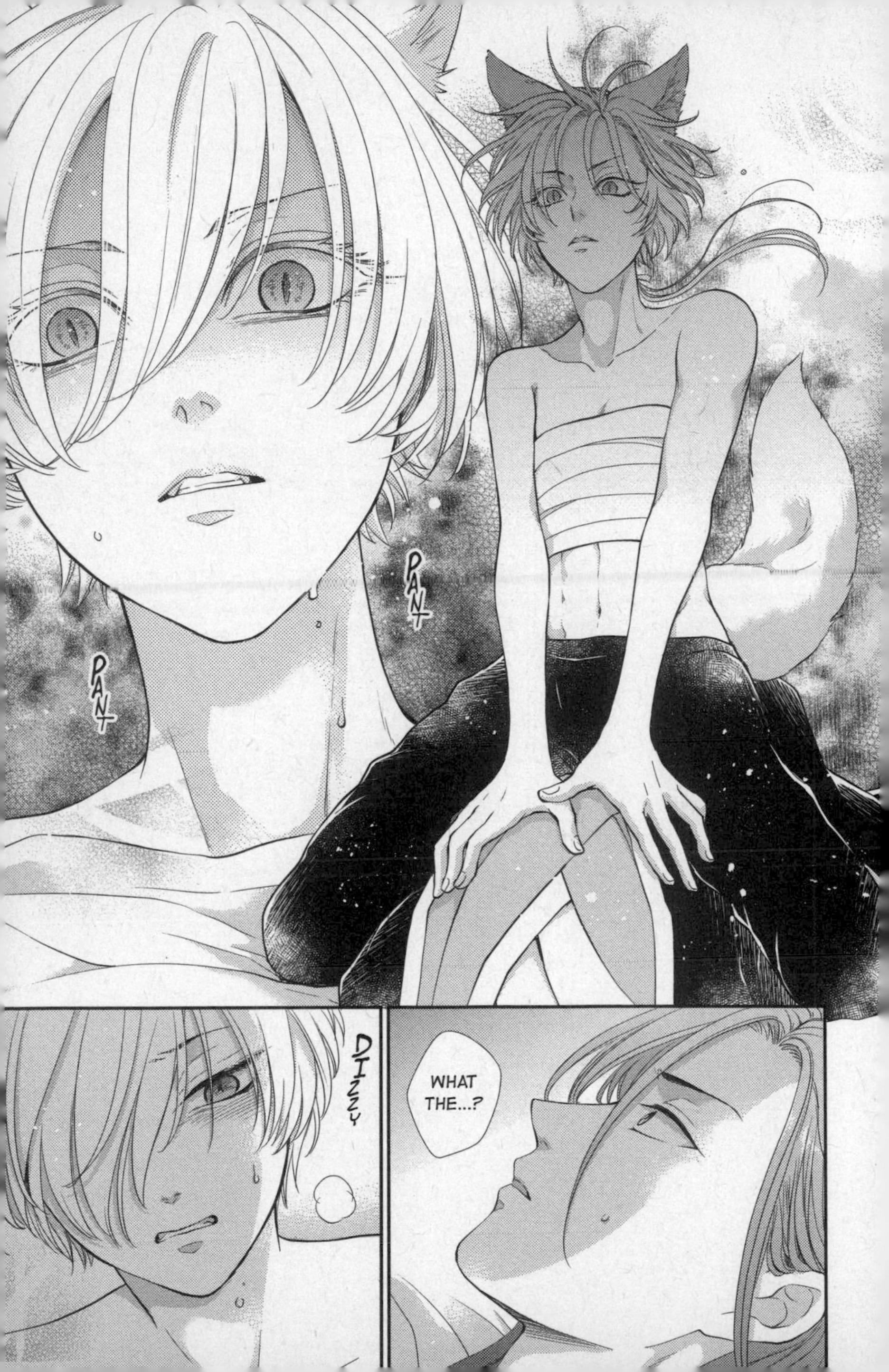
PANT
PANT
WHAT THE...?
DIZZY

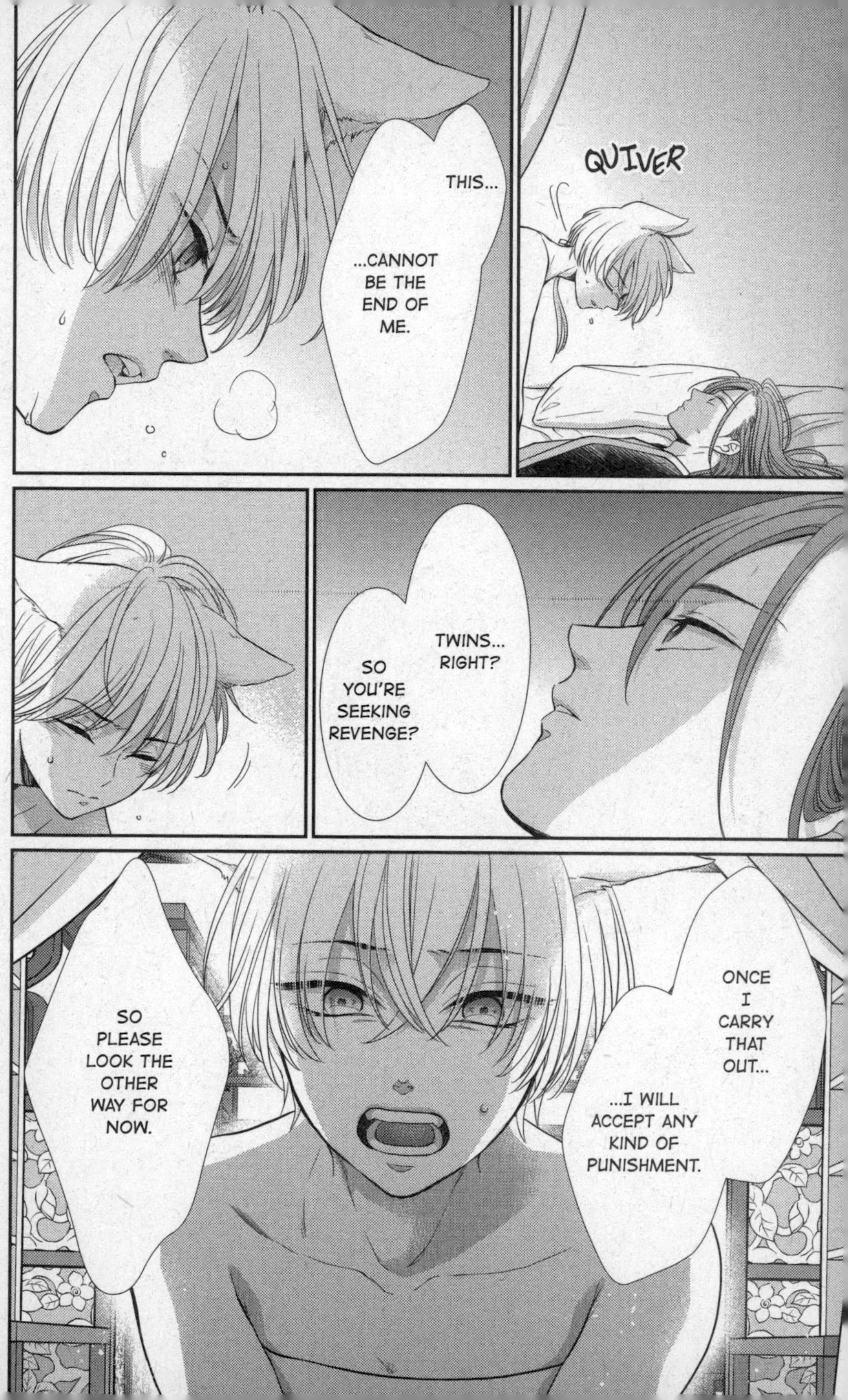
QUIVER
THIS...
...CANNOT BE THE END OF ME.
TWINS... RIGHT?
SO YOU'RE SEEKING REVENGE?
ONCE I CARRY THAT OUT...
...I WILL ACCEPT ANY KIND OF PUNISHMENT.
SO PLEASE LOOK THE OTHER WAY FOR NOW.

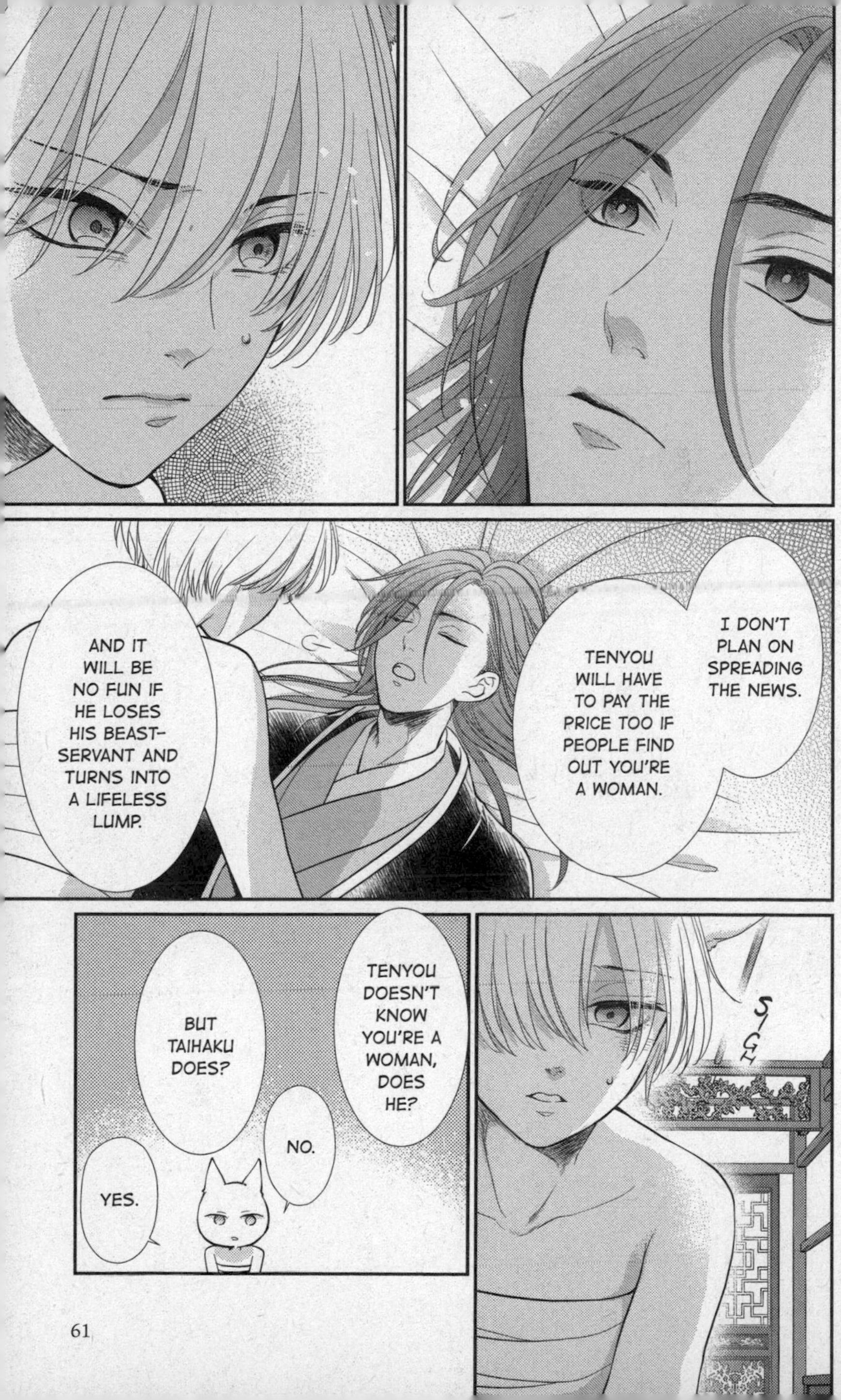
I DON'T PLAN ON SPREADING THE NEWS.
TENYOU WILL HAVE TO PAY THE PRICE TOO IF PEOPLE FIND OUT YOU'RE A WOMAN.
AND IT WILL BE NO FUN IF HE LOSES HIS BEAST-SERVANT AND TURNS INTO A LIFELESS LUMP.
SIGH
TENYOU DOESN'T KNOW YOU'RE A WOMAN, DOES HE?
BUT TAIHAKU DOES?
NO.
YES.

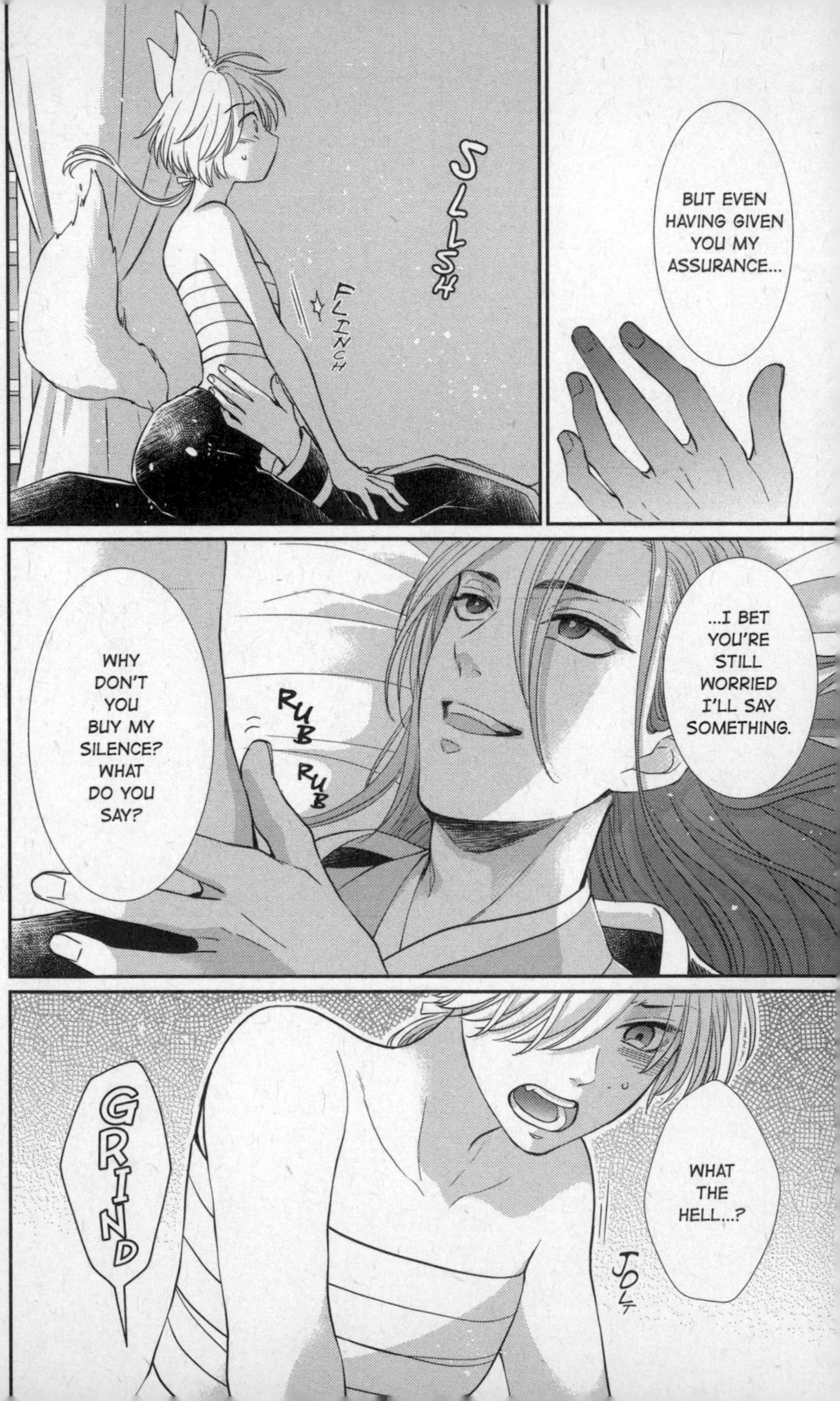
BUT EVEN HAVING GIVEN YOU MY ASSURANCE...
SLLSH
FLINCH
...I BET YOU'RE STILL WORRIED I'LL SAY SOMETHING.
RUB RUB
WHY DON'T YOU BUY MY SILENCE? WHAT DO YOU SAY?
WHAT THE HELL...?
JOLT
GRIND

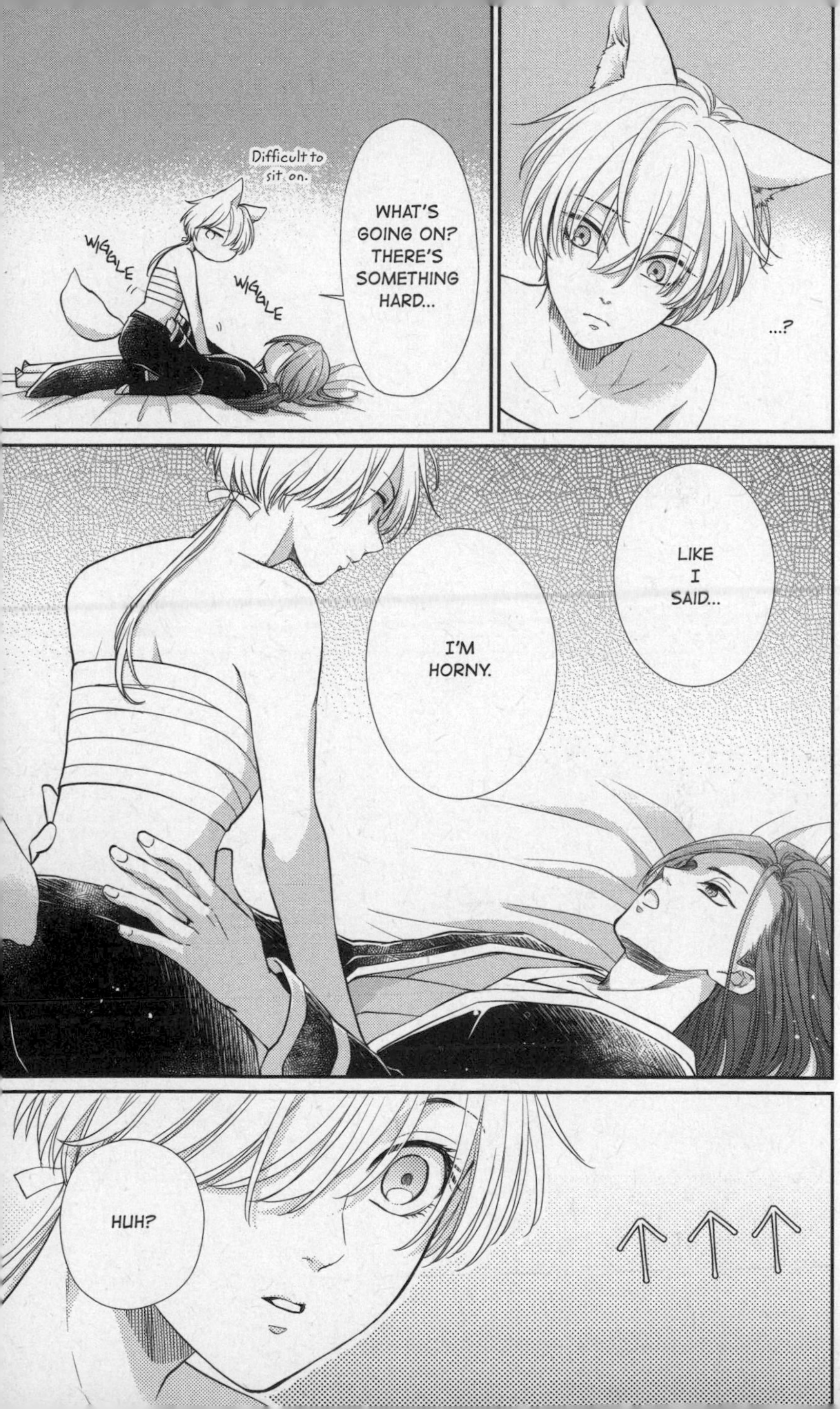
...?
WHAT'S GOING ON? THERE'S SOMETHING HARD...
Difficult to sit on.
WIGGLE
WIGGLE
LIKE I SAID...
I'M HORNY.
HUH?

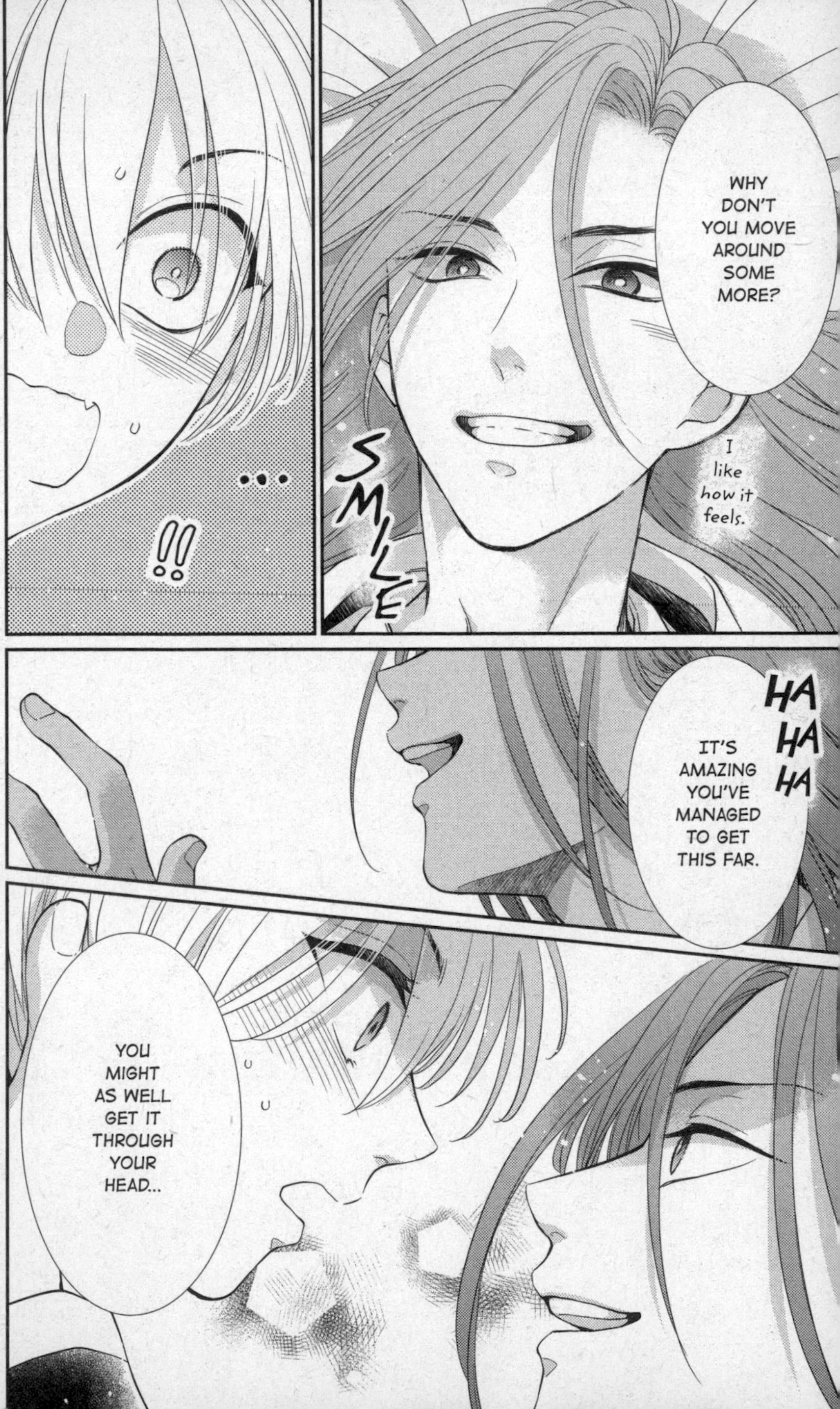
WHY DON'T YOU MOVE AROUND SOME MORE?
I like how it feels.
SMILE
...
!!
HA HA HA
IT'S AMAZING YOU'VE MANAGED TO GET THIS FAR.
YOU MIGHT AS WELL GET IT THROUGH YOUR HEAD...

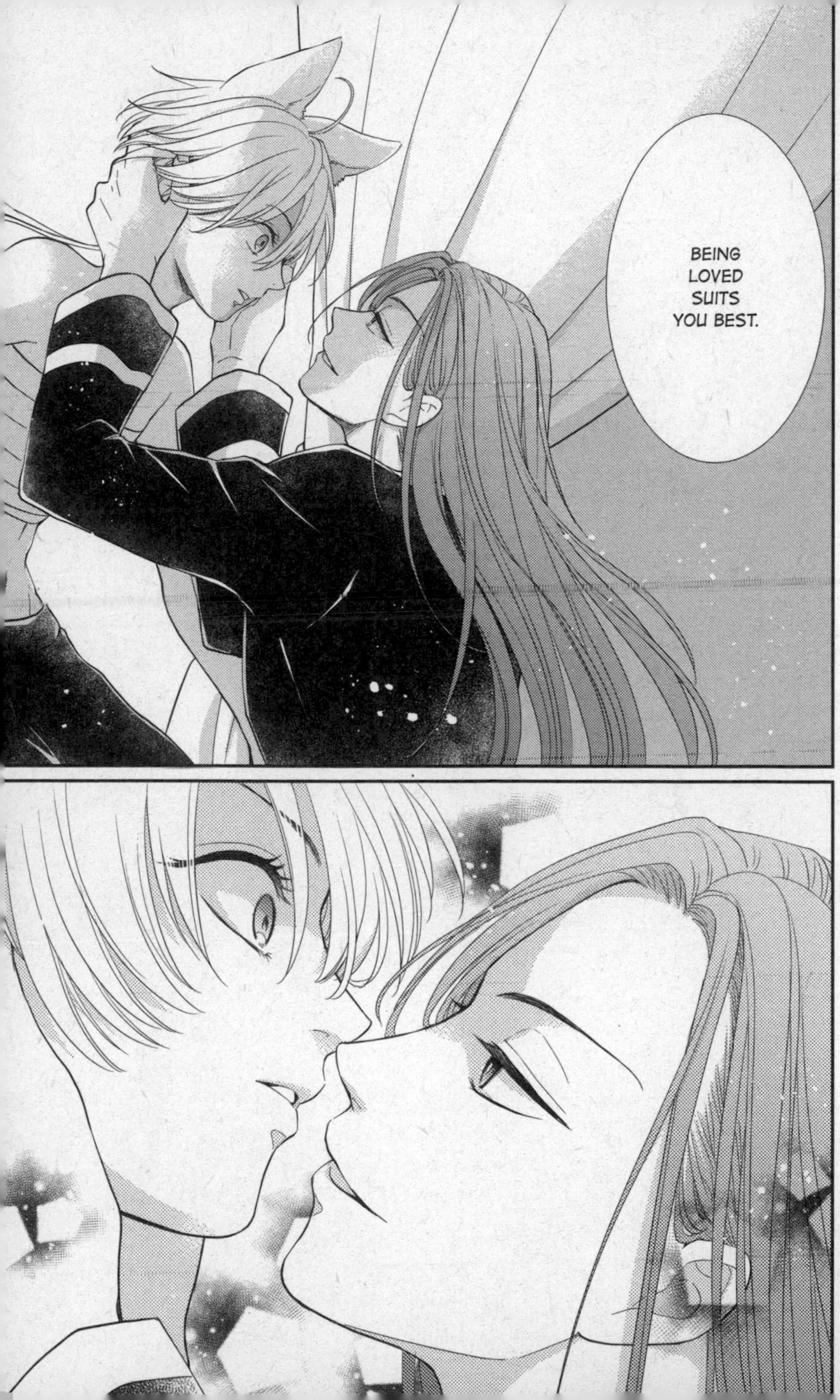
BEING LOVED SUITS YOU BEST.

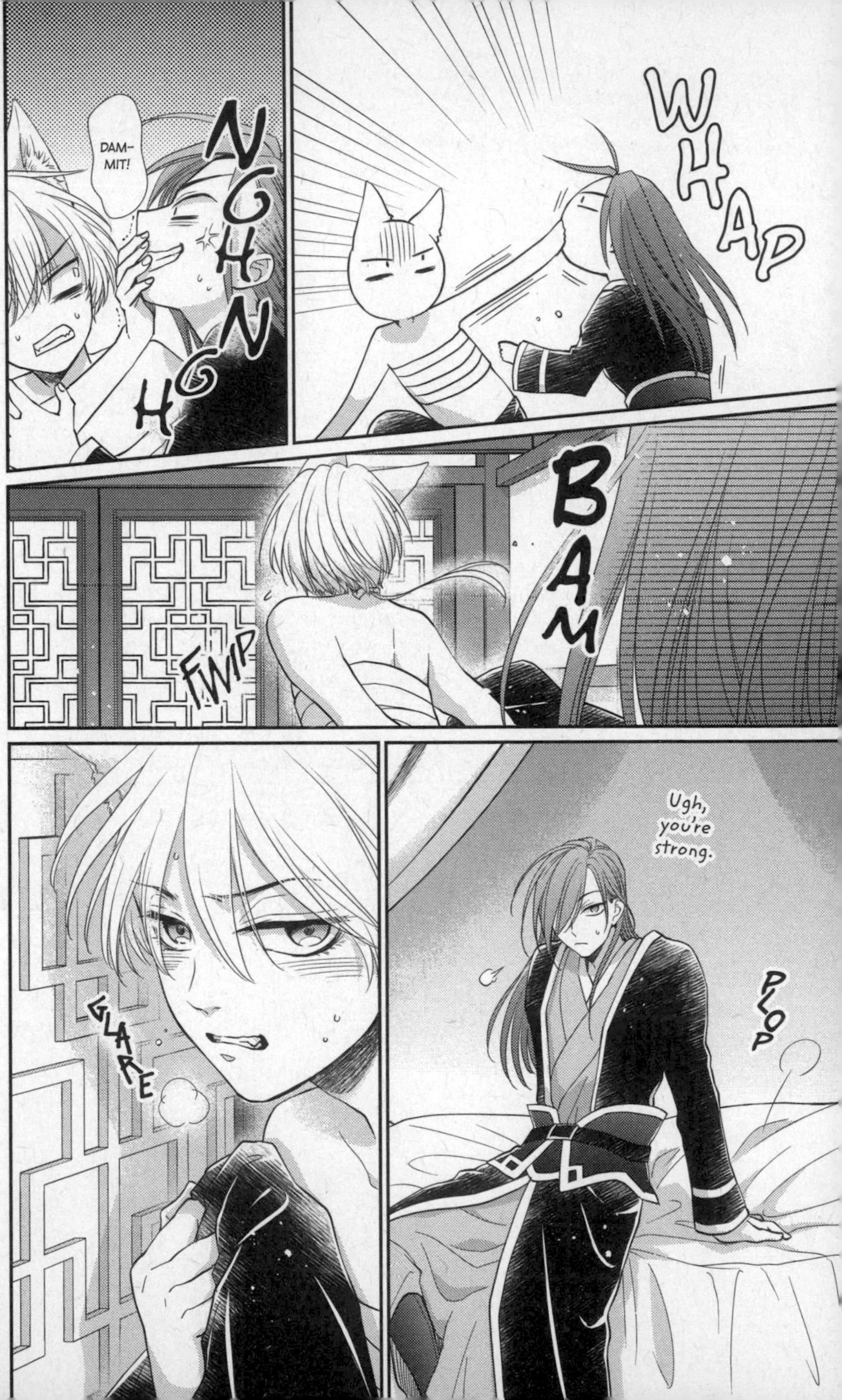
WHAP
DAM-MIT!
NGHNGH
BAM
FWIP
Ugh, you're strong.
PLOP
GLARE

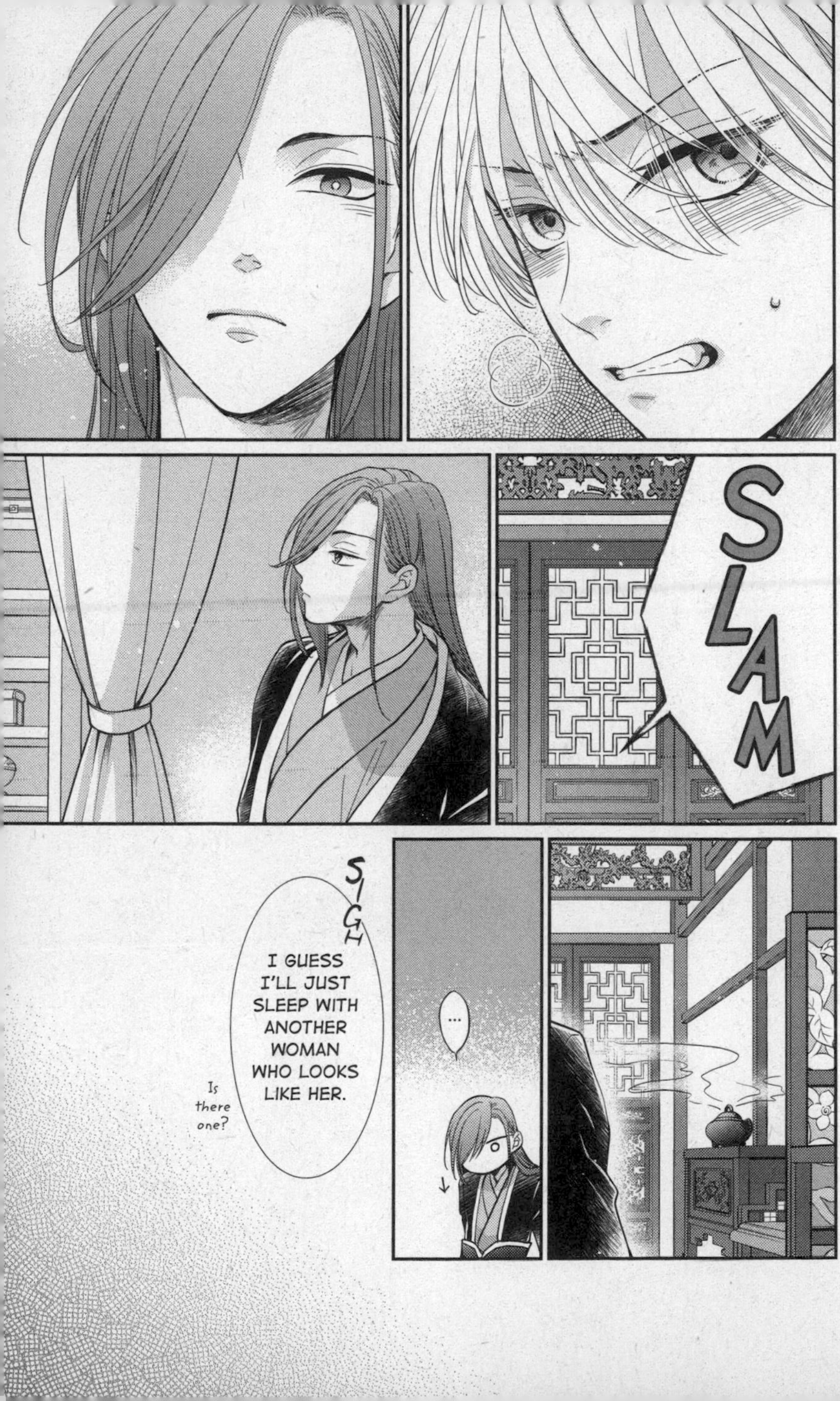
SLAM
...
SIGH
I GUESS I'LL JUST SLEEP WITH ANOTHER WOMAN WHO LOOKS LIKE HER.
Is there one?

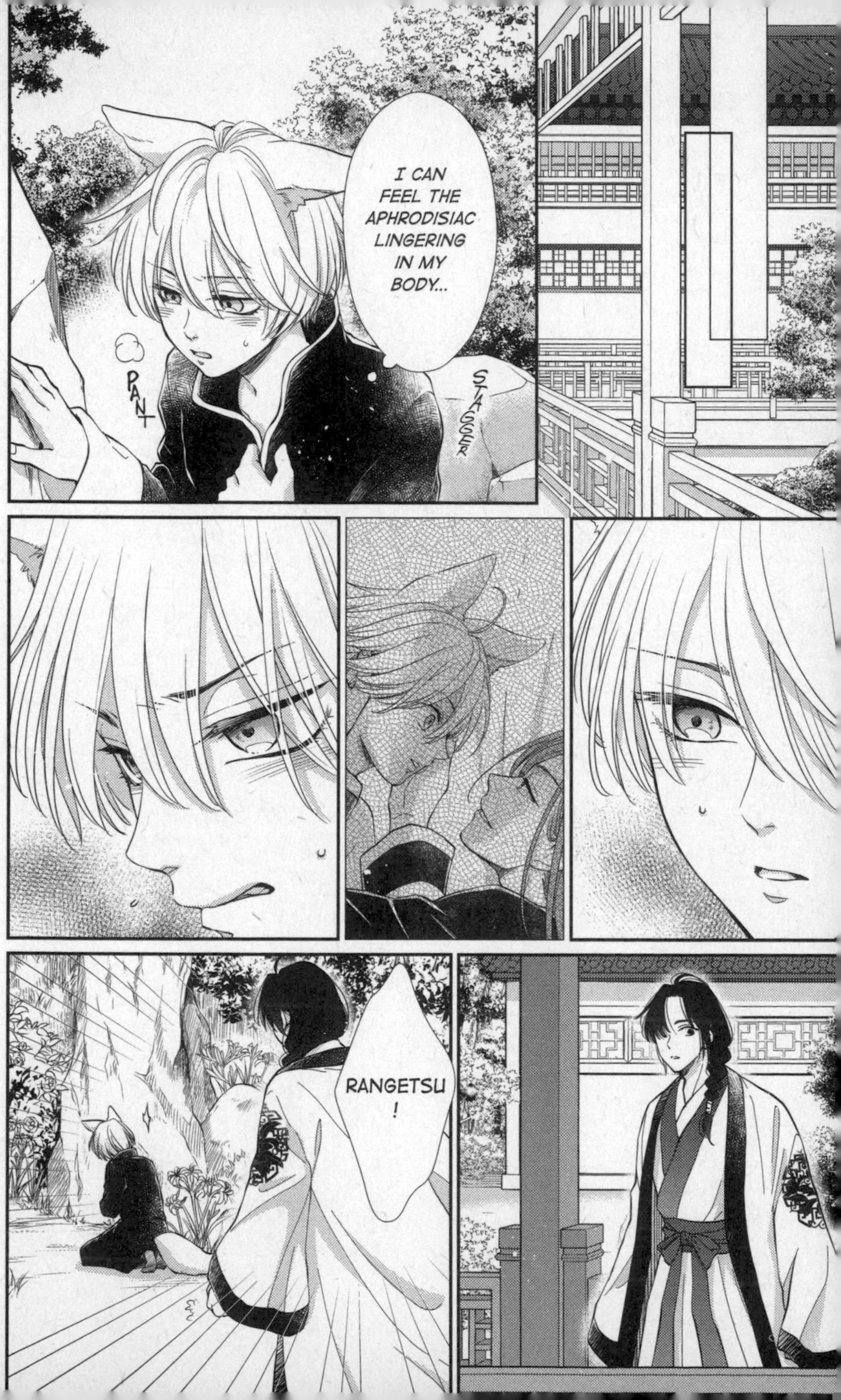
STAGGER
I CAN FEEL THE APHRODISIAC LINGERING IN MY BODY...
PANT
RANGETSU!

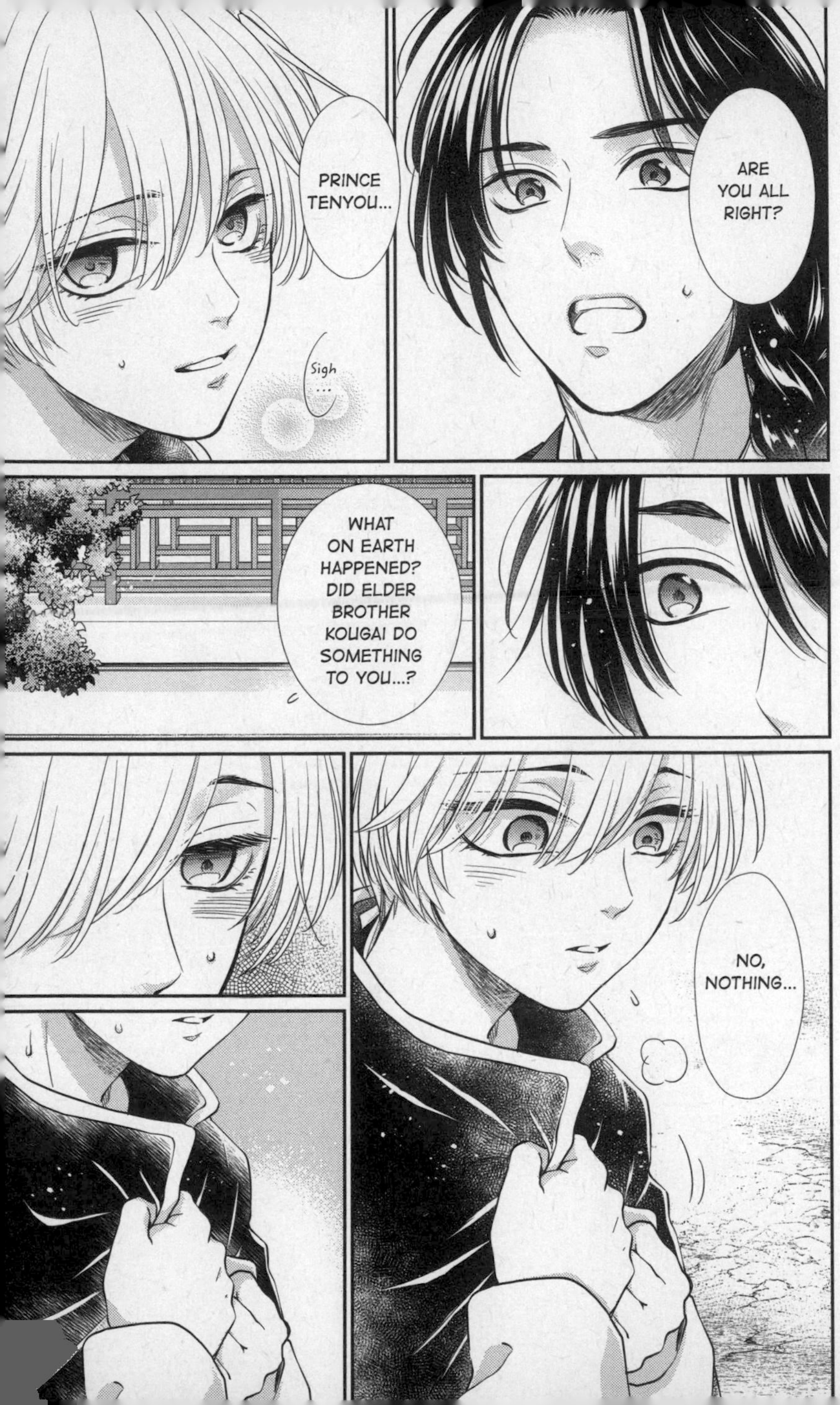
ARE YOU ALL RIGHT?
PRINCE TENYOU...
Sigh ...
WHAT ON EARTH HAPPENED? DID ELDER BROTHER KOUGAI DO SOMETHING TO YOU...?
NO, NOTHING...

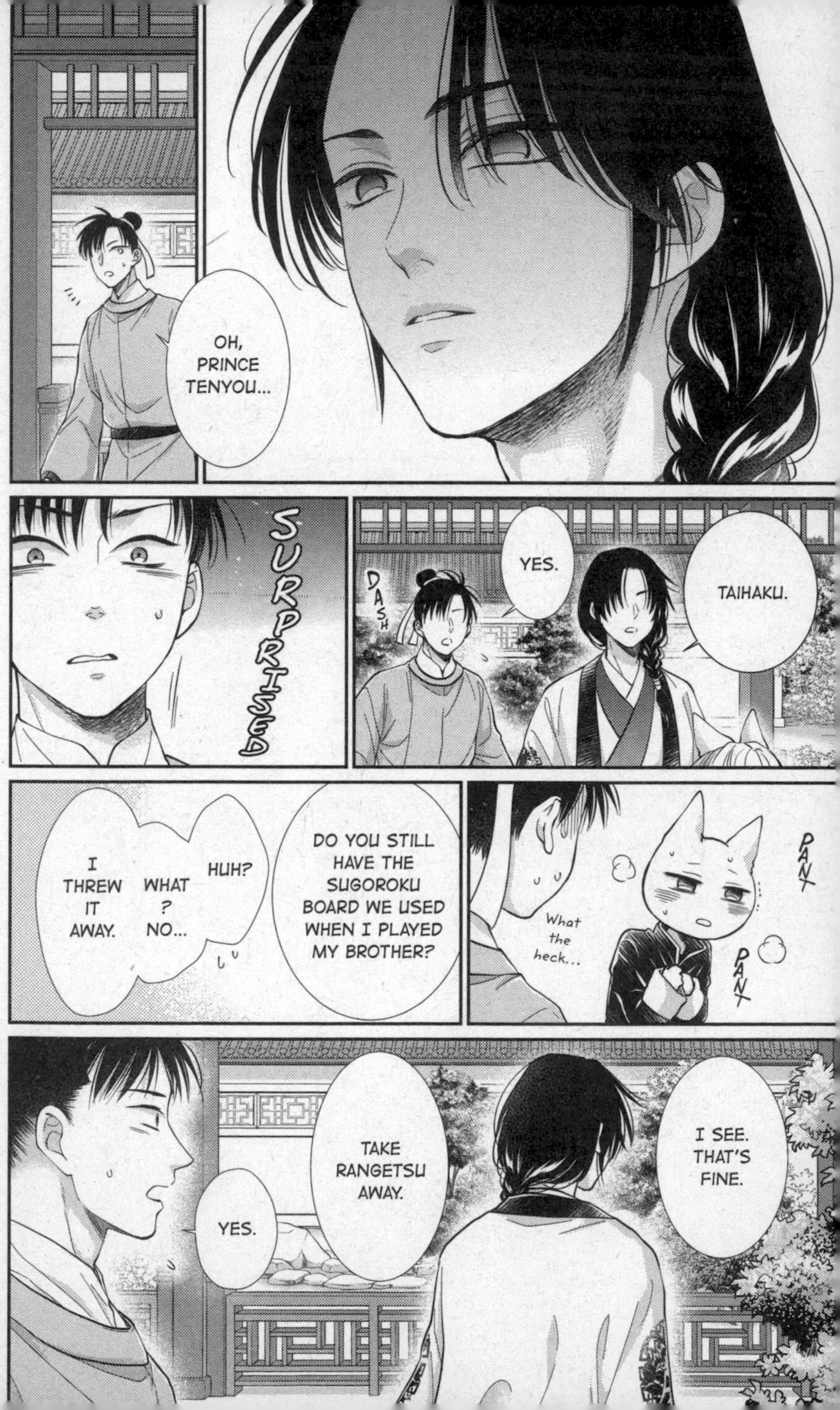
OH, PRINCE TENYOU...
TAIHAKU.
YES.
DASH
SURPRISED
PANT
PANT
What the heck...
DO YOU STILL HAVE THE SUGOROKU BOARD WE USED WHEN I PLAYED MY BROTHER?
HUH?
WHAT? NO...
I THREW IT AWAY.
I SEE. THAT'S FINE.
TAKE RANGETSU AWAY.
YES.

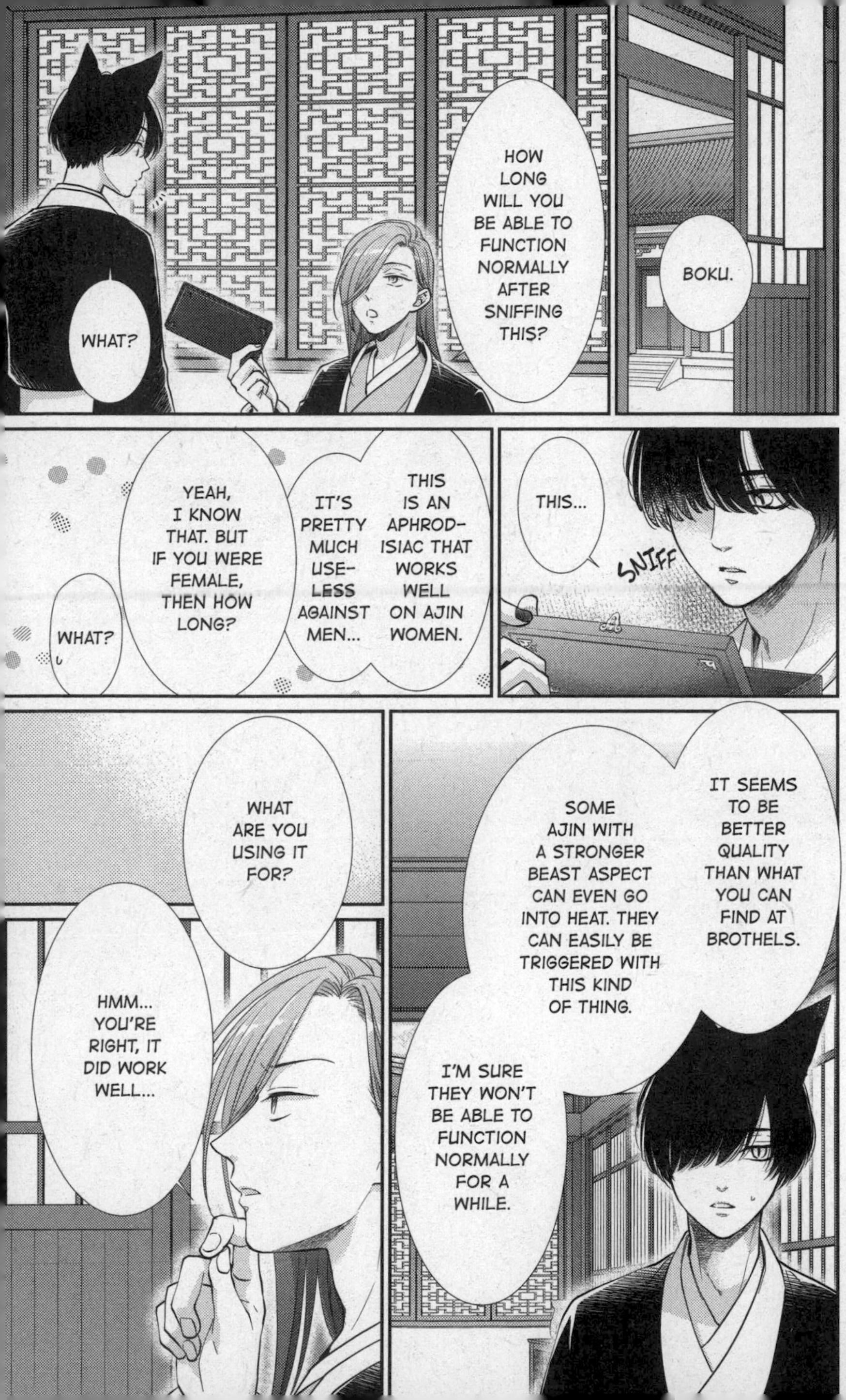
BOKU.
HOW LONG WILL YOU BE ABLE TO FUNCTION NORMALLY AFTER SNIFFING THIS?
WHAT?
THIS...
SNIFF
THIS IS AN APHROD-ISIAC THAT WORKS WELL ON AJIN WOMEN.
IT'S PRETTY MUCH USE-LESS AGAINST MEN...
YEAH, I KNOW THAT. BUT IF YOU WERE FEMALE, THEN HOW LONG?
WHAT?
IT SEEMS TO BE BETTER QUALITY THAN WHAT YOU CAN FIND AT BROTHELS.
SOME AJIN WITH A STRONGER BEAST ASPECT CAN EVEN GO INTO HEAT. THEY CAN EASILY BE TRIGGERED WITH THIS KIND OF THING.
I'M SURE THEY WON'T BE ABLE TO FUNCTION NORMALLY FOR A WHILE.
WHAT ARE YOU USING IT FOR?
HMM... YOU'RE RIGHT, IT DID WORK WELL...

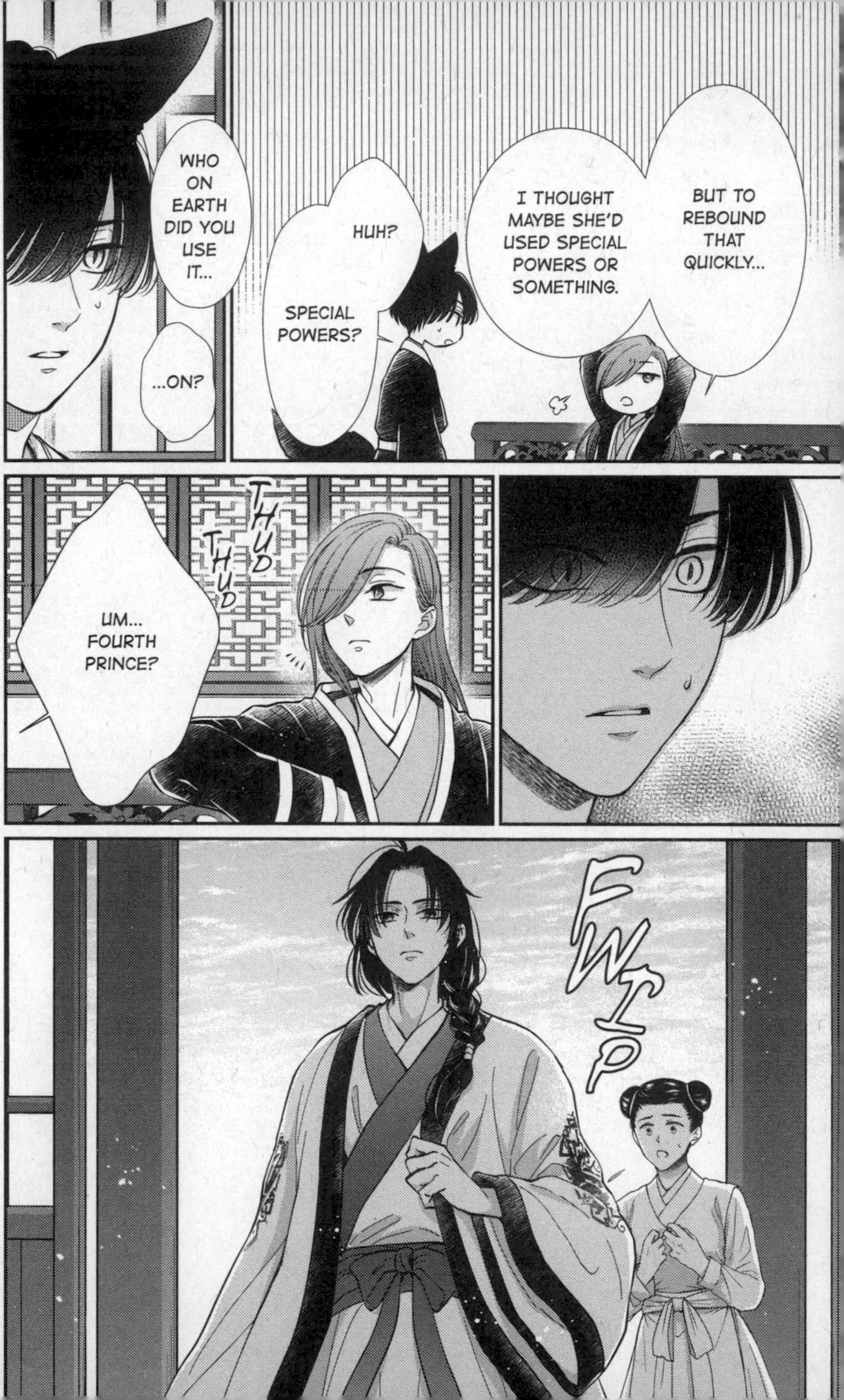
BUT TO REBOUND THAT QUICKLY...
I THOUGHT MAYBE SHE'D USED SPECIAL POWERS OR SOMETHING.
HUH?
SPECIAL POWERS?
WHO ON EARTH DID YOU USE IT...
...ON?
THUD
THUD
UM... FOURTH PRINCE?
FWIP

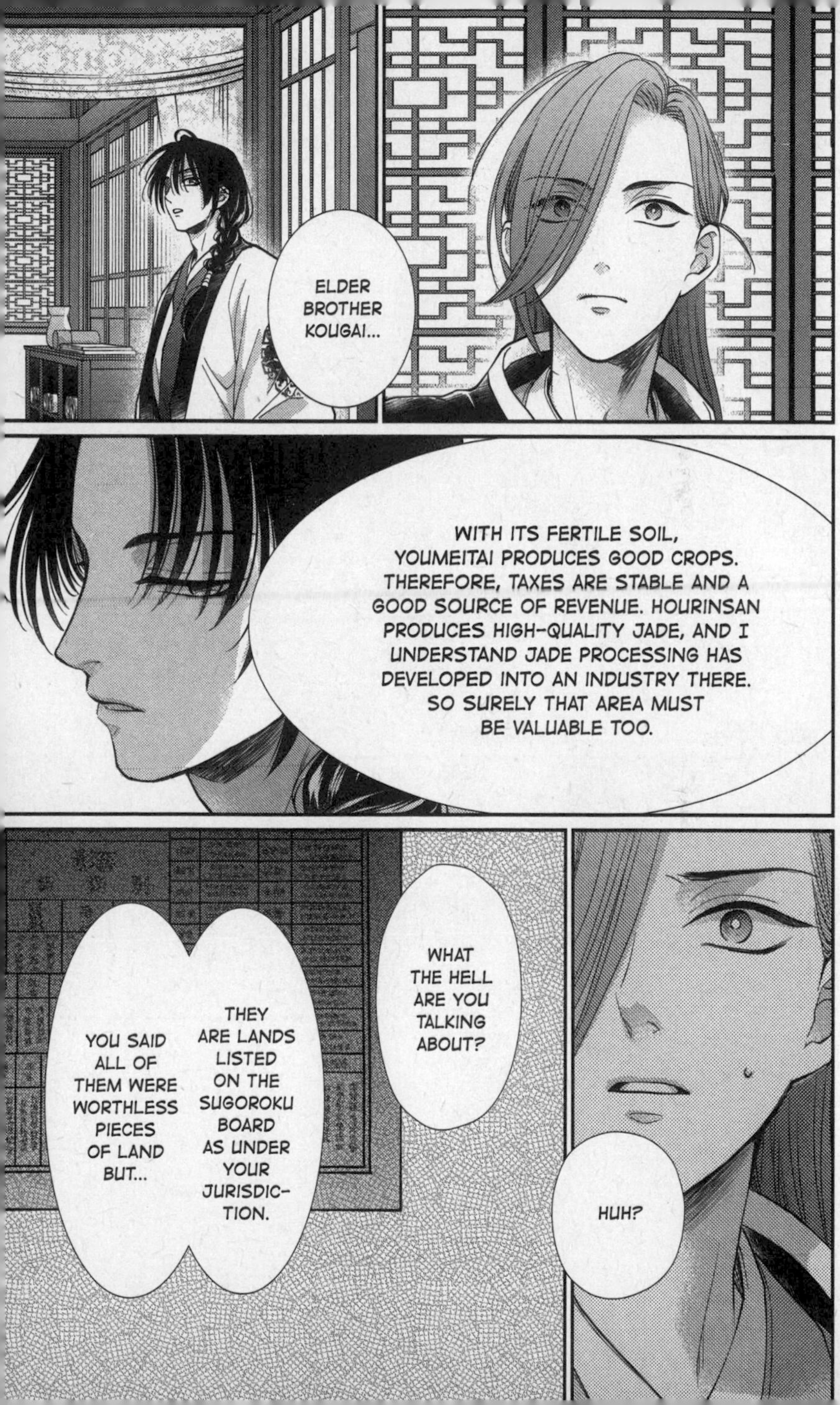
ELDER BROTHER KOUGAI...
WITH ITS FERTILE SOIL, YOUMEITAI PRODUCES GOOD CROPS. THEREFORE, TAXES ARE STABLE AND A GOOD SOURCE OF REVENUE. HOURINSAN PRODUCES HIGH-QUALITY JADE, AND I UNDERSTAND JADE PROCESSING HAS DEVELOPED INTO AN INDUSTRY THERE. SO SURELY THAT AREA MUST BE VALUABLE TOO.
HUH?
WHAT THE HELL ARE YOU TALKING ABOUT?
THEY ARE LANDS LISTED ON THE SUGOROKU BOARD AS UNDER YOUR JURISDIC-TION.
YOU SAID ALL OF THEM WERE WORTHLESS PIECES OF LAND BUT...

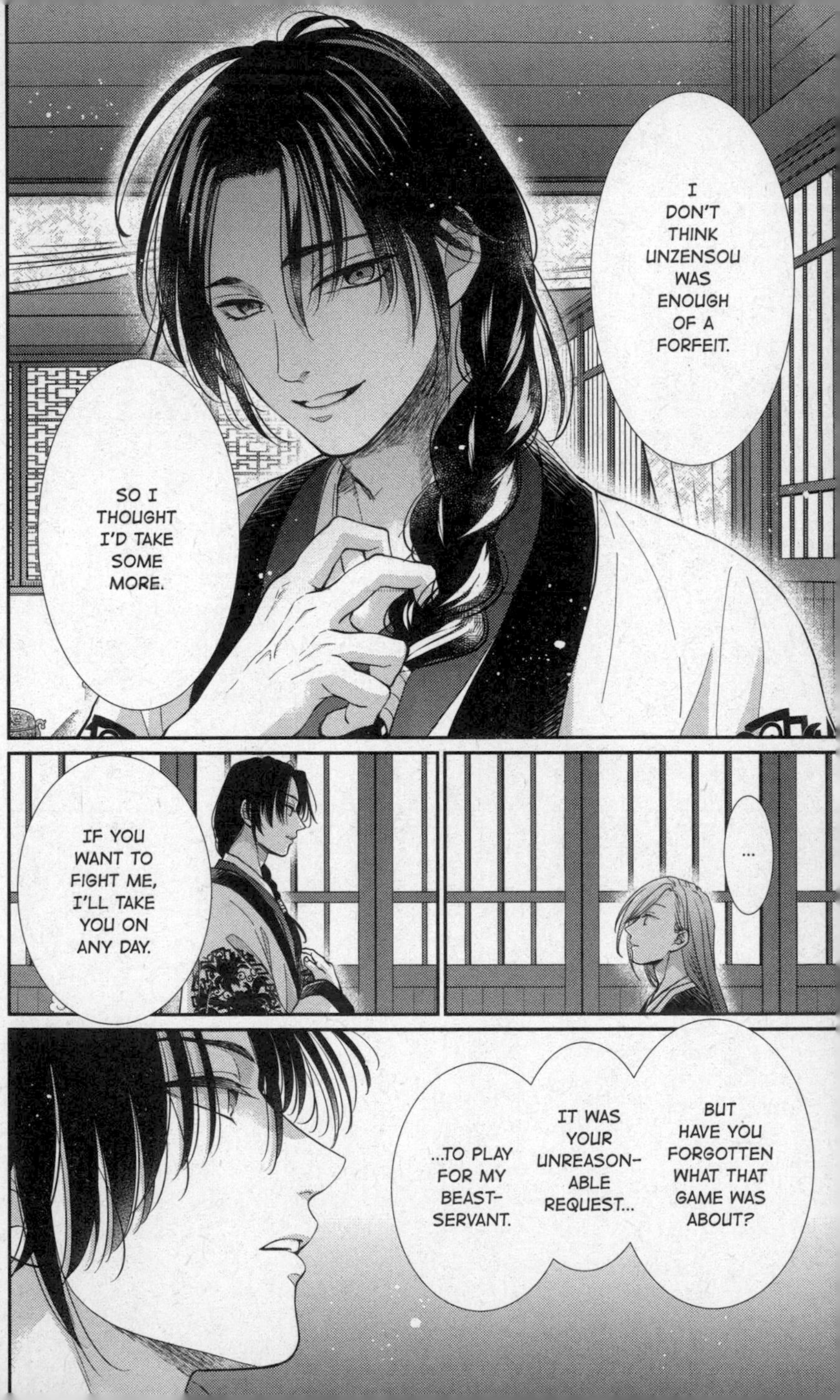
I DON'T THINK UNZENSOU WAS ENOUGH OF A FORFEIT.
SO I THOUGHT I'D TAKE SOME MORE.
...
IF YOU WANT TO FIGHT ME, I'LL TAKE YOU ON ANY DAY.
BUT HAVE YOU FORGOTTEN WHAT THAT GAME WAS ABOUT?
IT WAS YOUR UNREASON-ABLE REQUEST...
...TO PLAY FOR MY BEAST-SERVANT.

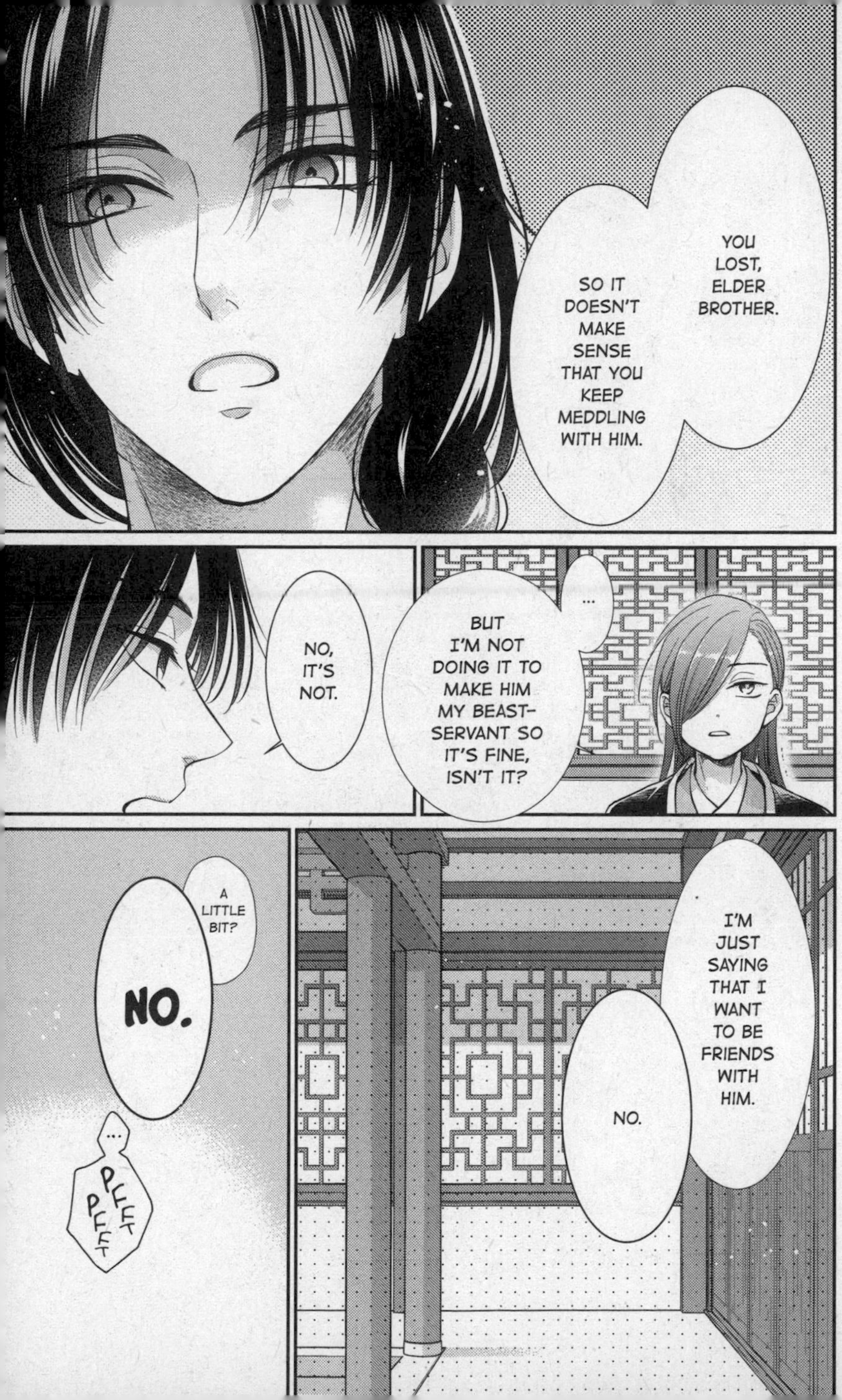
YOU LOST, ELDER BROTHER.
SO IT DOESN'T MAKE SENSE THAT YOU KEEP MEDDLING WITH HIM.
...
BUT I'M NOT DOING IT TO MAKE HIM MY BEAST-SERVANT SO IT'S FINE, ISN'T IT?
NO, IT'S NOT.
I'M JUST SAYING THAT I WANT TO BE FRIENDS WITH HIM.
NO.
A LITTLE BIT?
NO.
...
PFFT PFFT

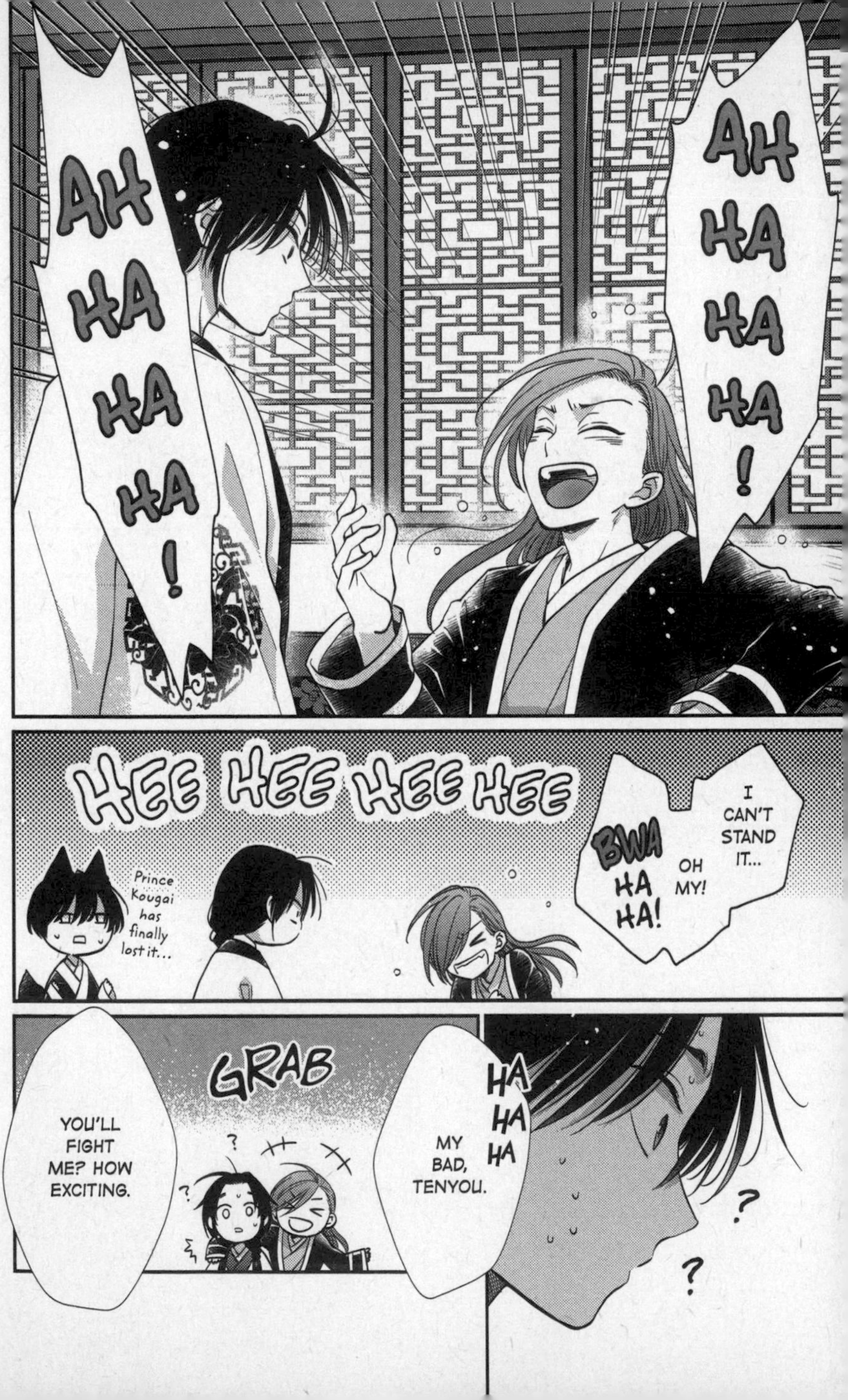
AH HA HA HA HA!
AH HA HA HA!
I CAN'T STAND IT...
OH MY!
BWA HA HA!
HEE HEE HEE HEE
Prince Kougai has finally lost it...
HA HA HA
MY BAD, TENYOU.
?
?
GRAB
?
?
YOU'LL FIGHT ME? HOW EXCITING.

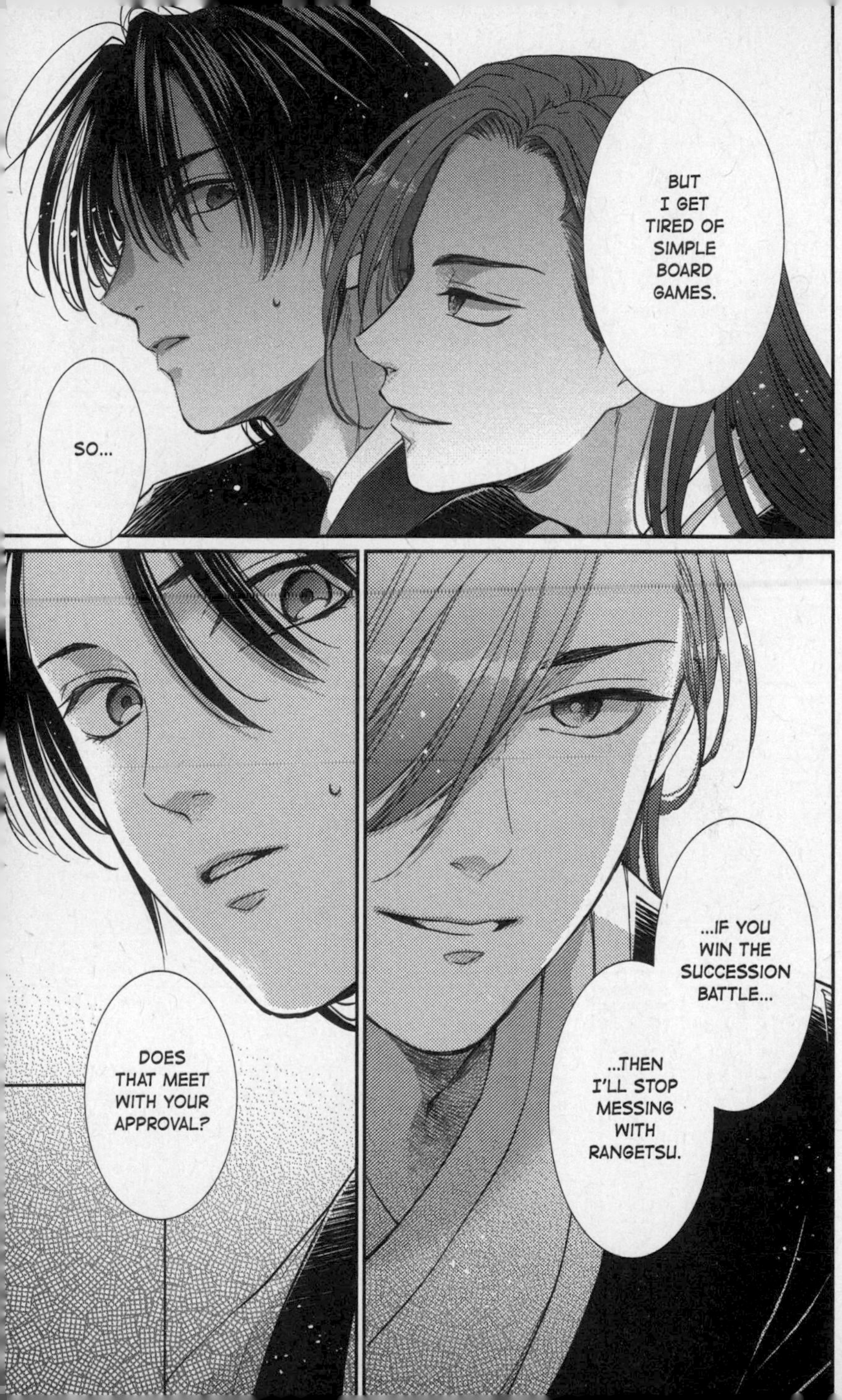
BUT I GET TIRED OF SIMPLE BOARD GAMES.
SO...
...IF YOU WIN THE SUCCESSION BATTLE...
...THEN I'LL STOP MESSING WITH RANGETSU.
DOES THAT MEET WITH YOUR APPROVAL?

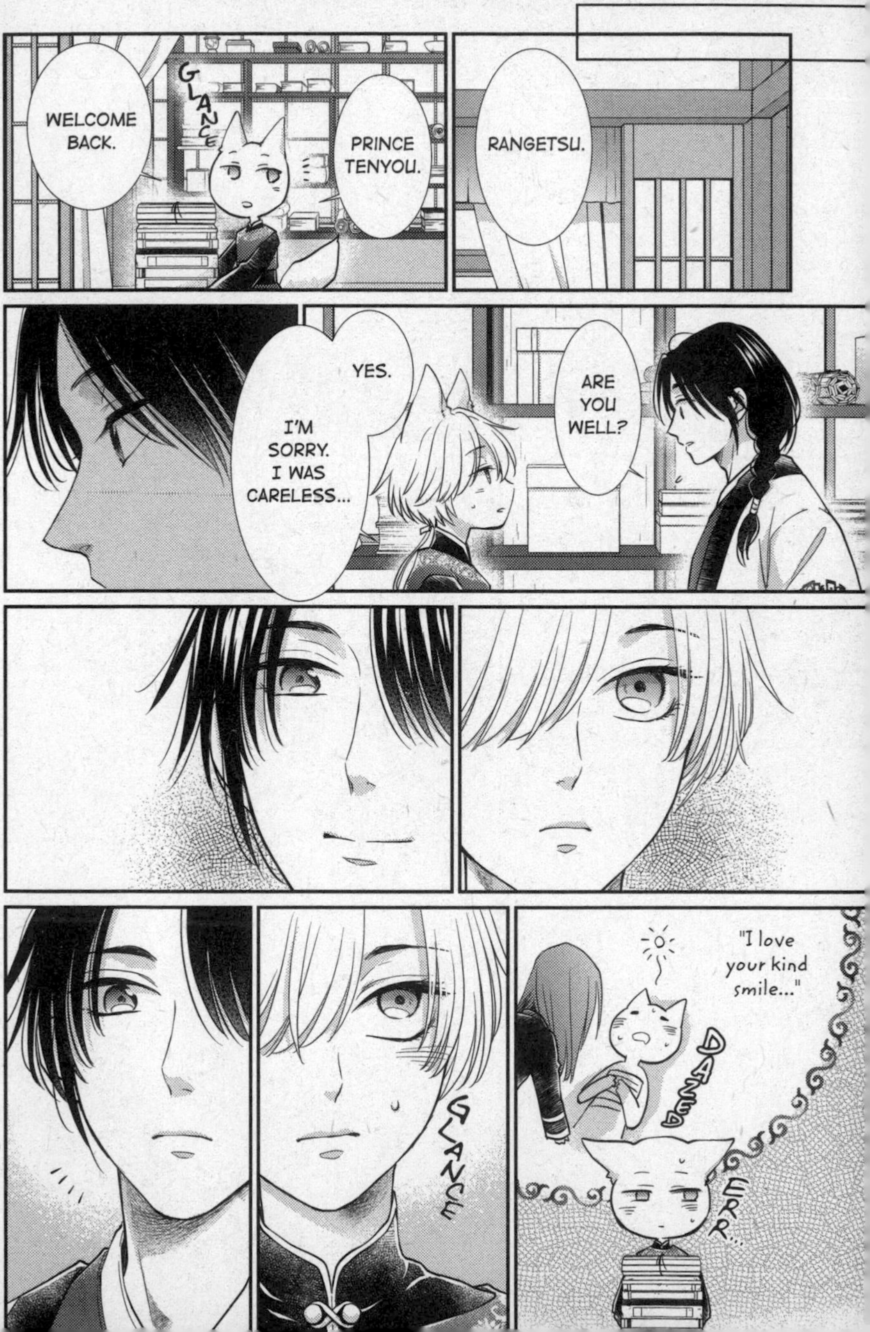
RANGETSU.
PRINCE TENYOU.
GLANCE
WELCOME BACK.
ARE YOU WELL?
YES.
I'M SORRY. I WAS CARELESS...
"I love your kind smile..."
ERRR...
GLANCE

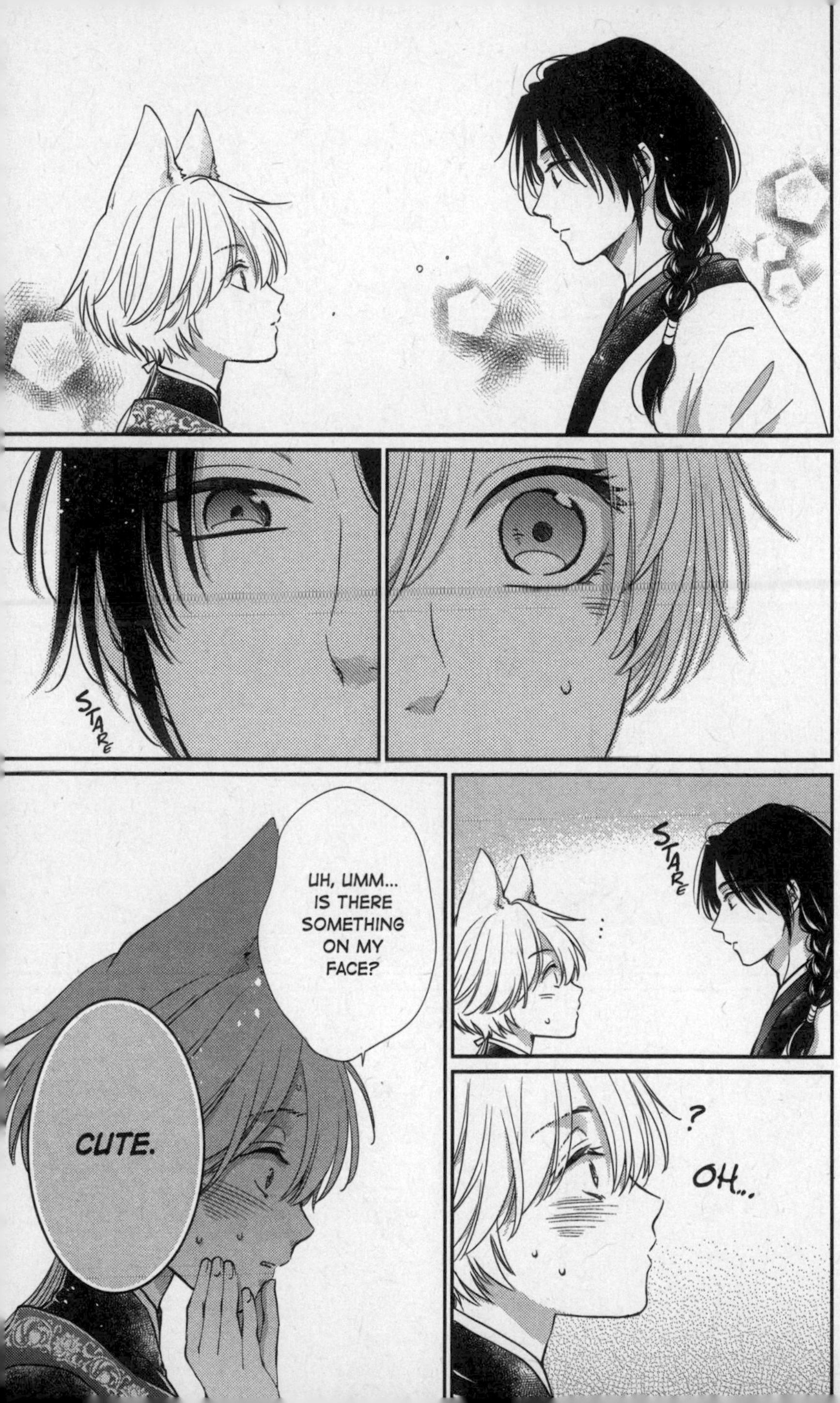
STARE
STARE
...
?
OH...
UH, UMM... IS THERE SOMETHING ON MY FACE?
CUTE.

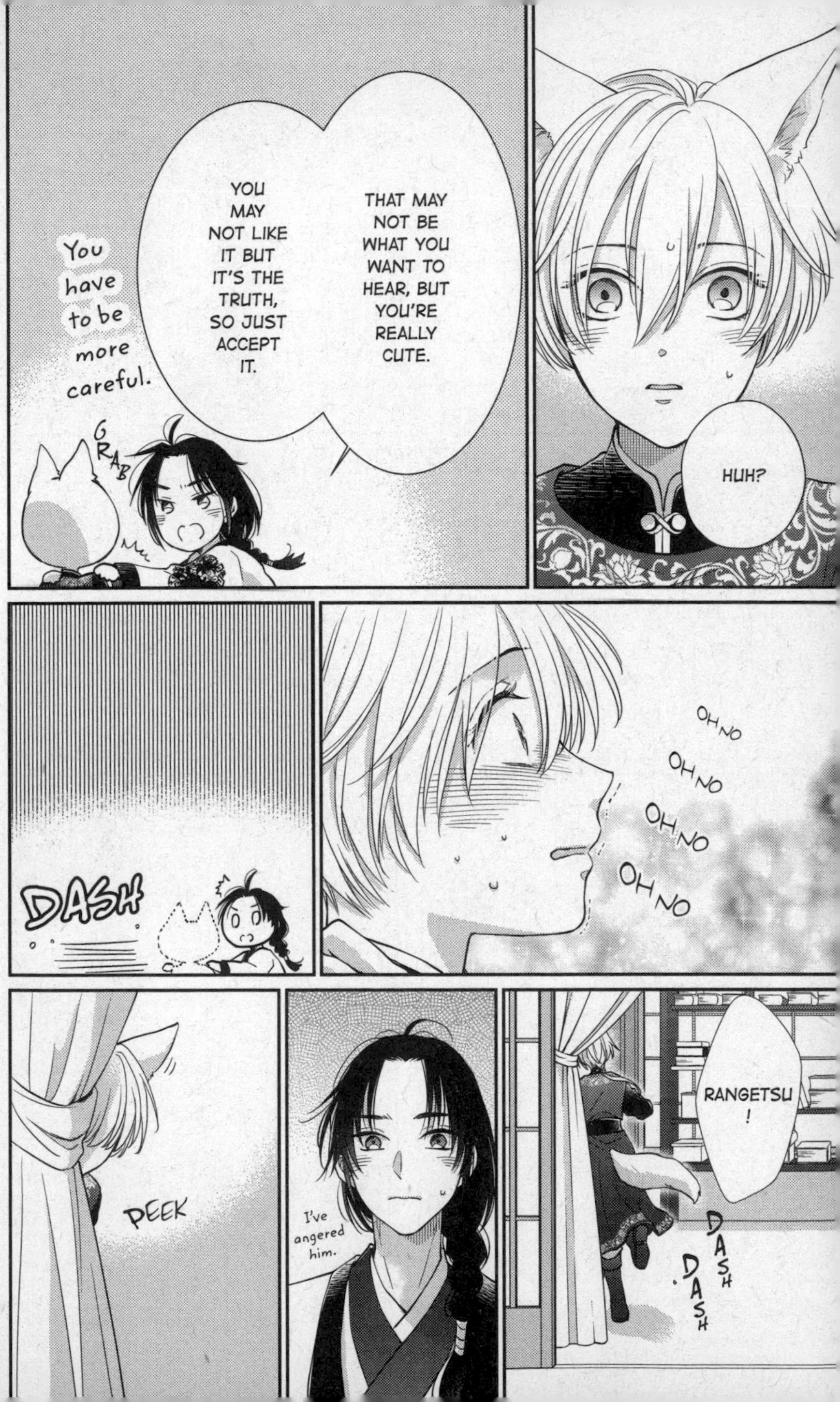
HUH?
THAT MAY NOT BE WHAT YOU WANT TO HEAR, BUT YOU'RE REALLY CUTE.
YOU MAY NOT LIKE IT BUT IT'S THE TRUTH, SO JUST ACCEPT IT.
You have to be more careful.
GRAB
OH NO
OH NO
OH NO
OH NO
DASH
RANGETSU!
DASH
DASH
I've angered him.
PEEK

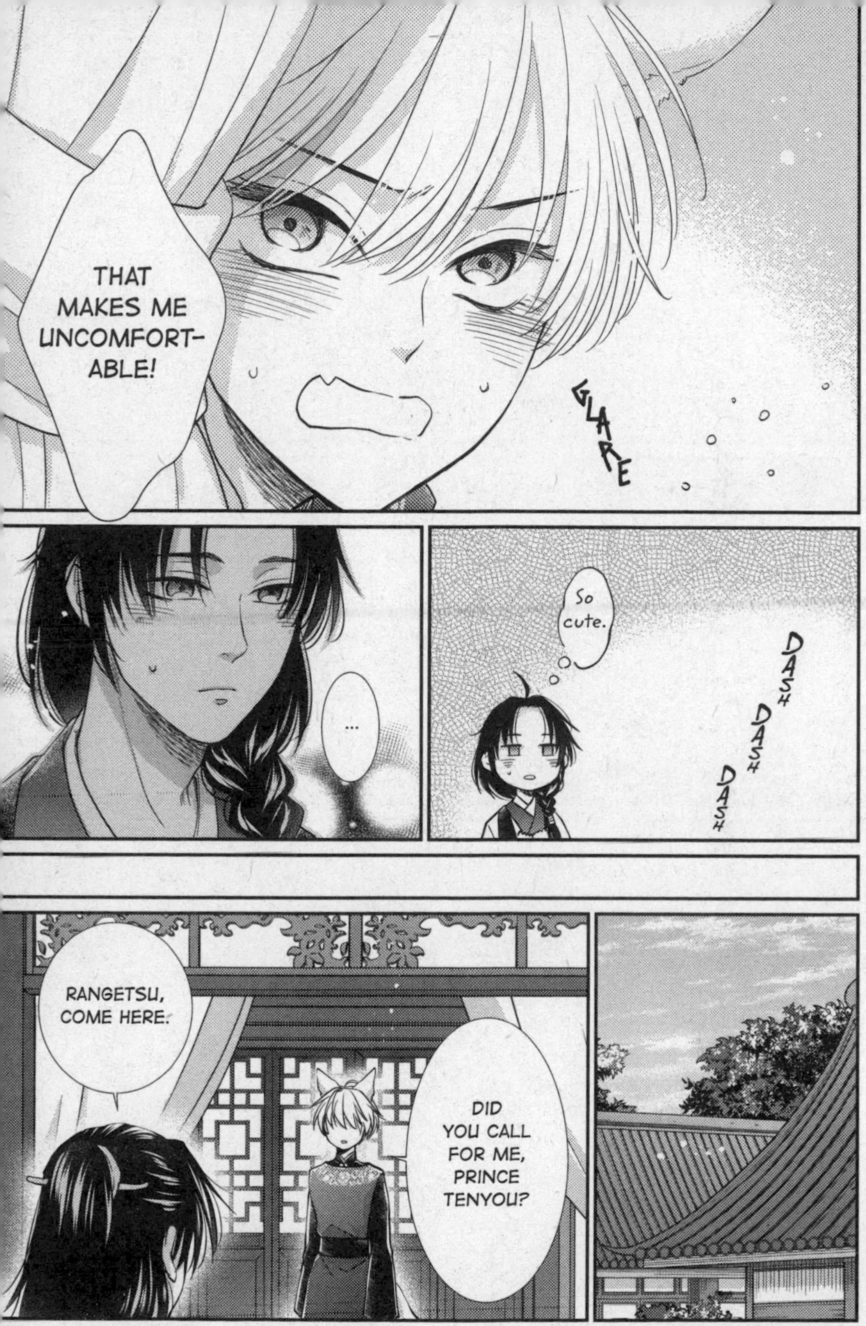
THAT MAKES ME UNCOMFORT-ABLE!
GLARE
So cute.
DASH DASH DASH
...
RANGETSU, COME HERE.
DID YOU CALL FOR ME, PRINCE TENYOU?

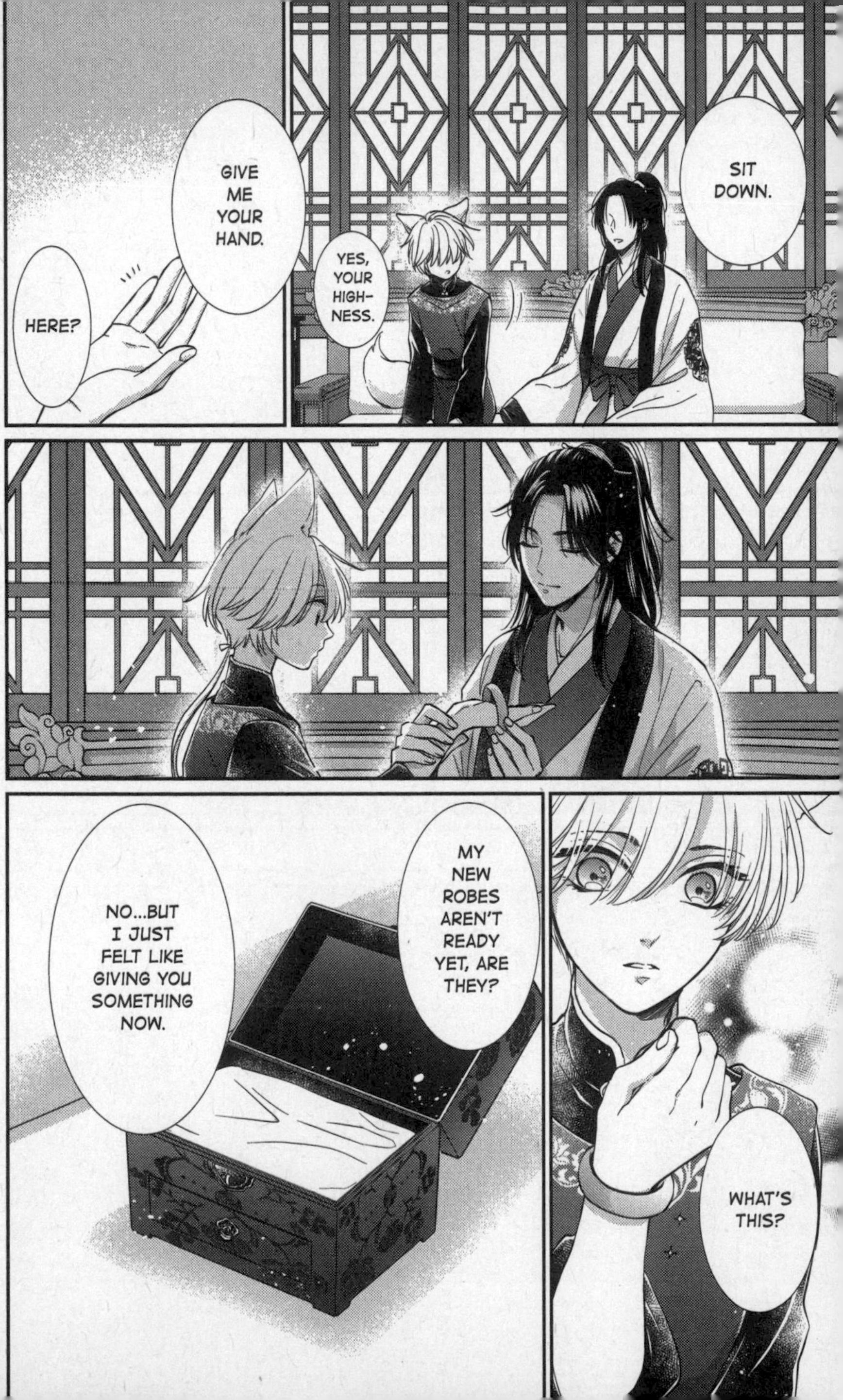
SIT DOWN.
YES, YOUR HIGH-NESS.
GIVE ME YOUR HAND.
HERE?
WHAT'S THIS?
MY NEW ROBES AREN'T READY YET, ARE THEY?
NO...BUT I JUST FELT LIKE GIVING YOU SOMETHING NOW.

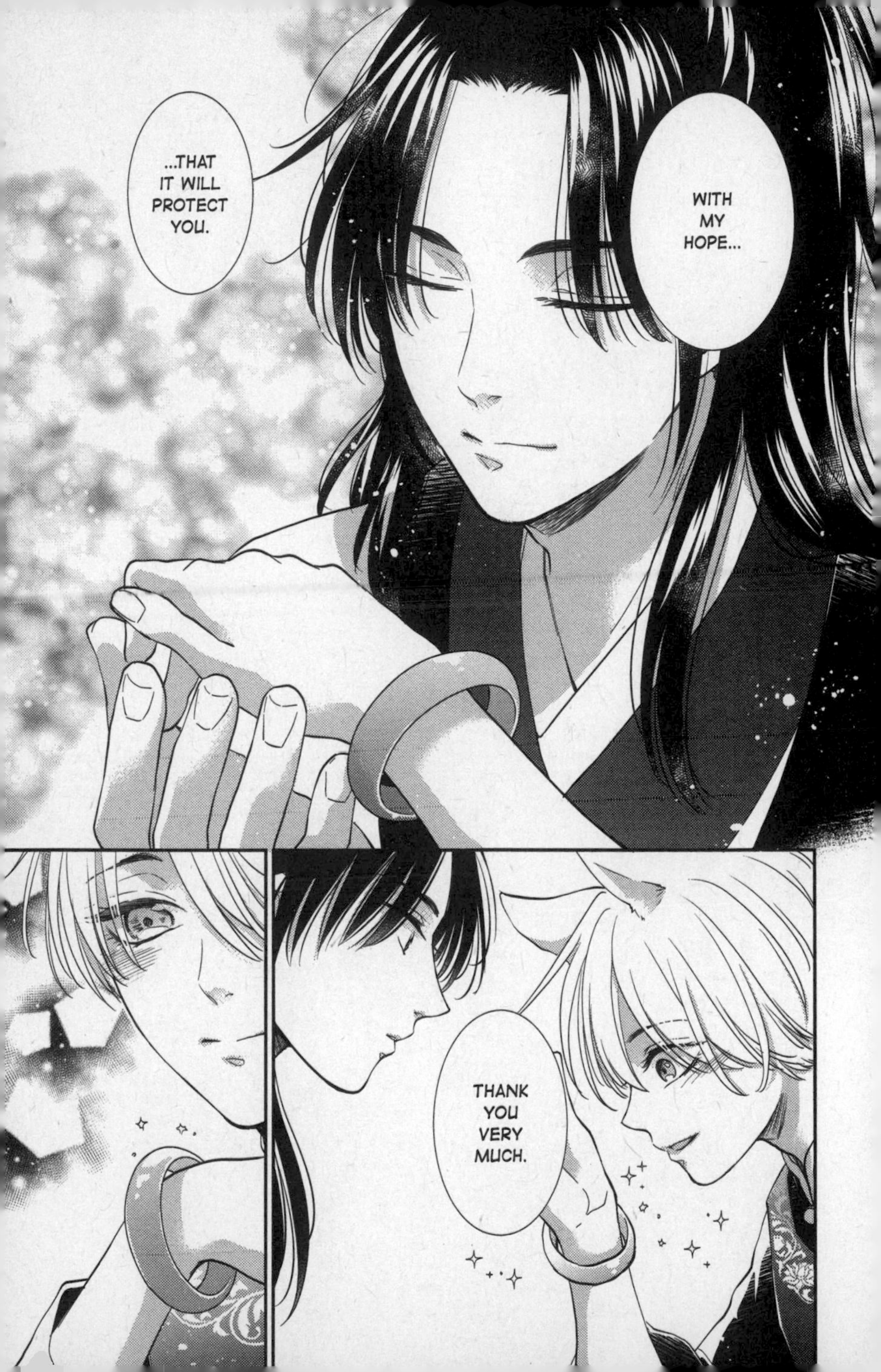
WITH MY HOPE...
...THAT IT WILL PROTECT YOU.
THANK YOU VERY MUCH.

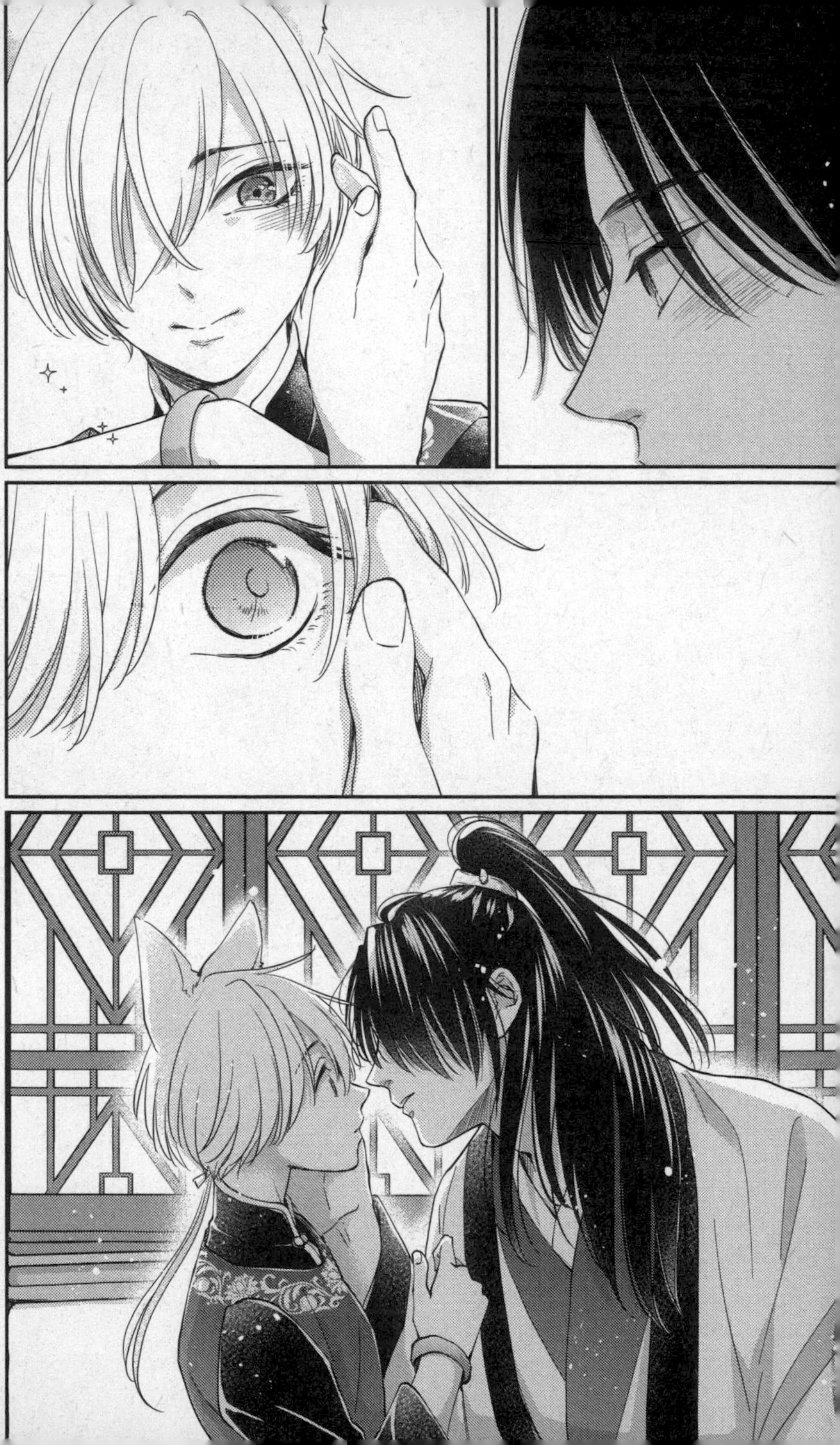

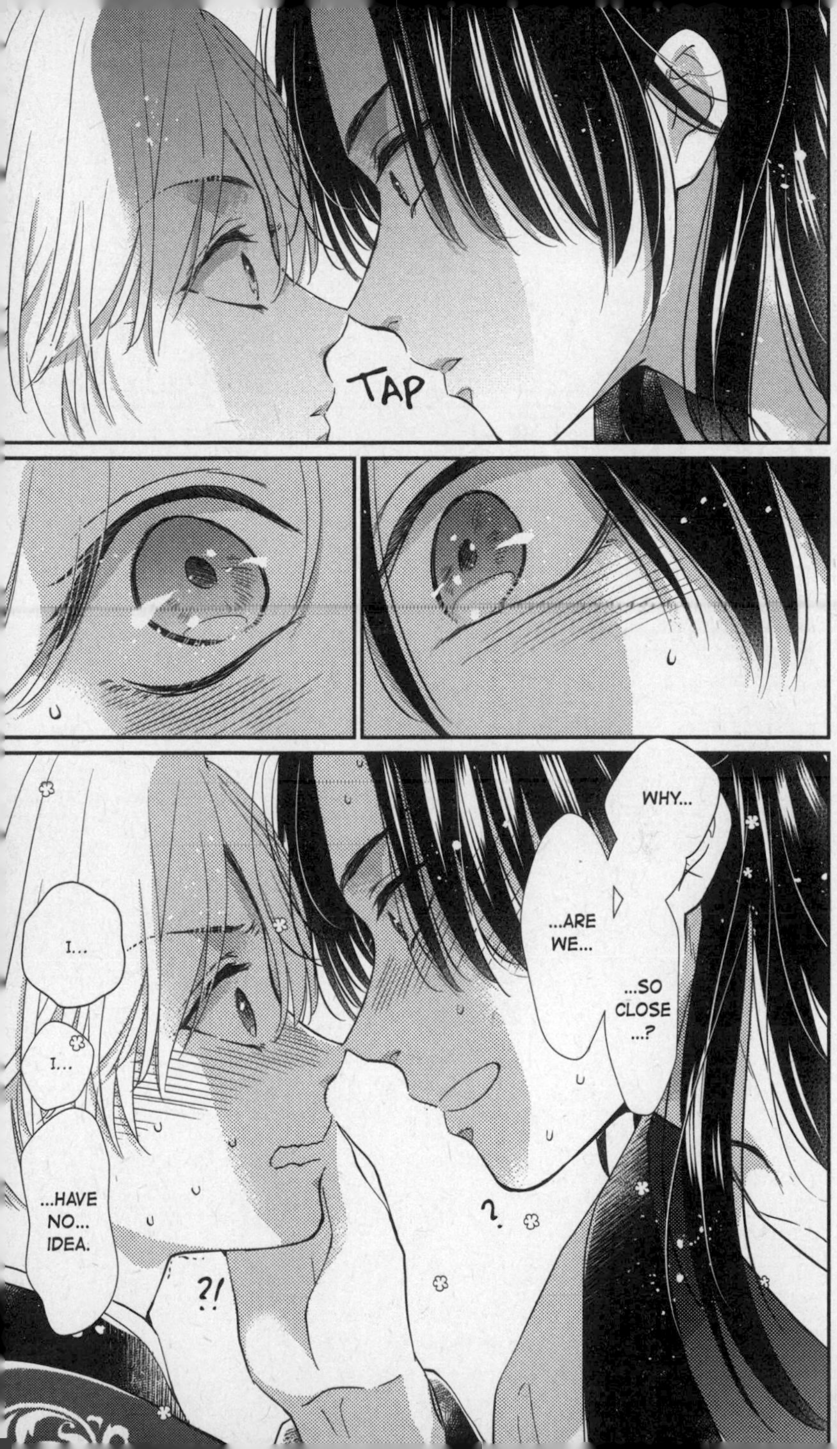
TAP
WHY...
...ARE WE...
...SO CLOSE ...?
?
I...
I...
...HAVE NO... IDEA.
?!

Extra! A Story That Happened Around Chapter 21

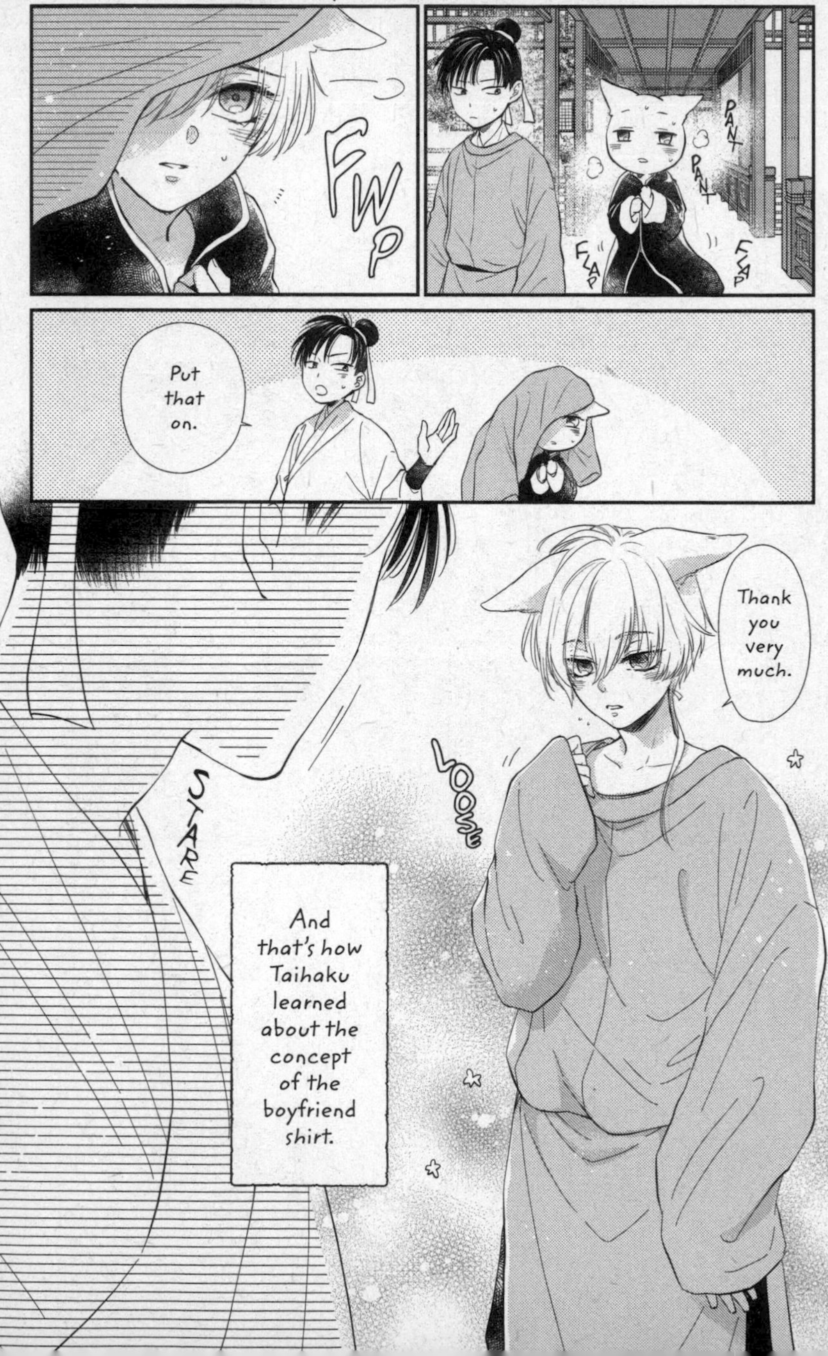
PANT
PANT
FLAP
FLAP
FWP
Put that on.
Thank you very much.
LOOSE
STARE
And that's how Taihaku learned about the concept of the boyfriend shirt.

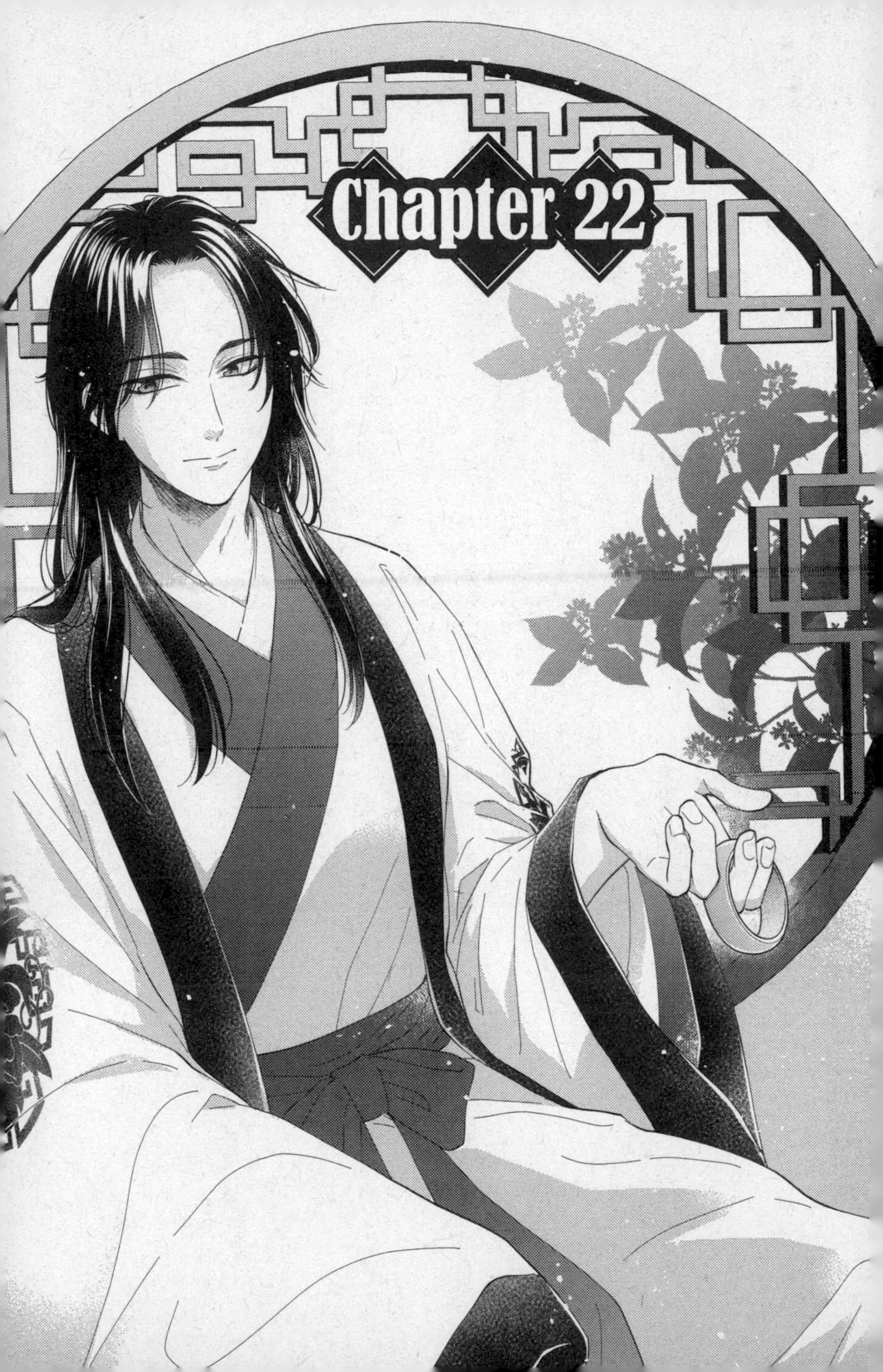
Chapter 22

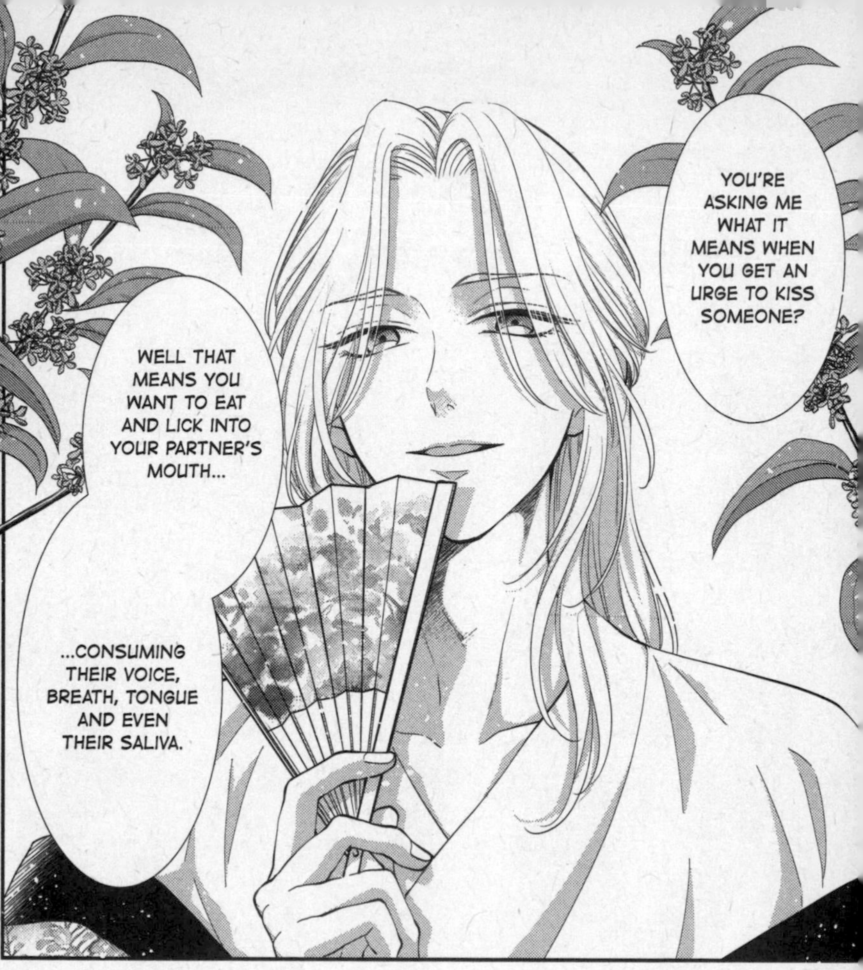
YOU'RE ASKING ME WHAT IT MEANS WHEN YOU GET AN URGE TO KISS SOMEONE?
WELL THAT MEANS YOU WANT TO EAT AND LICK INTO YOUR PARTNER'S MOUTH...
...CONSUMING THEIR VOICE, BREATH, TONGUE AND EVEN THEIR SALIVA.

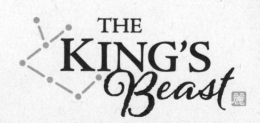

THE KING'S *Beast*

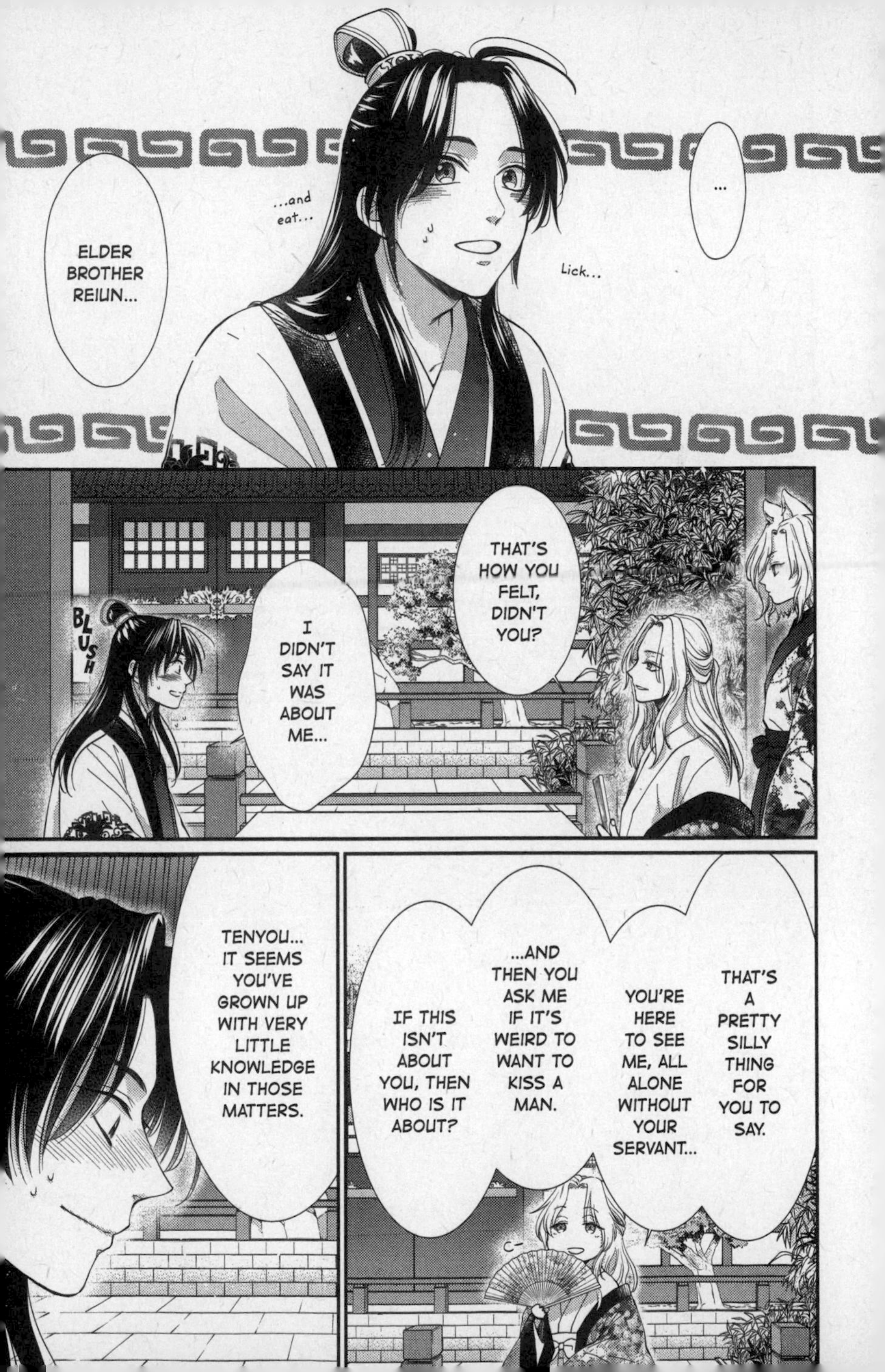
...
...and eat...
Lick...
ELDER BROTHER REIUN...
THAT'S HOW YOU FELT, DIDN'T YOU?
I DIDN'T SAY IT WAS ABOUT ME...
BLUSH
THAT'S A PRETTY SILLY THING FOR YOU TO SAY.
YOU'RE HERE TO SEE ME, ALL ALONE WITHOUT YOUR SERVANT...
...AND THEN YOU ASK ME IF IT'S WEIRD TO WANT TO KISS A MAN.
IF THIS ISN'T ABOUT YOU, THEN WHO IS IT ABOUT?
C-
TENYOU... IT SEEMS YOU'VE GROWN UP WITH VERY LITTLE KNOWLEDGE IN THOSE MATTERS.

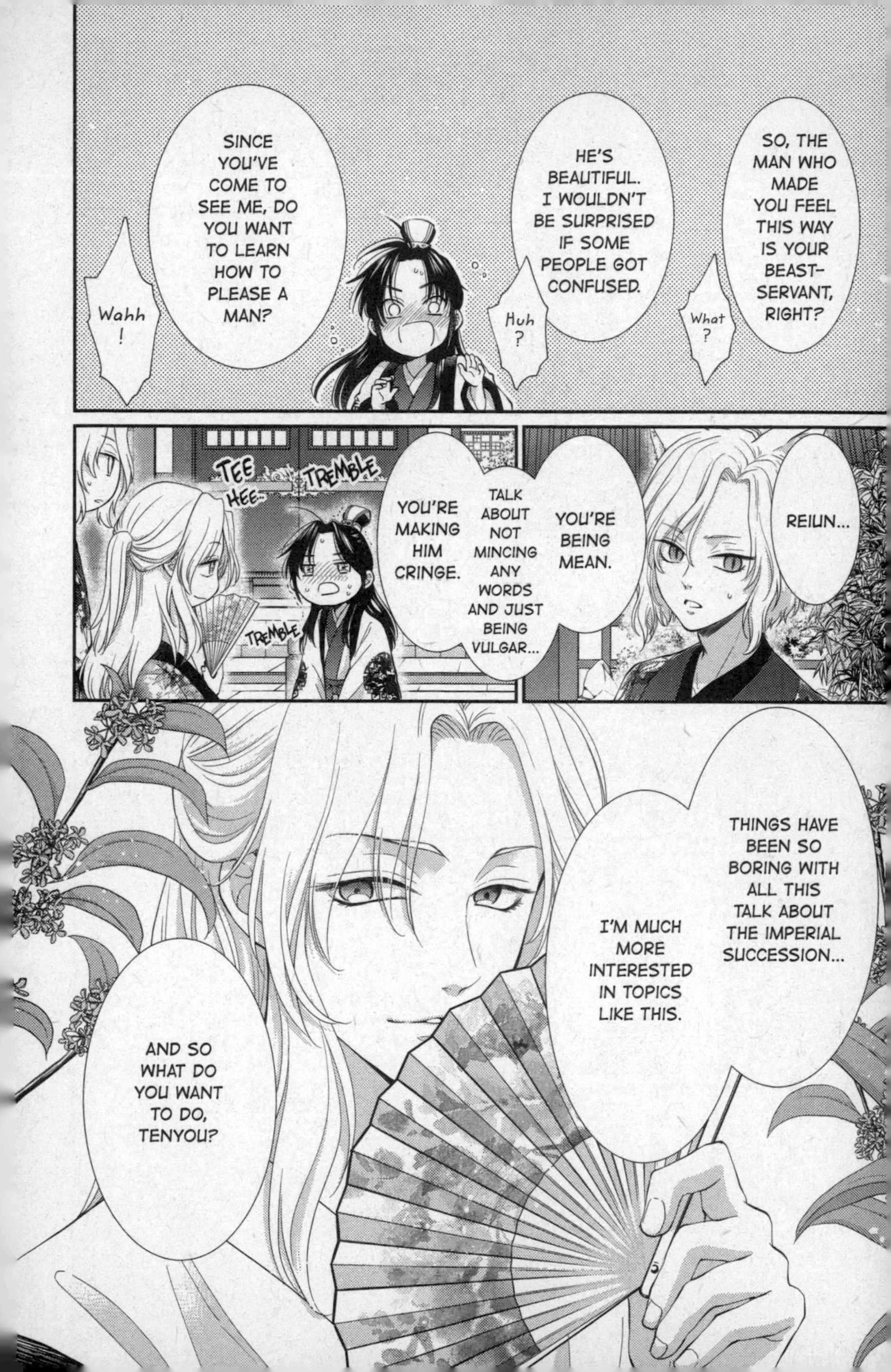
SO, THE MAN WHO MADE YOU FEEL THIS WAY IS YOUR BEAST-SERVANT, RIGHT?
What?
HE'S BEAUTIFUL. I WOULDN'T BE SURPRISED IF SOME PEOPLE GOT CONFUSED.
Huh?
SINCE YOU'VE COME TO SEE ME, DO YOU WANT TO LEARN HOW TO PLEASE A MAN?
Wahh!
REIUN...
YOU'RE BEING MEAN.
TALK ABOUT NOT MINCING ANY WORDS AND JUST BEING VULGAR...
YOU'RE MAKING HIM CRINGE.
TREMBLE
TEE HEE..
TREMBLE
THINGS HAVE BEEN SO BORING WITH ALL THIS TALK ABOUT THE IMPERIAL SUCCESSION...
I'M MUCH MORE INTERESTED IN TOPICS LIKE THIS.
AND SO WHAT DO YOU WANT TO DO, TENYOU?

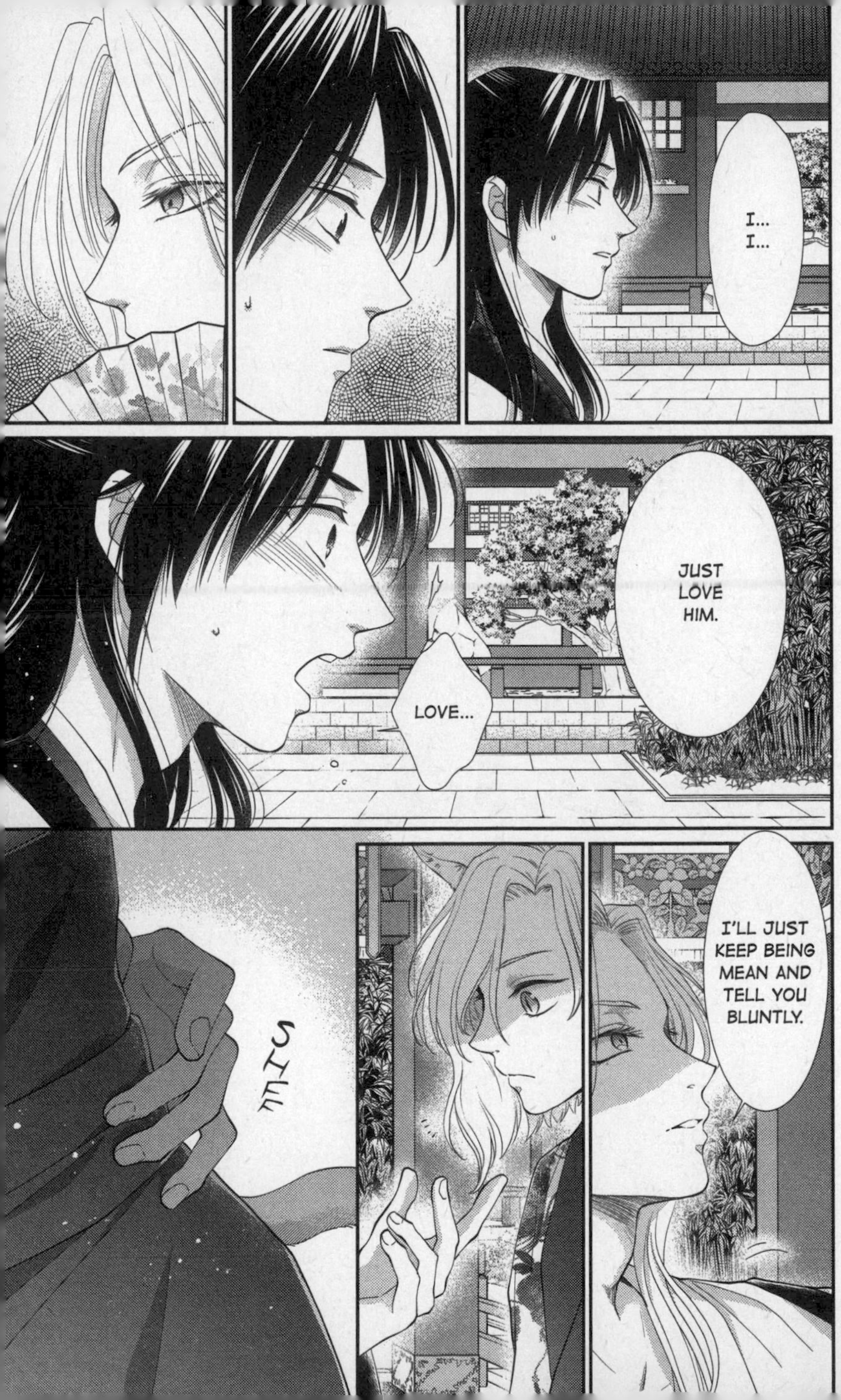
I...
I...
JUST LOVE HIM.
LOVE...
I'LL JUST KEEP BEING MEAN AND TELL YOU BLUNTLY.
SHFF

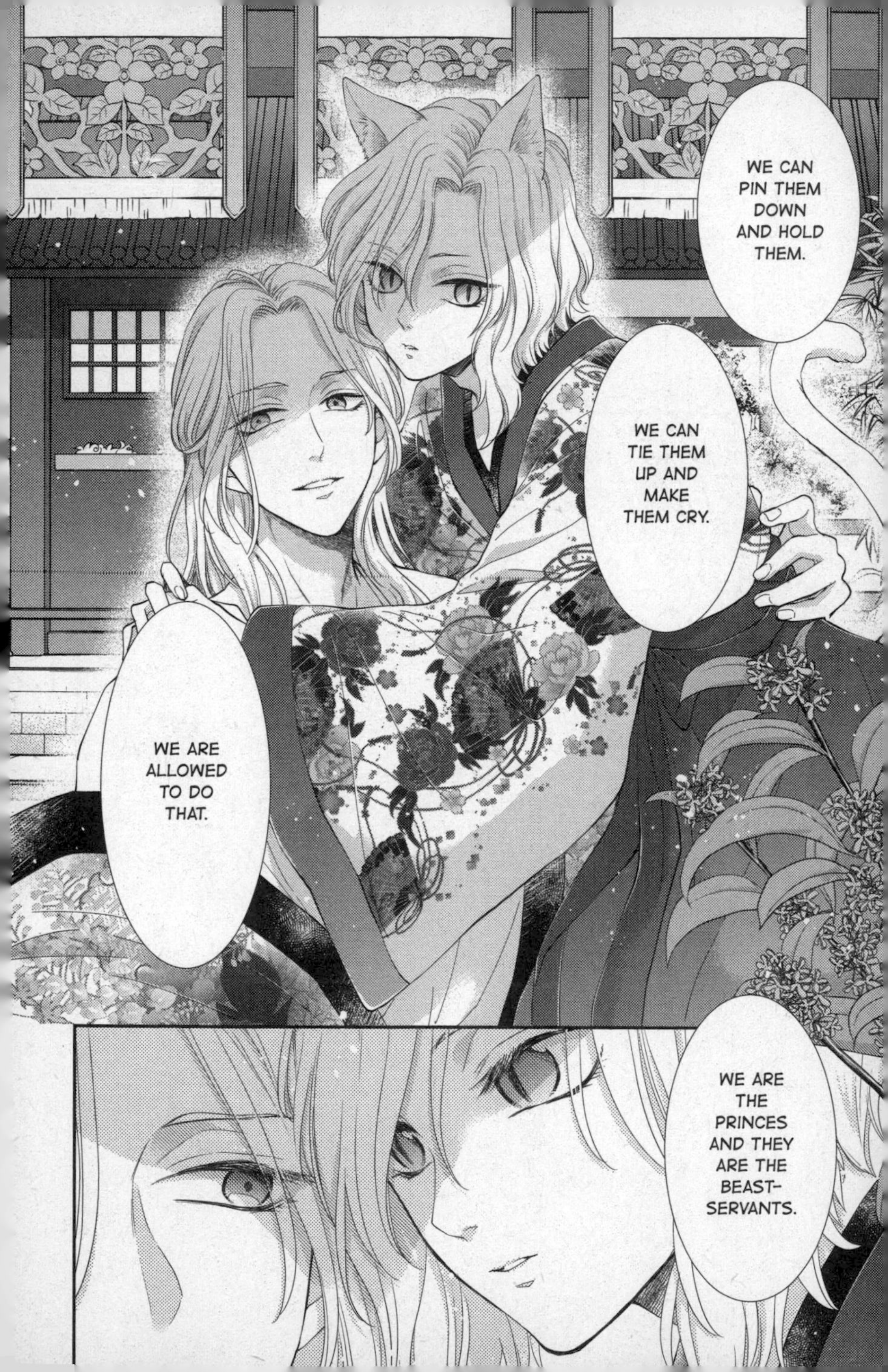
WE CAN PIN THEM DOWN AND HOLD THEM.
WE CAN TIE THEM UP AND MAKE THEM CRY.
WE ARE ALLOWED TO DO THAT.
WE ARE THE PRINCES AND THEY ARE THE BEAST-SERVANTS.

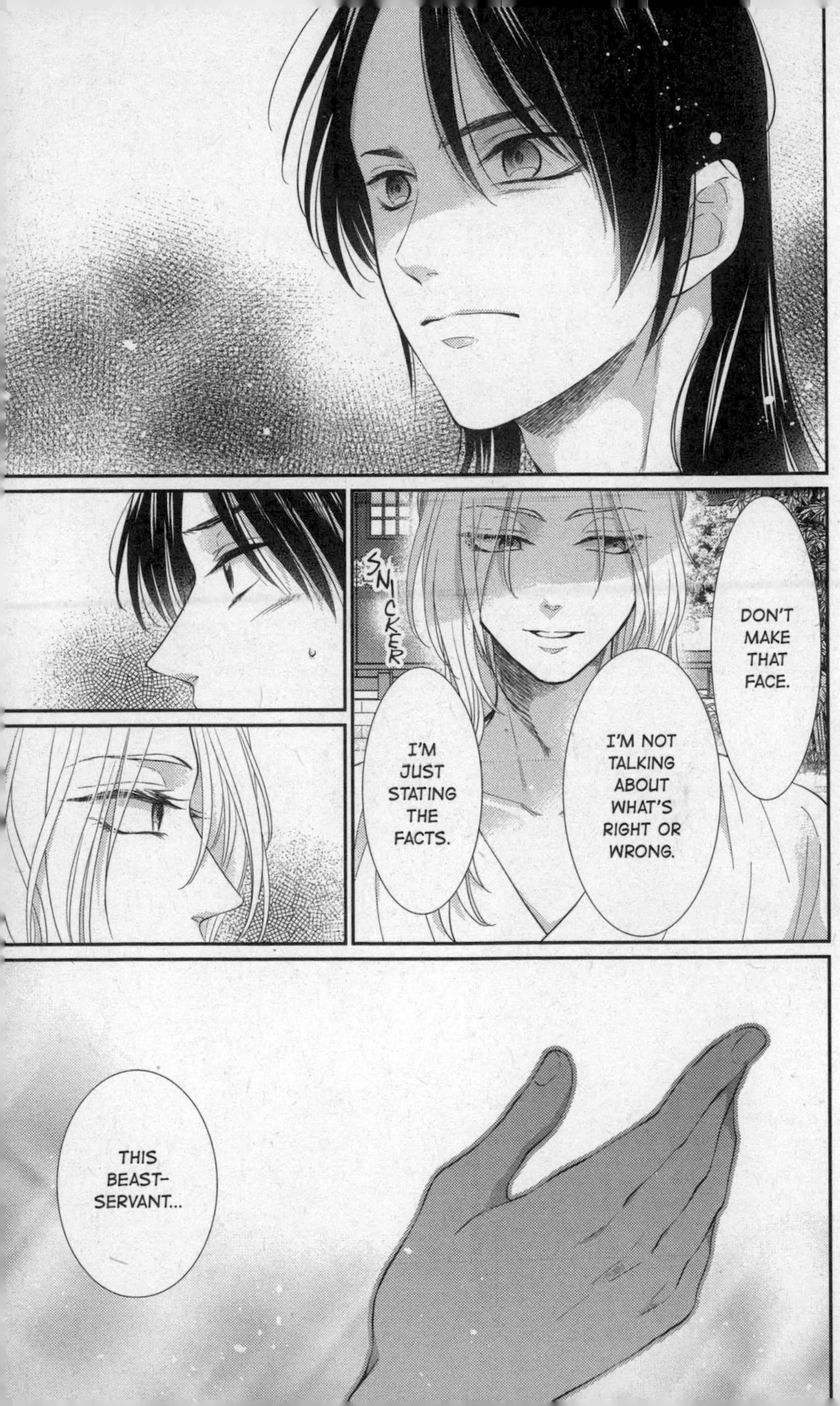
DON'T MAKE THAT FACE.
SNICKER
I'M NOT TALKING ABOUT WHAT'S RIGHT OR WRONG.
I'M JUST STATING THE FACTS.
THIS BEAST-SERVANT...

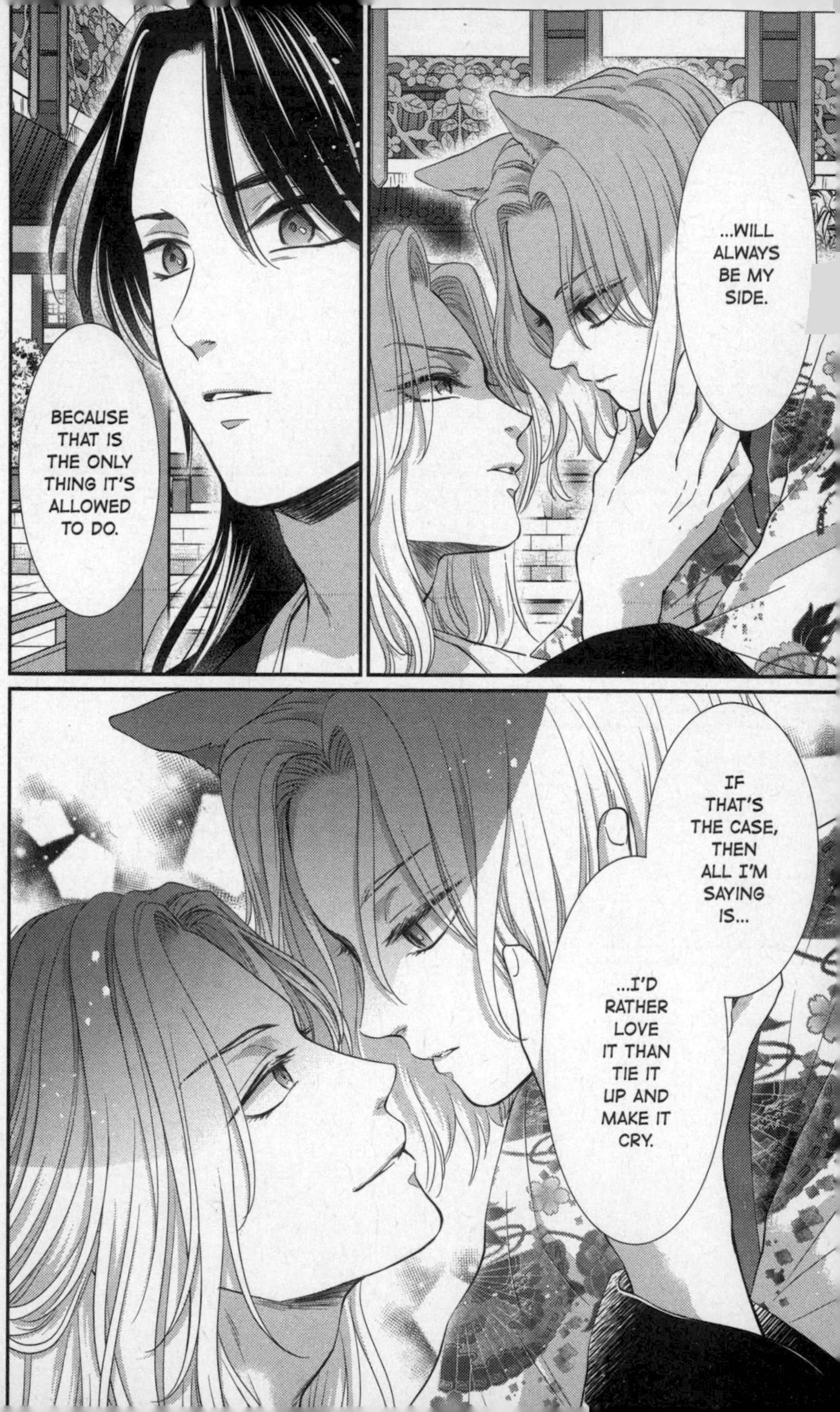
...WILL ALWAYS BE MY SIDE.
BECAUSE THAT IS THE ONLY THING IT'S ALLOWED TO DO.
IF THAT'S THE CASE, THEN ALL I'M SAYING IS...
...I'D RATHER LOVE IT THAN TIE IT UP AND MAKE IT CRY.

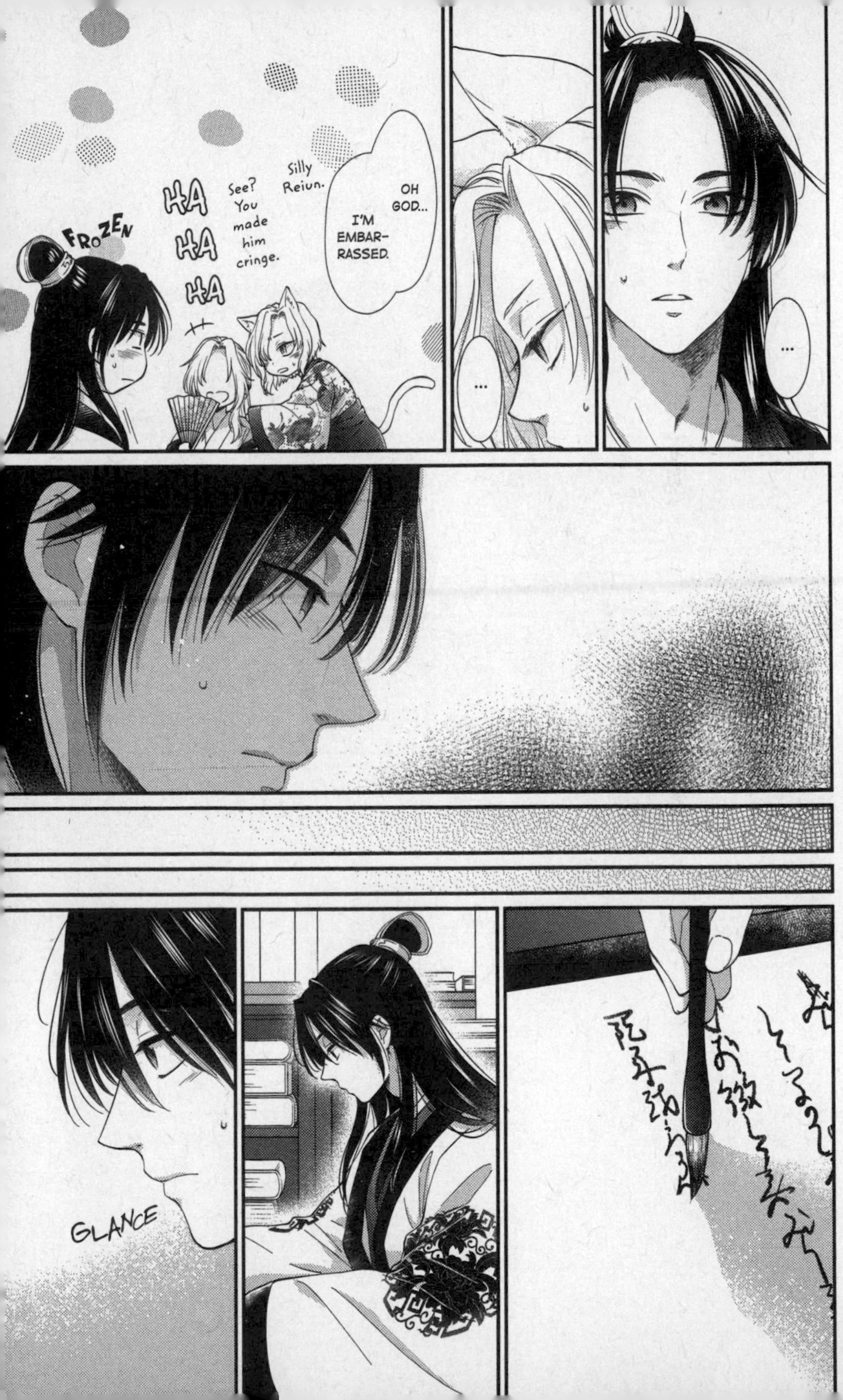
...
...
OH GOD... I'M EMBARRASSED.
Silly Reiun.
See? You made him cringe.
HA HA HA
FROZEN
GLANCE

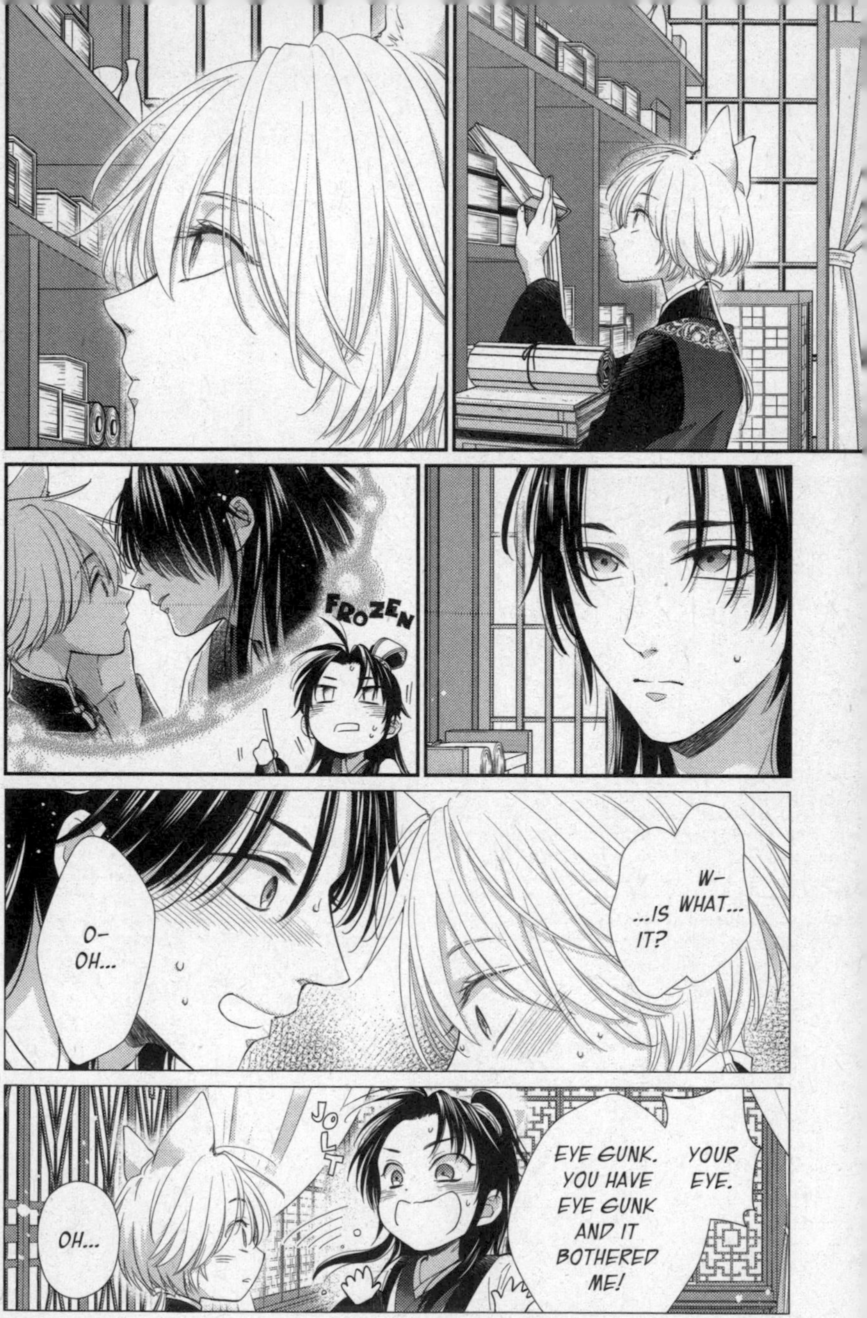
FROZEN
W-WHAT...
...IS IT?
O-OH...
YOUR EYE.
EYE GUNK. YOU HAVE EYE GUNK AND IT BOTHERED ME!
JOLT
OH...

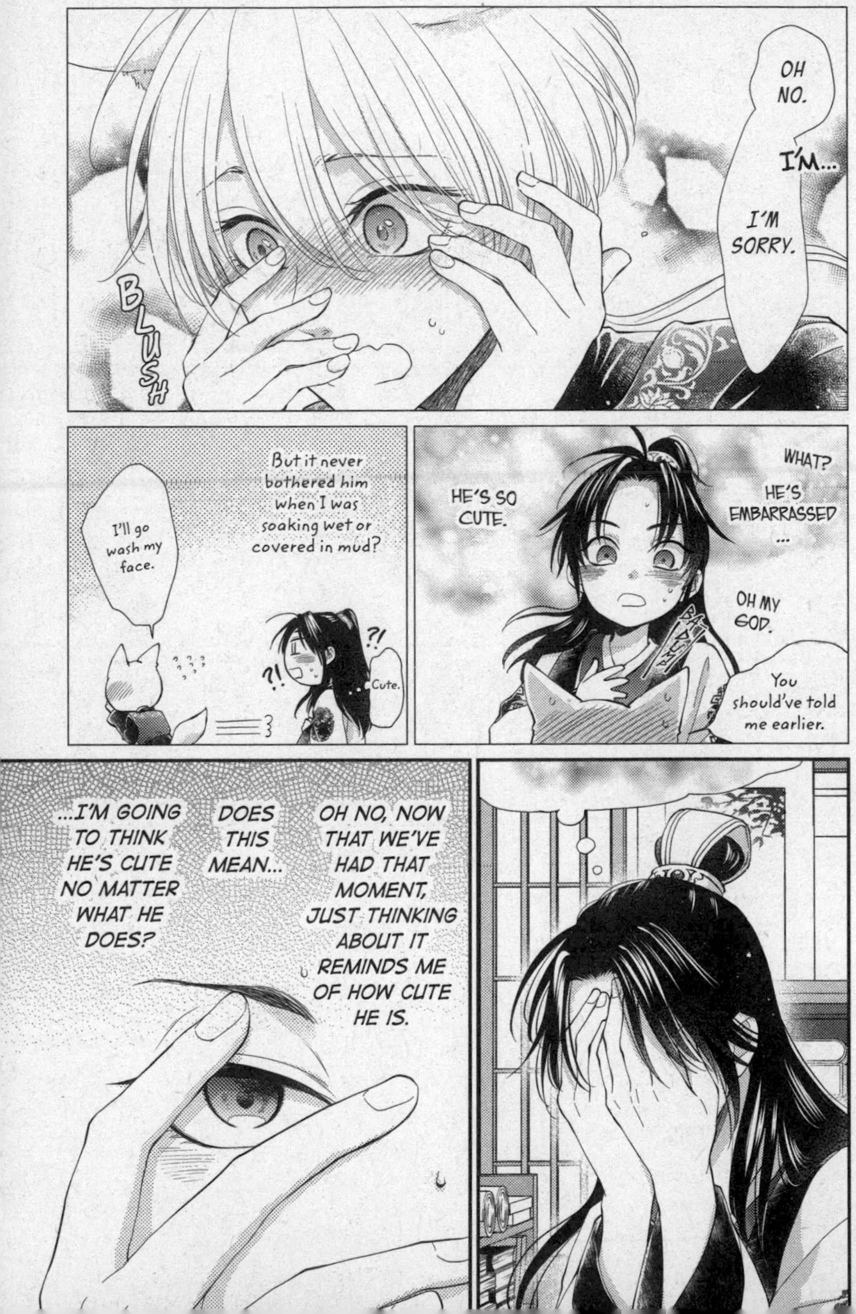
OH NO.
I'M...
I'M SORRY.
BLUSH
WHAT?
HE'S EMBARRASSED...
HE'S SO CUTE.
OH MY GOD.
You should've told me earlier.
But it never bothered him when I was soaking wet or covered in mud?
I'll go wash my face.
?!
Cute.
?!
OH NO, NOW THAT WE'VE HAD THAT MOMENT, JUST THINKING ABOUT IT REMINDS ME OF HOW CUTE HE IS.
DOES THIS MEAN...
...I'M GOING TO THINK HE'S CUTE NO MATTER WHAT HE DOES?

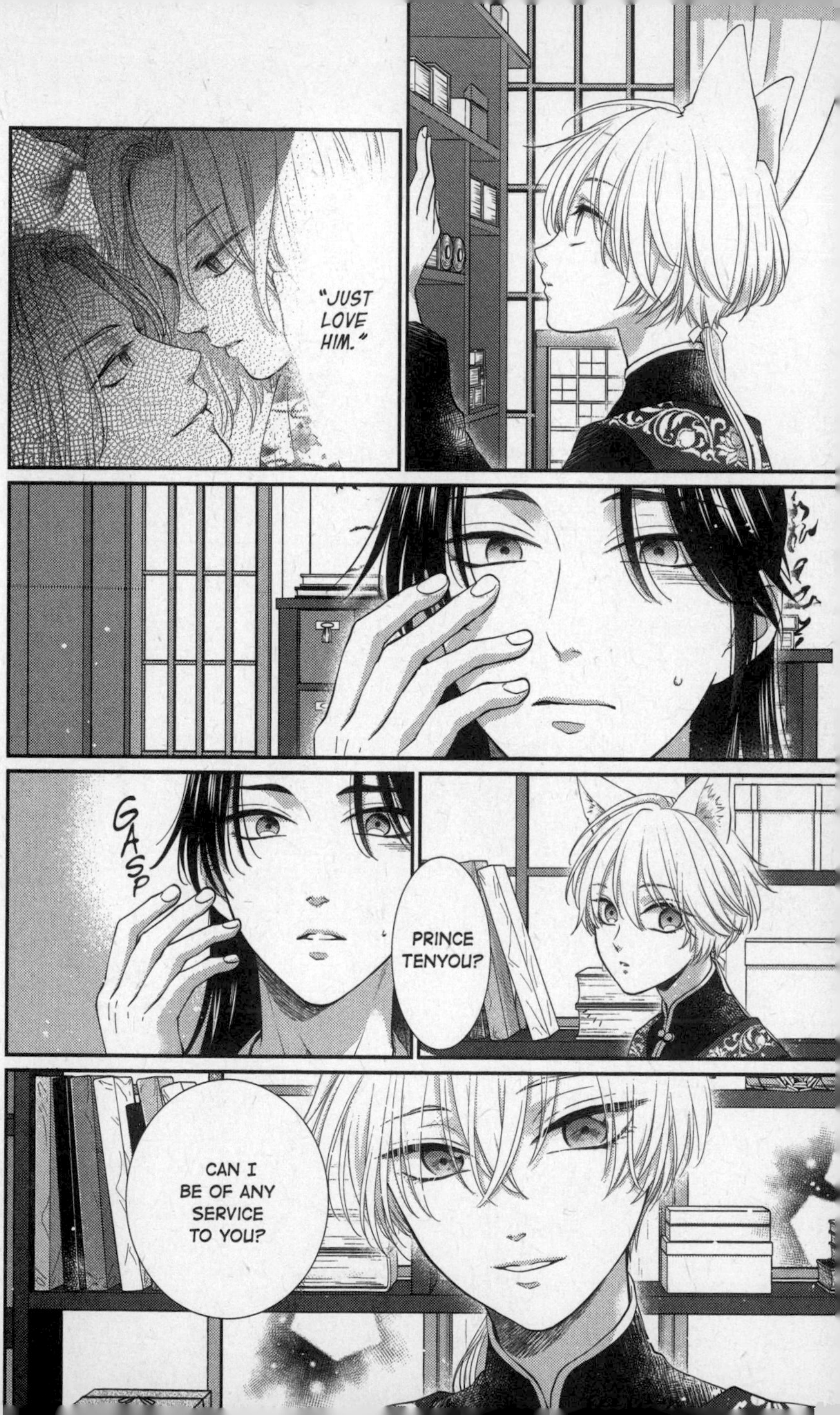
"JUST LOVE HIM."
GASP
PRINCE TENYOU?
CAN I BE OF ANY SERVICE TO YOU?

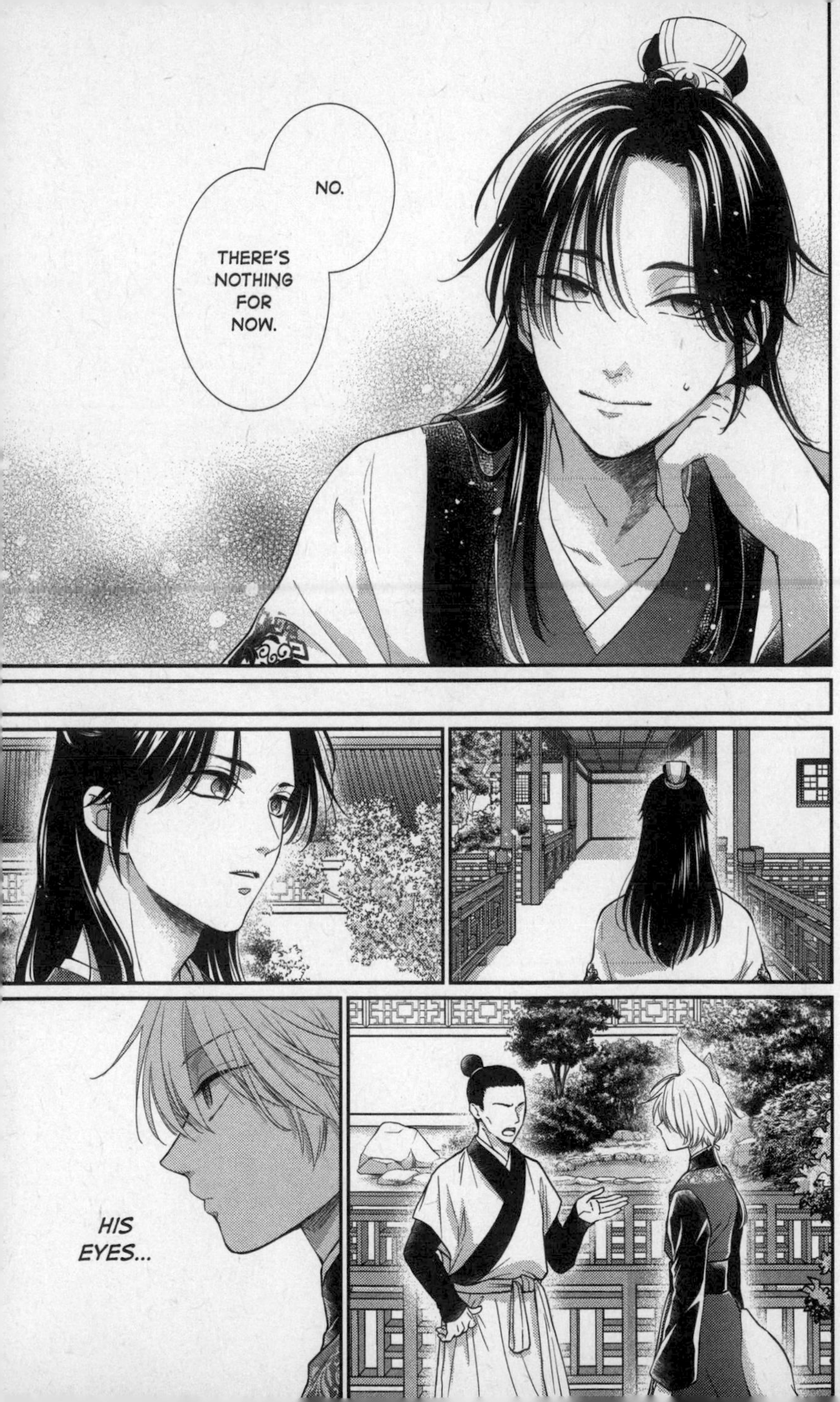
NO.
THERE'S NOTHING FOR NOW.
HIS EYES...

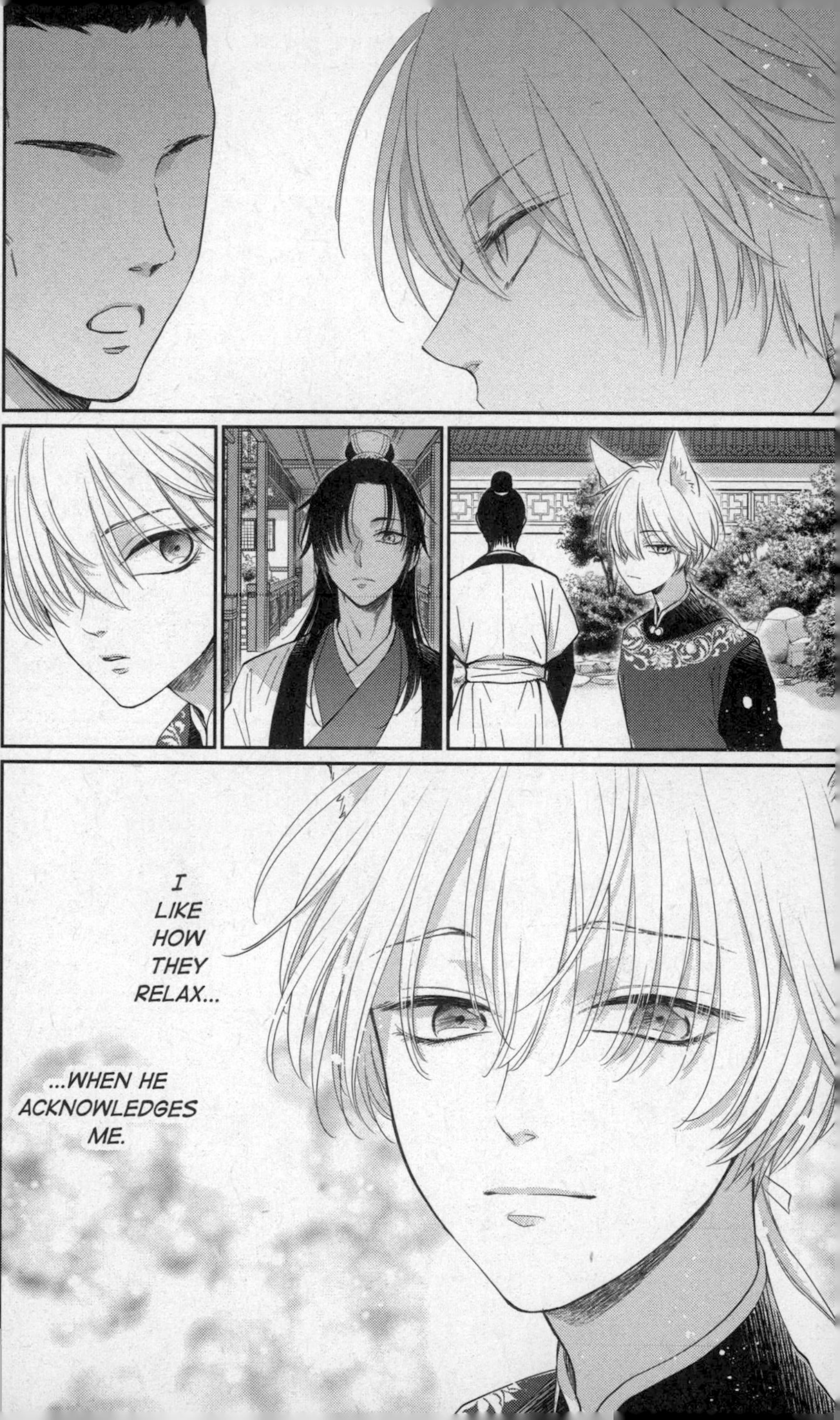
I LIKE HOW THEY RELAX...
...WHEN HE ACKNOWLEDGES ME.

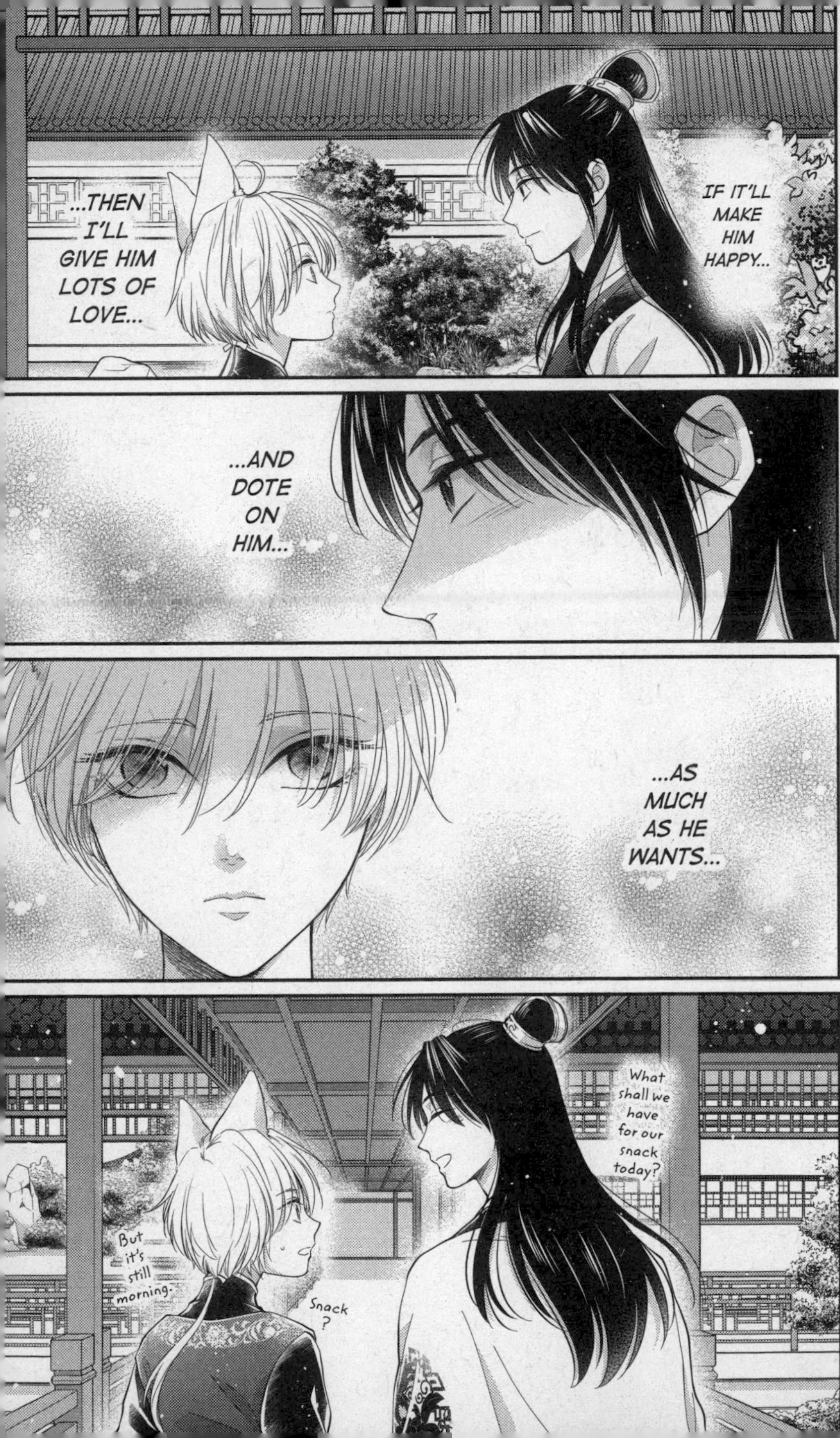
IF IT'LL MAKE HIM HAPPY...
...THEN I'LL GIVE HIM LOTS OF LOVE...
...AND DOTE ON HIM...
...AS MUCH AS HE WANTS...
What shall we have for our snack today?
Snack?
But it's still morning.

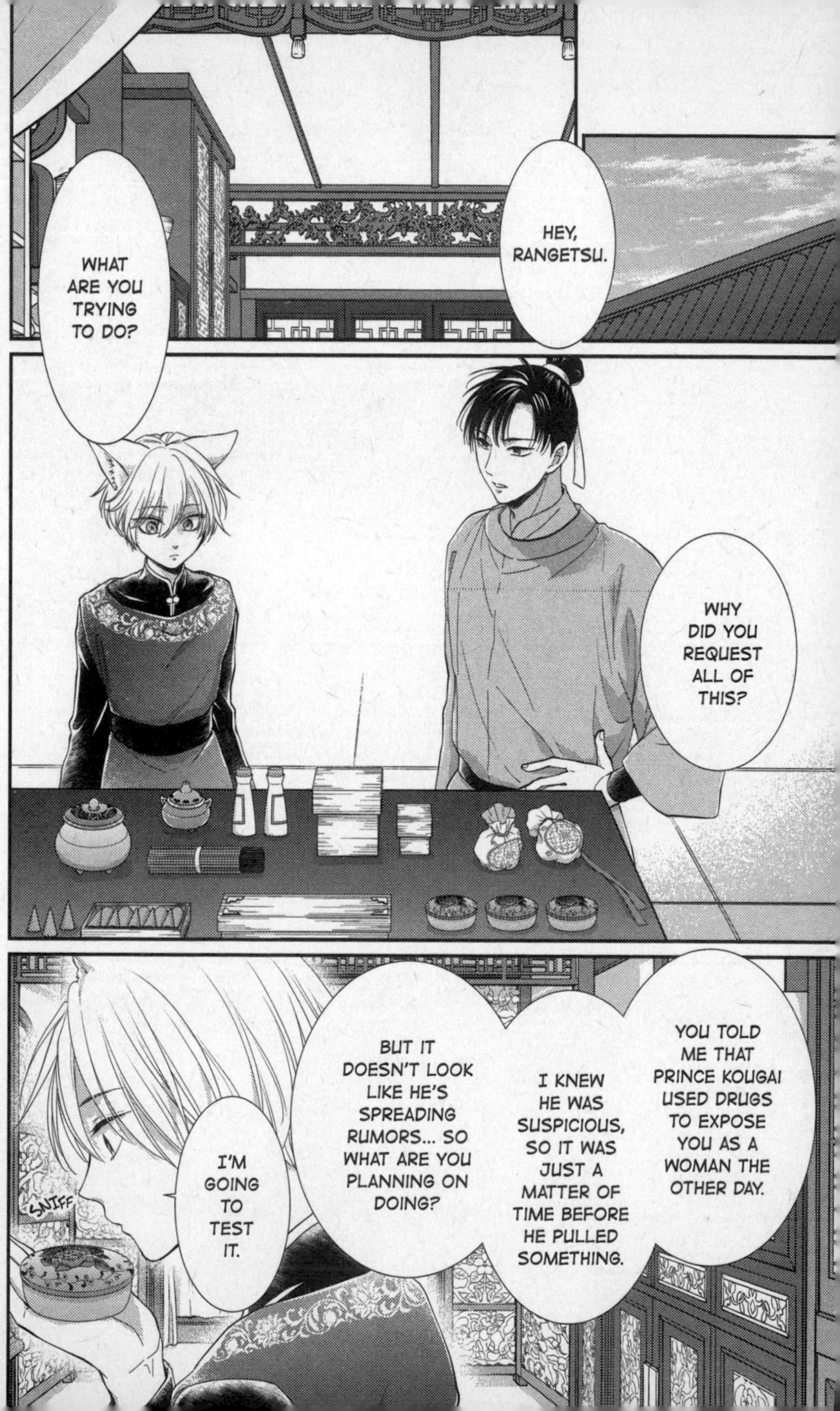
HEY, RANGETSU.
WHAT ARE YOU TRYING TO DO?
WHY DID YOU REQUEST ALL OF THIS?
YOU TOLD ME THAT PRINCE KOUGAI USED DRUGS TO EXPOSE YOU AS A WOMAN THE OTHER DAY.
I KNEW HE WAS SUSPICIOUS, SO IT WAS JUST A MATTER OF TIME BEFORE HE PULLED SOMETHING.
BUT IT DOESN'T LOOK LIKE HE'S SPREADING RUMORS... SO WHAT ARE YOU PLANNING ON DOING?
I'M GOING TO TEST IT.
SNIFF

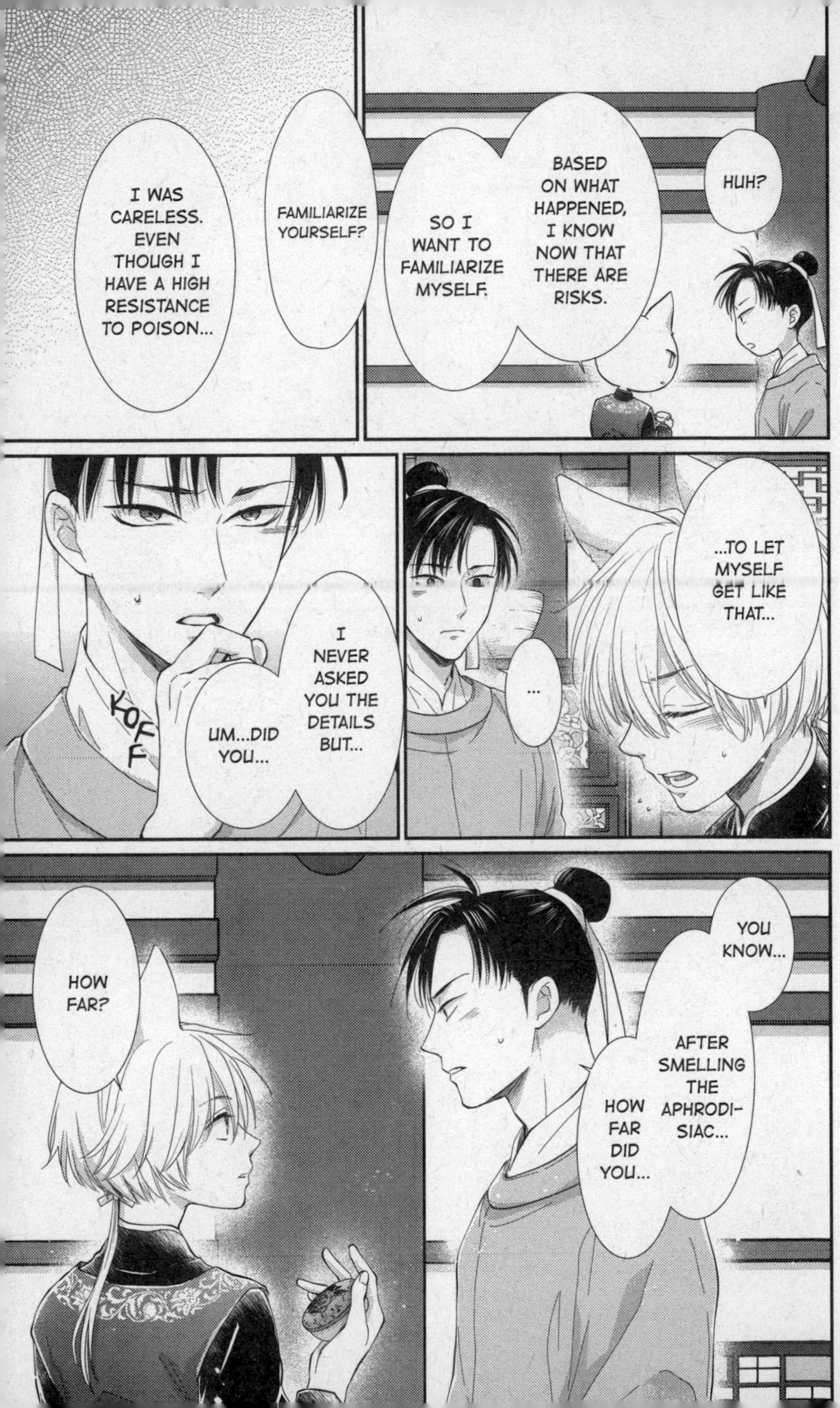
HUH?
BASED ON WHAT HAPPENED, I KNOW NOW THAT THERE ARE RISKS.
SO I WANT TO FAMILIARIZE MYSELF.
FAMILIARIZE YOURSELF?
I WAS CARELESS. EVEN THOUGH I HAVE A HIGH RESISTANCE TO POISON...
...TO LET MYSELF GET LIKE THAT...
...
I NEVER ASKED YOU THE DETAILS BUT...
UM...DID YOU...
KOFF
YOU KNOW...
AFTER SMELLING THE APHRODISIAC...
HOW FAR DID YOU...
HOW FAR?

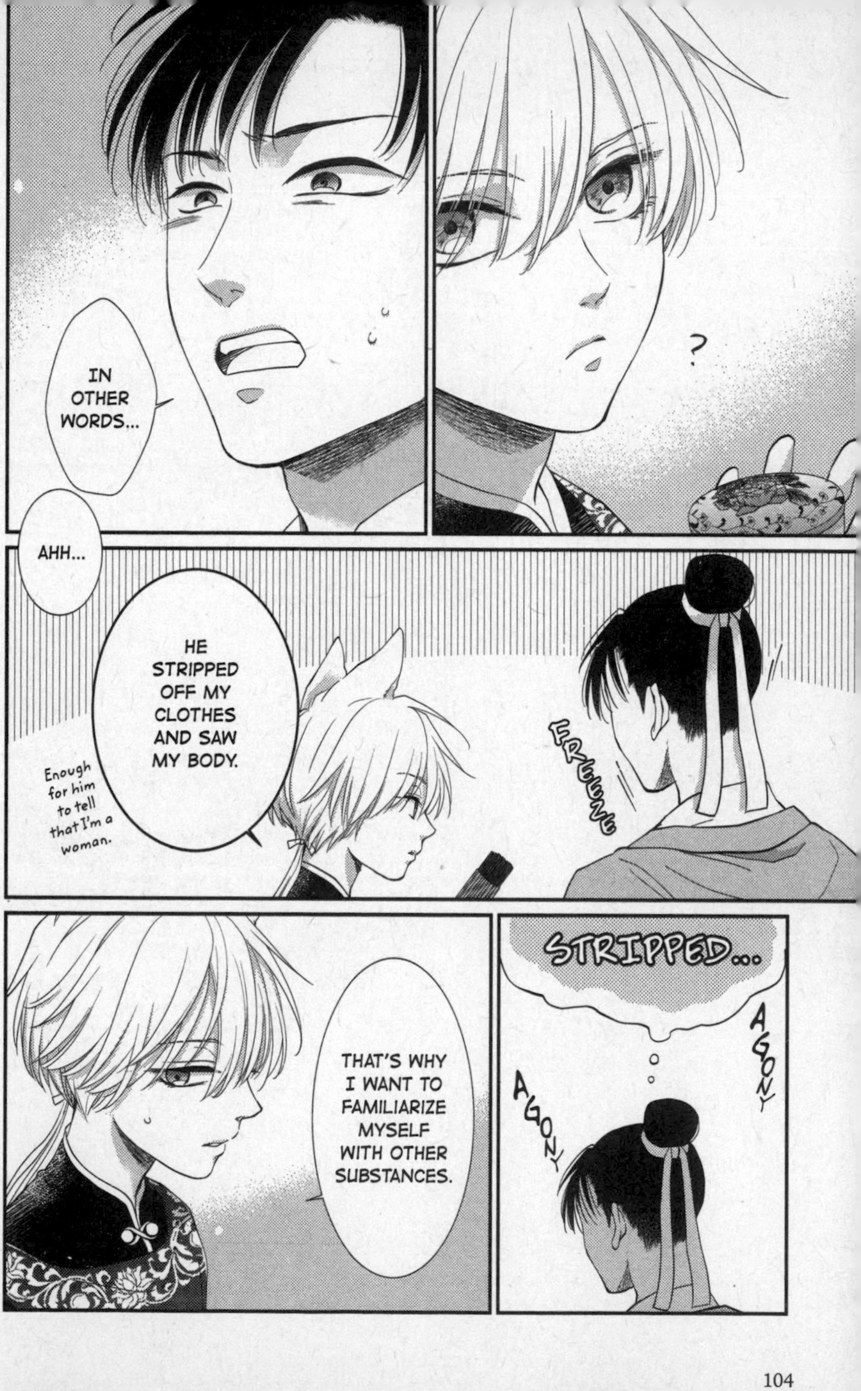
?
IN OTHER WORDS...
AHH...
HE STRIPPED OFF MY CLOTHES AND SAW MY BODY.
FREEZE
Enough for him to tell that I'm a woman.
STRIPPED...
AGONY
AGONY
THAT'S WHY I WANT TO FAMILIARIZE MYSELF WITH OTHER SUBSTANCES.

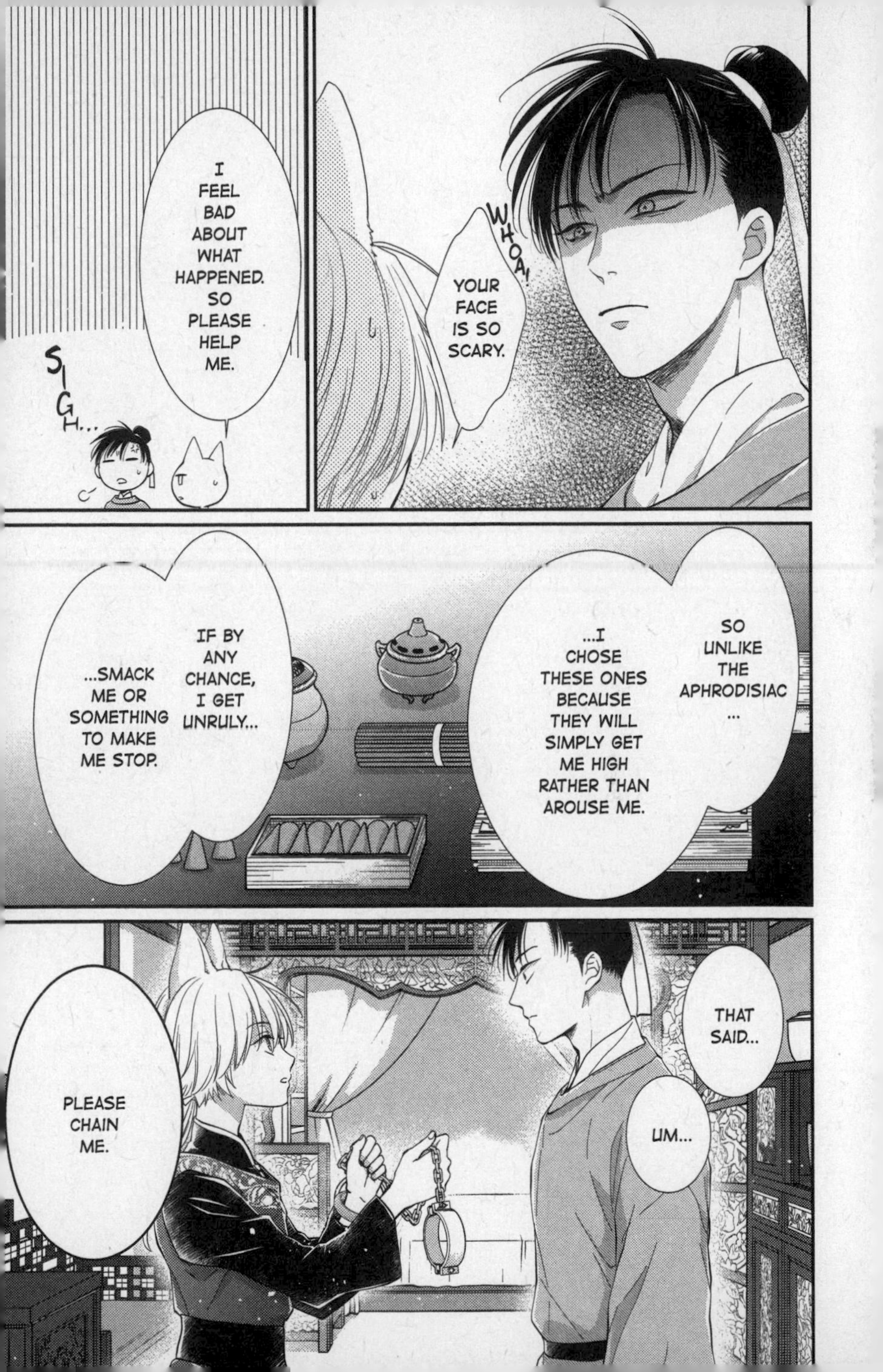
WHOA!
YOUR FACE IS SO SCARY.
I FEEL BAD ABOUT WHAT HAPPENED. SO PLEASE HELP ME.
SIGH...
SO UNLIKE THE APHRODISIAC...
...I CHOSE THESE ONES BECAUSE THEY WILL SIMPLY GET ME HIGH RATHER THAN AROUSE ME.
IF BY ANY CHANCE, I GET UNRULY...
...SMACK ME OR SOMETHING TO MAKE ME STOP.
THAT SAID...
UM...
PLEASE CHAIN ME.

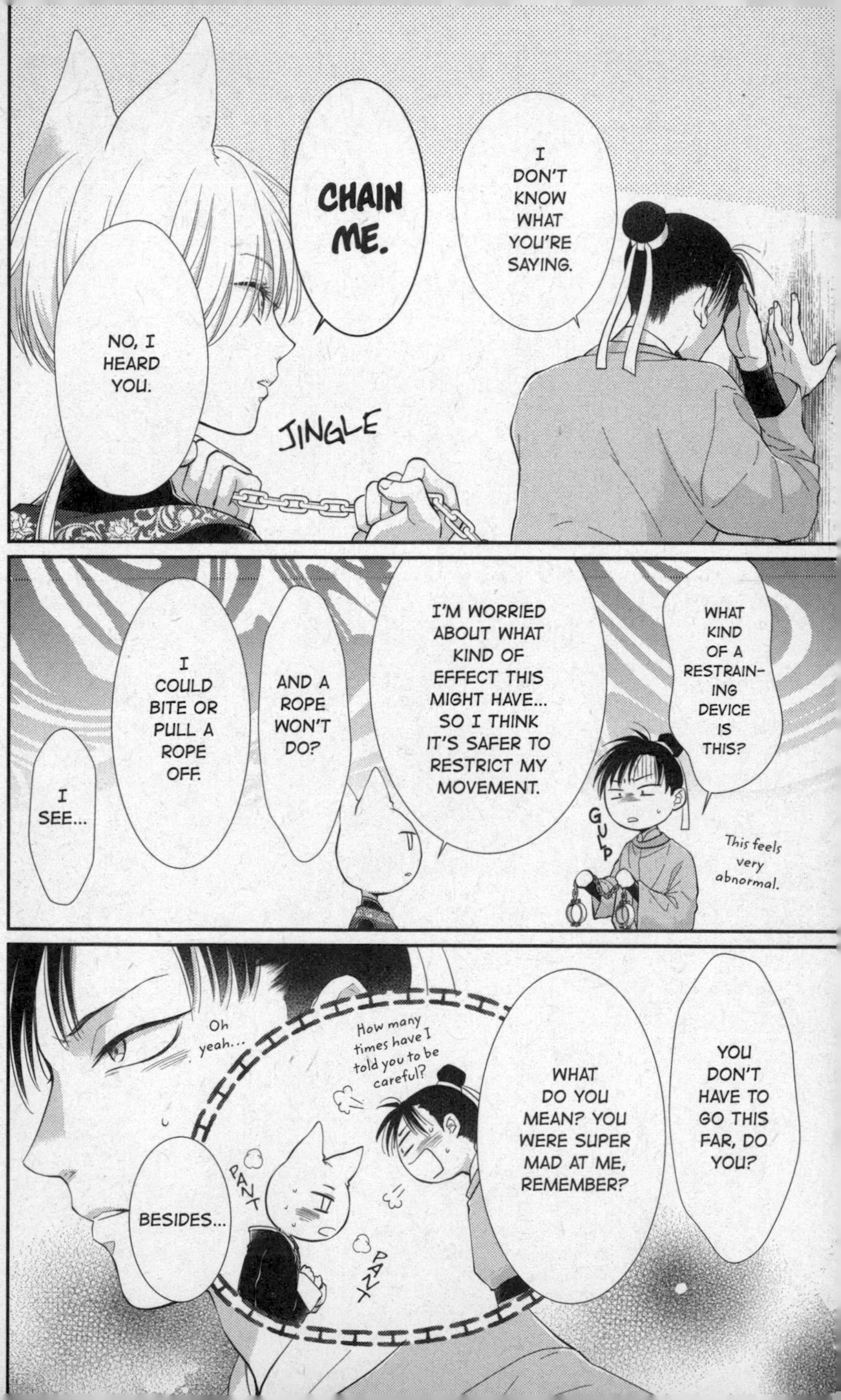
I DON'T KNOW WHAT YOU'RE SAYING.
CHAIN ME.
NO, I HEARD YOU.
JINGLE
WHAT KIND OF A RESTRAIN-ING DEVICE IS THIS?
This feels very abnormal.
GULP
I'M WORRIED ABOUT WHAT KIND OF EFFECT THIS MIGHT HAVE... SO I THINK IT'S SAFER TO RESTRICT MY MOVEMENT.
AND A ROPE WON'T DO?
I COULD BITE OR PULL A ROPE OFF.
I SEE...
YOU DON'T HAVE TO GO THIS FAR, DO YOU?
WHAT DO YOU MEAN? YOU WERE SUPER MAD AT ME, REMEMBER?
How many times have I told you to be careful?
PANT
PANT
Oh yeah...
BESIDES...

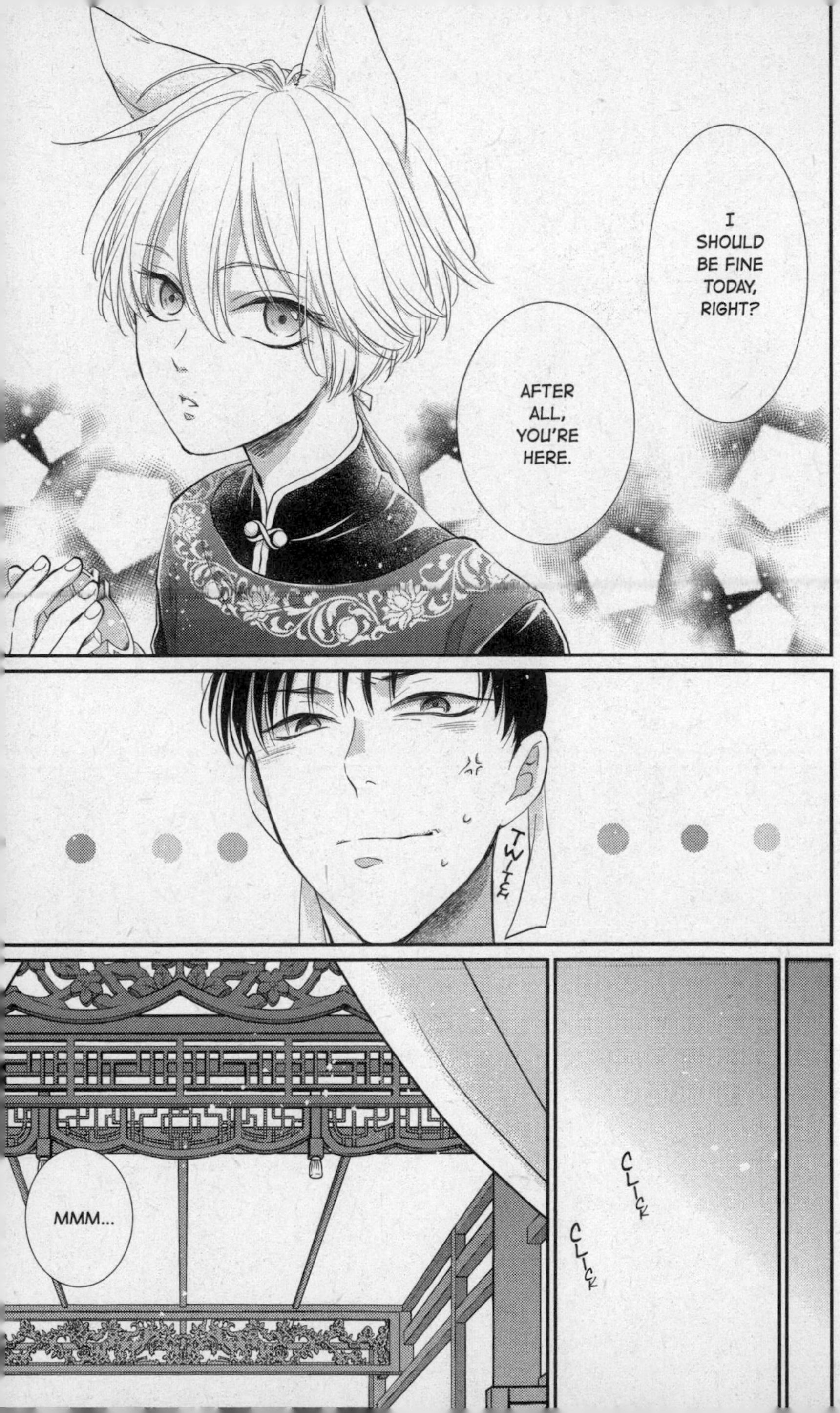
I SHOULD BE FINE TODAY, RIGHT?
AFTER ALL, YOU'RE HERE.
TWITCH
CLICK
CLICK
MMM...

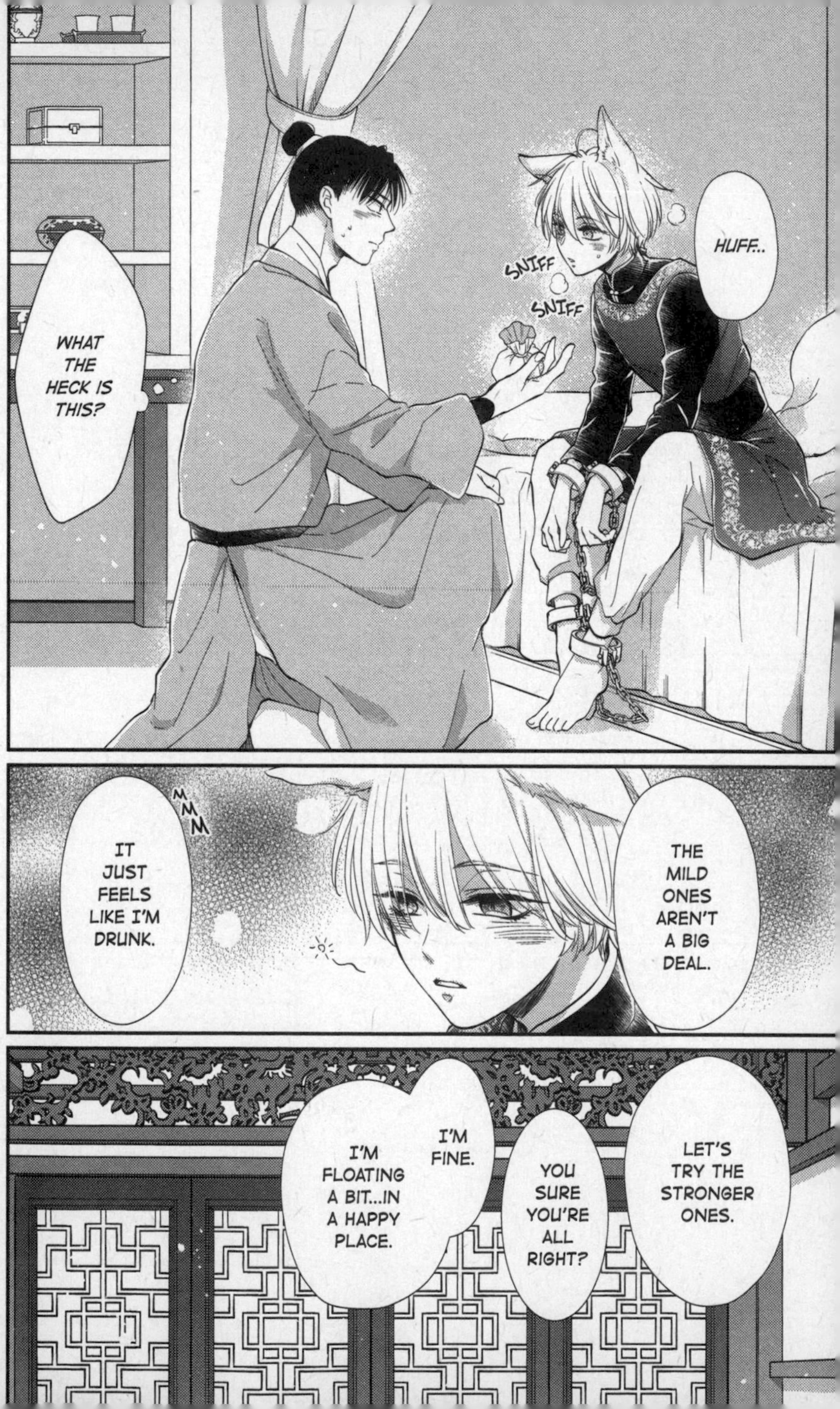
HUFF...
SNIFF
SNIFF
WHAT THE HECK IS THIS?
THE MILD ONES AREN'T A BIG DEAL.
MMM
IT JUST FEELS LIKE I'M DRUNK.
LET'S TRY THE STRONGER ONES.
YOU SURE YOU'RE ALL RIGHT?
I'M FINE.
I'M FLOATING A BIT...IN A HAPPY PLACE.

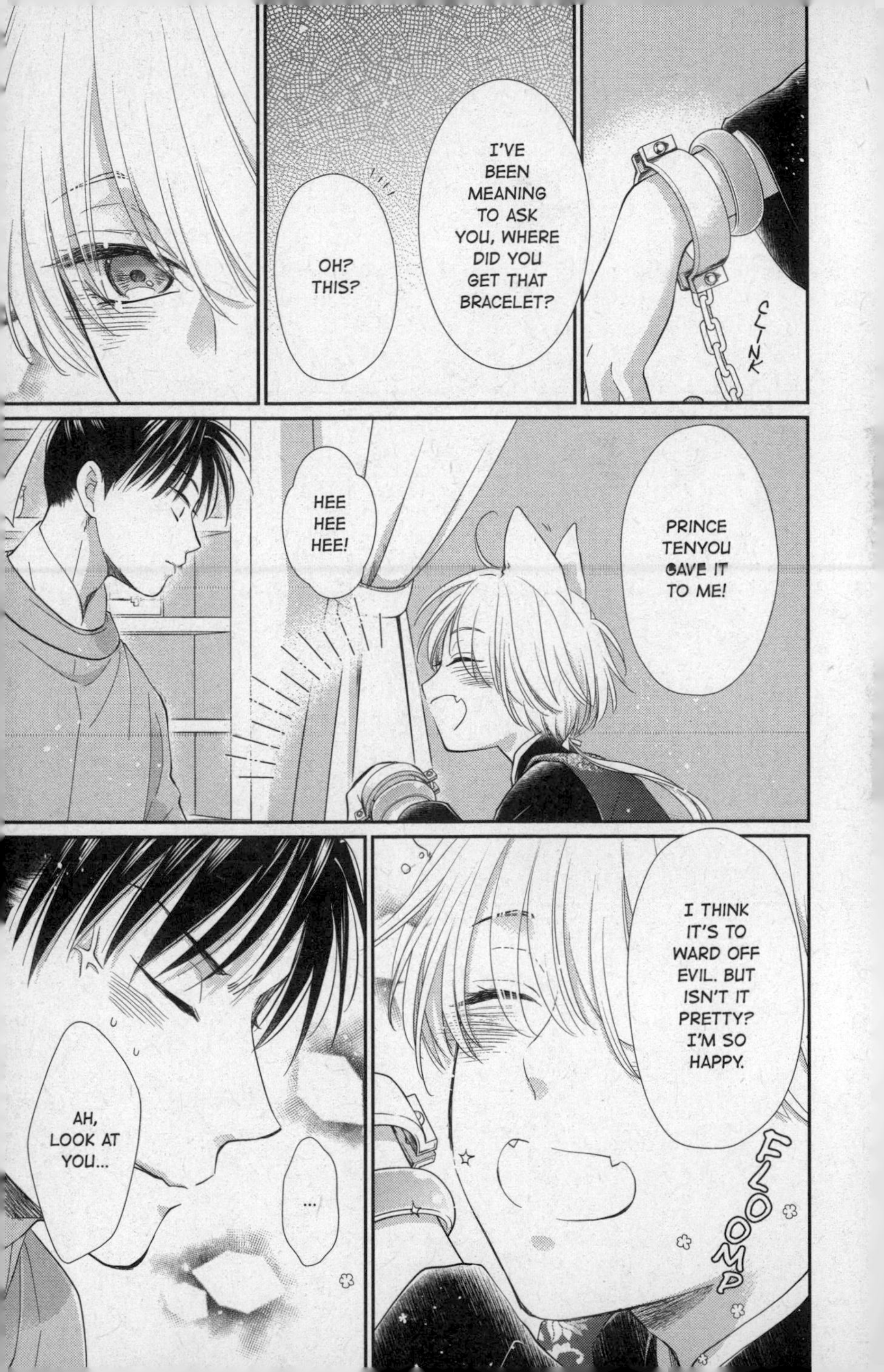
CLINK
I'VE BEEN MEANING TO ASK YOU, WHERE DID YOU GET THAT BRACELET?
OH? THIS?
PRINCE TENYOU GAVE IT TO ME!
HEE HEE HEE!
I THINK IT'S TO WARD OFF EVIL. BUT ISN'T IT PRETTY? I'M SO HAPPY.
FLOOMP
AH, LOOK AT YOU...
...

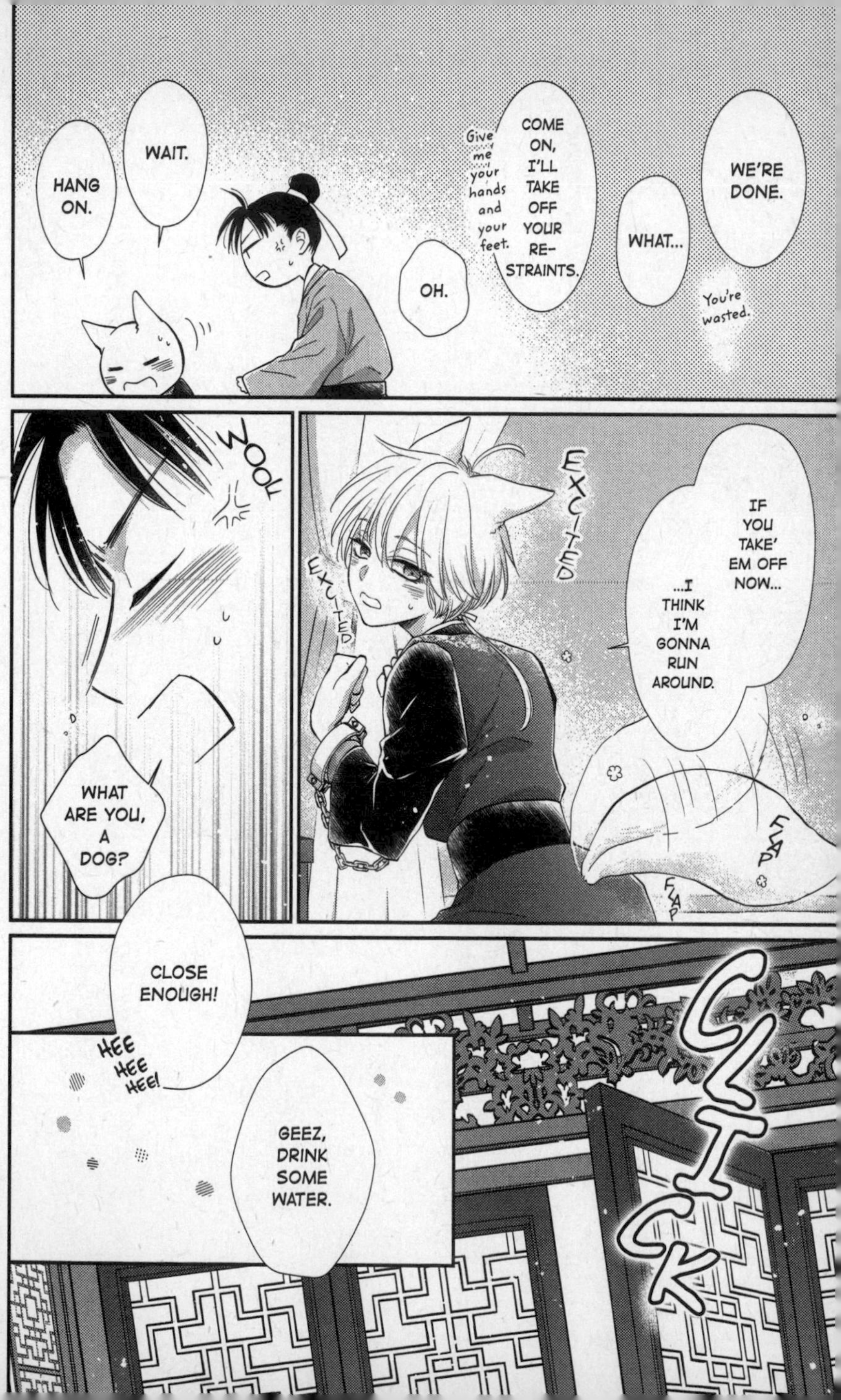
WE'RE DONE.
You're wasted.
WHAT...
COME ON, I'LL TAKE OFF YOUR RE-STRAINTS.
Give me your hands and your feet.
OH.
WAIT.
HANG ON.
EXCITED
IF YOU TAKE' EM OFF NOW...
...I THINK I'M GONNA RUN AROUND.
EXCITED
FLAP
FLAP
WOOF
WHAT ARE YOU, A DOG?
CLICK
CLOSE ENOUGH!
HEE HEE HEE!
GEEZ, DRINK SOME WATER.

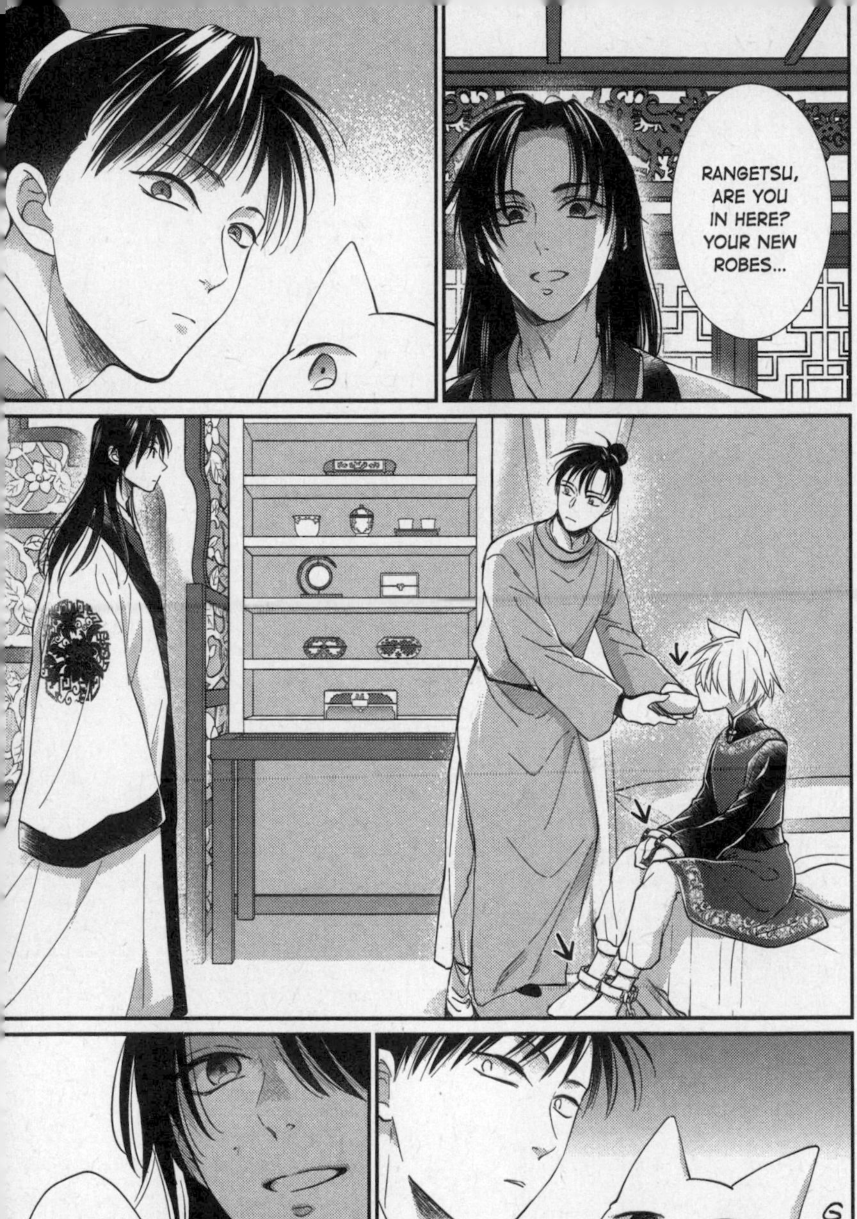
RANGETSU, ARE YOU IN HERE? YOUR NEW ROBES...
GULP GULP
YOUR H—

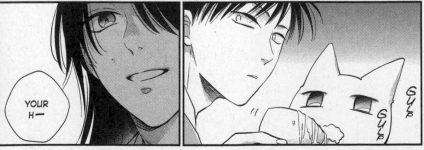

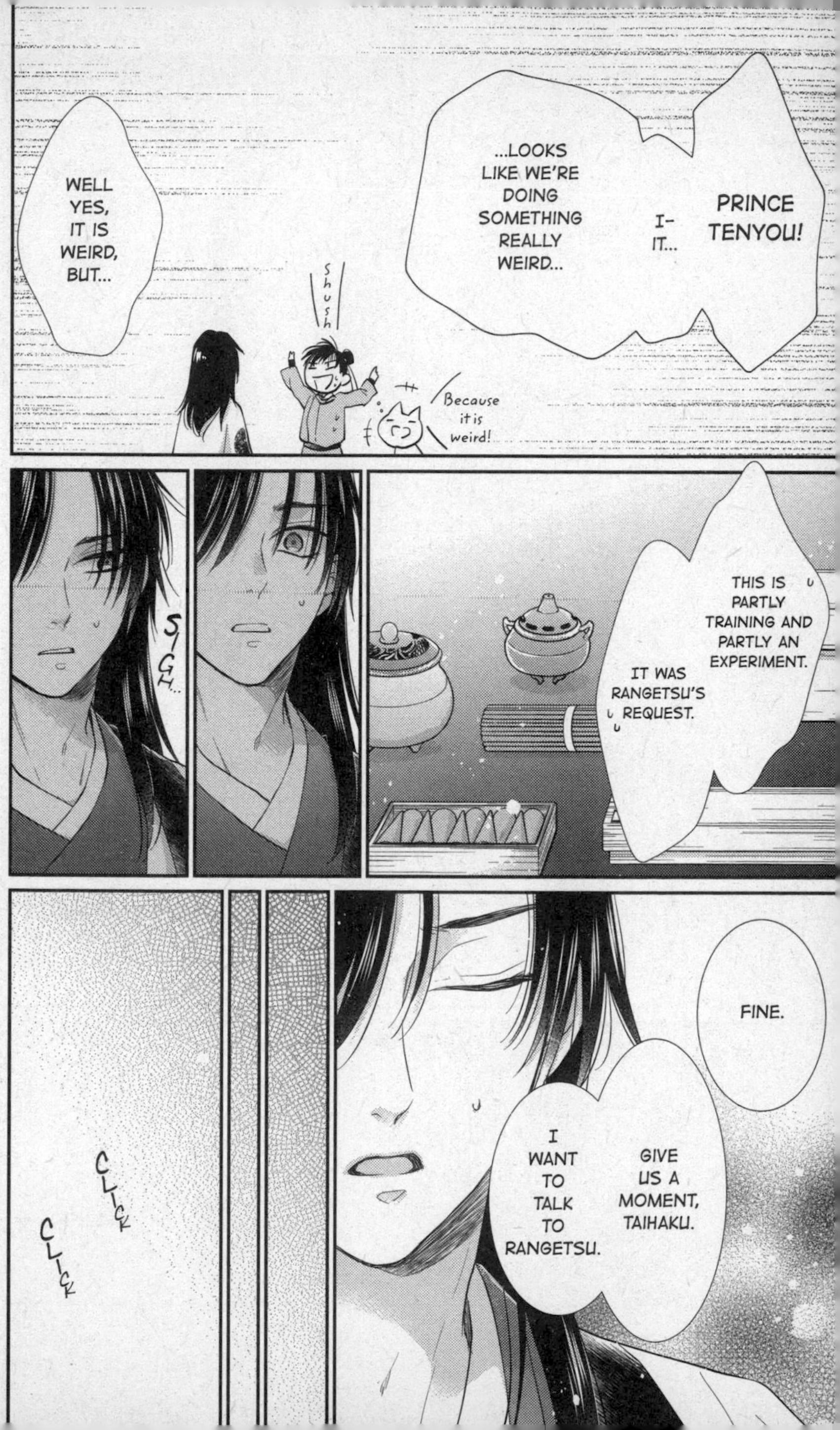
PRINCE TENYOU!
I- IT...
...LOOKS LIKE WE'RE DOING SOMETHING REALLY WEIRD...
WELL YES, IT IS WEIRD, BUT...
Shush
Because it is weird!
THIS IS PARTLY TRAINING AND PARTLY AN EXPERIMENT.
IT WAS RANGETSU'S REQUEST.
SIGH...
FINE.
GIVE US A MOMENT, TAIHAKU.
I WANT TO TALK TO RANGETSU.
CLICK
CLICK

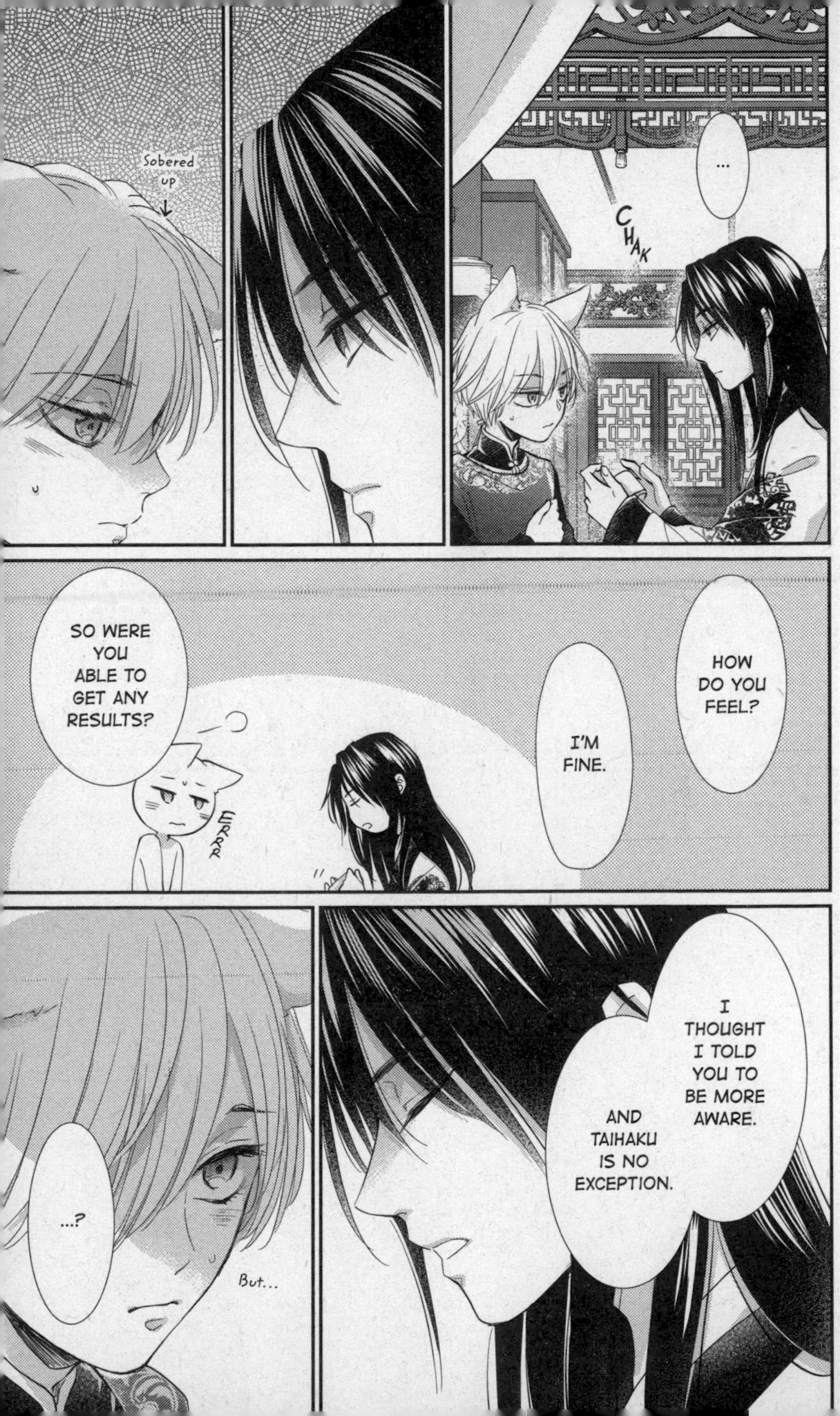
...
CHAK
Sobered up
SO WERE YOU ABLE TO GET ANY RESULTS?
HOW DO YOU FEEL?
I'M FINE.
ERRR
I THOUGHT I TOLD YOU TO BE MORE AWARE.
AND TAIHAKU IS NO EXCEPTION.
...?
But...

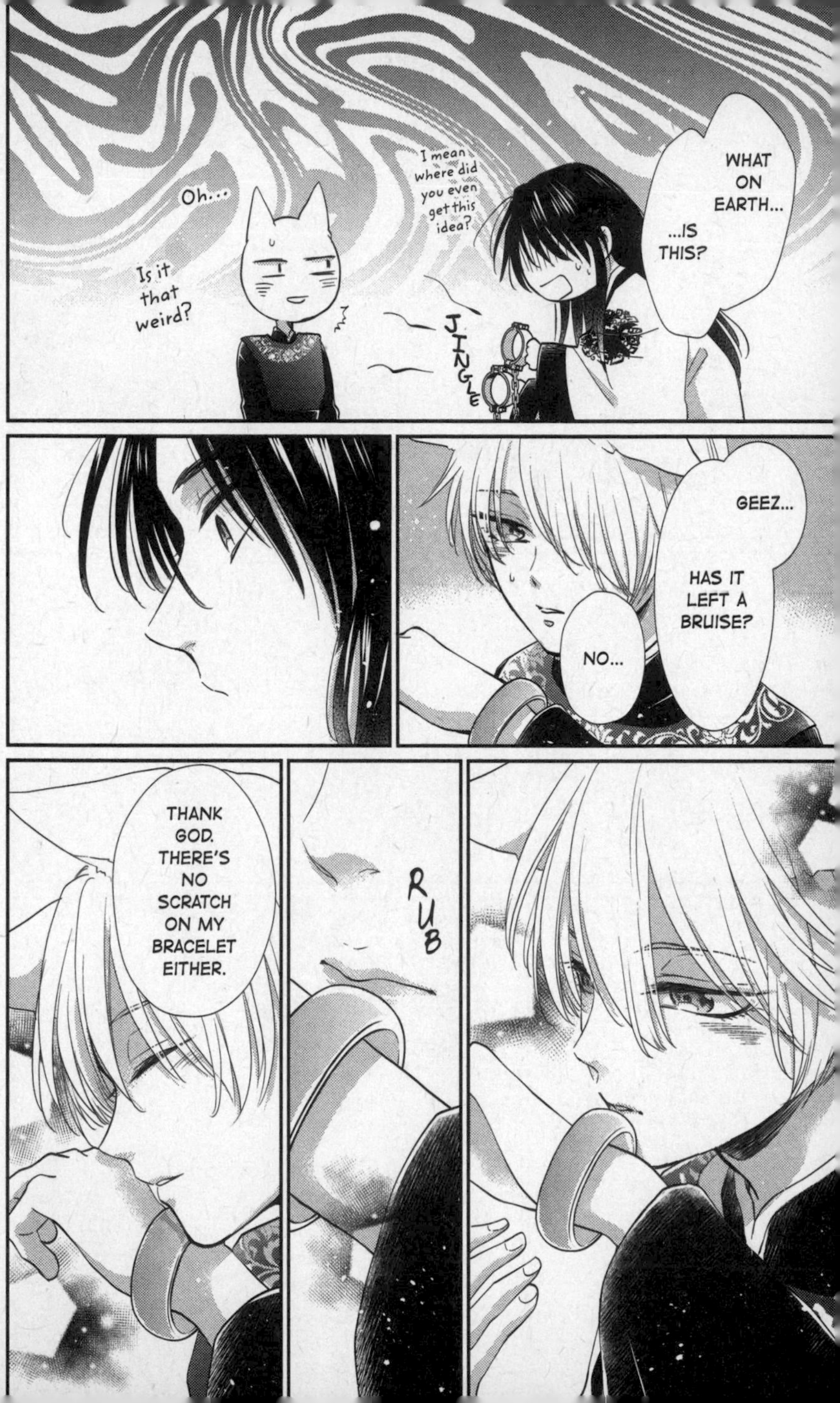

WHAT ON EARTH...
...IS THIS?
I mean where did you even get this idea?
Oh...
JINGLE
Is it that weird?
GEEZ...
HAS IT LEFT A BRUISE?
NO...
RUB
THANK GOD. THERE'S NO SCRATCH ON MY BRACELET EITHER.

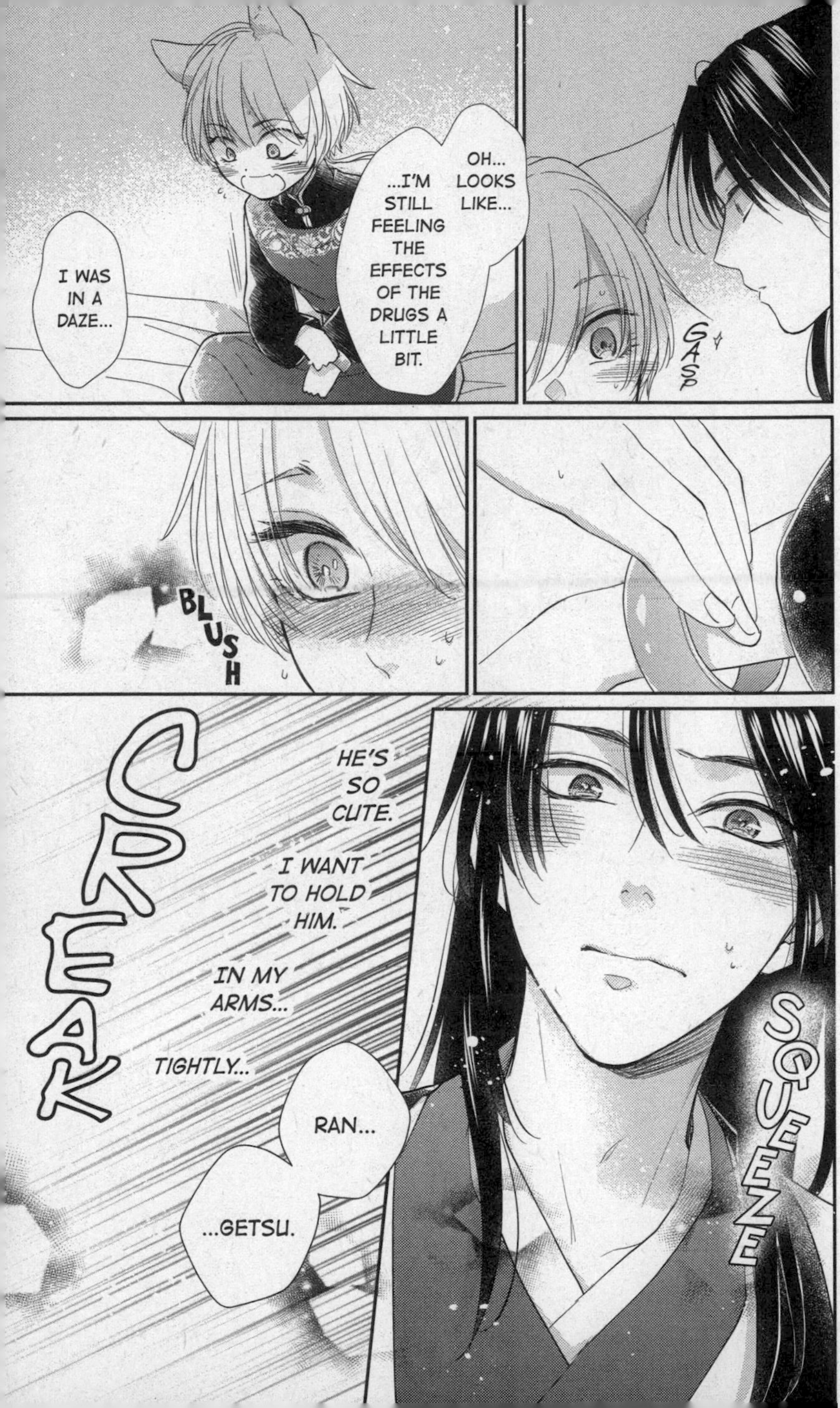
GASP
OH... LOOKS LIKE...
...I'M STILL FEELING THE EFFECTS OF THE DRUGS A LITTLE BIT.
I WAS IN A DAZE...
BLUSH
SQUEEZE
HE'S SO CUTE.
I WANT TO HOLD HIM.
IN MY ARMS...
TIGHTLY...
RAN...
...GETSU.
CREAK

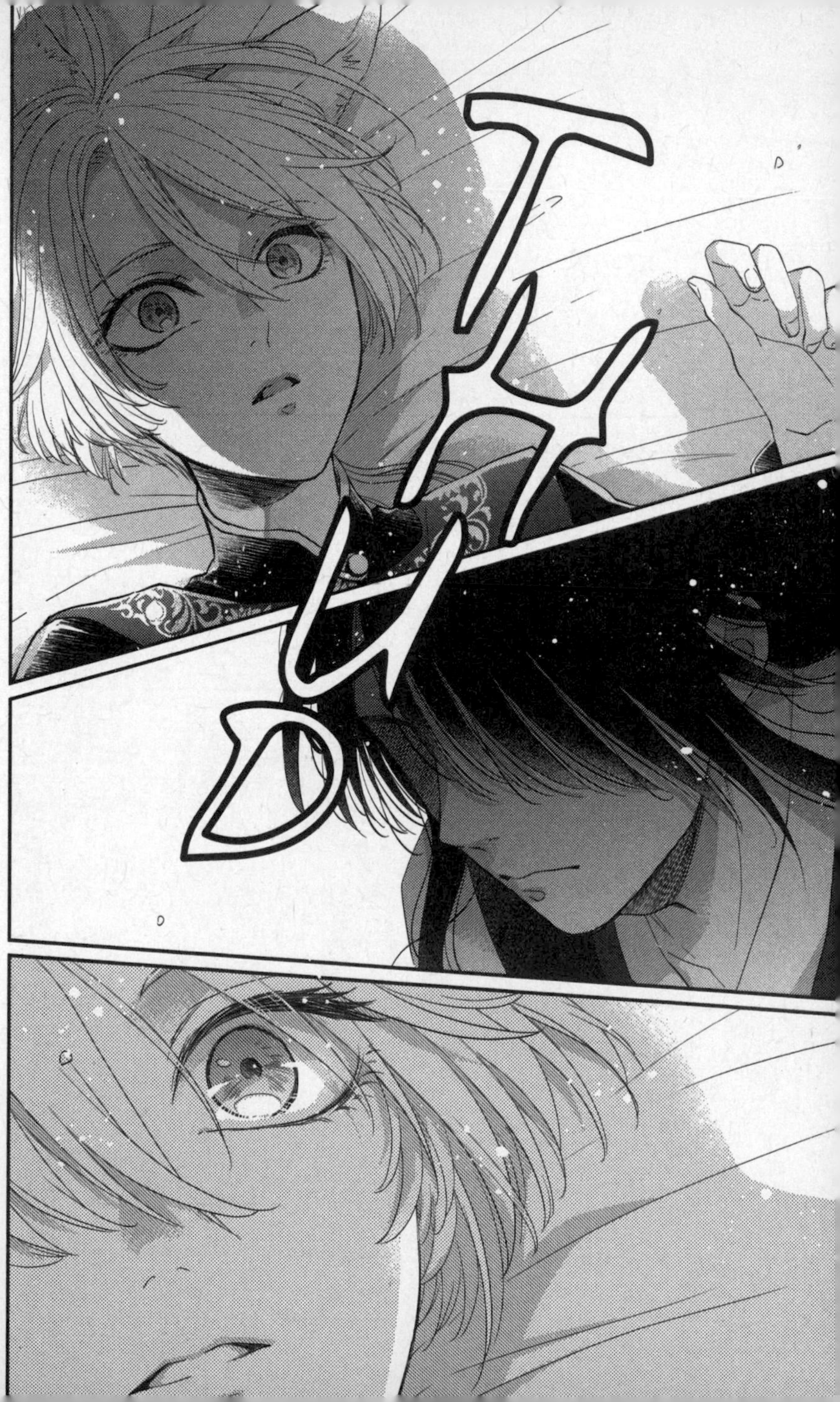
THUD

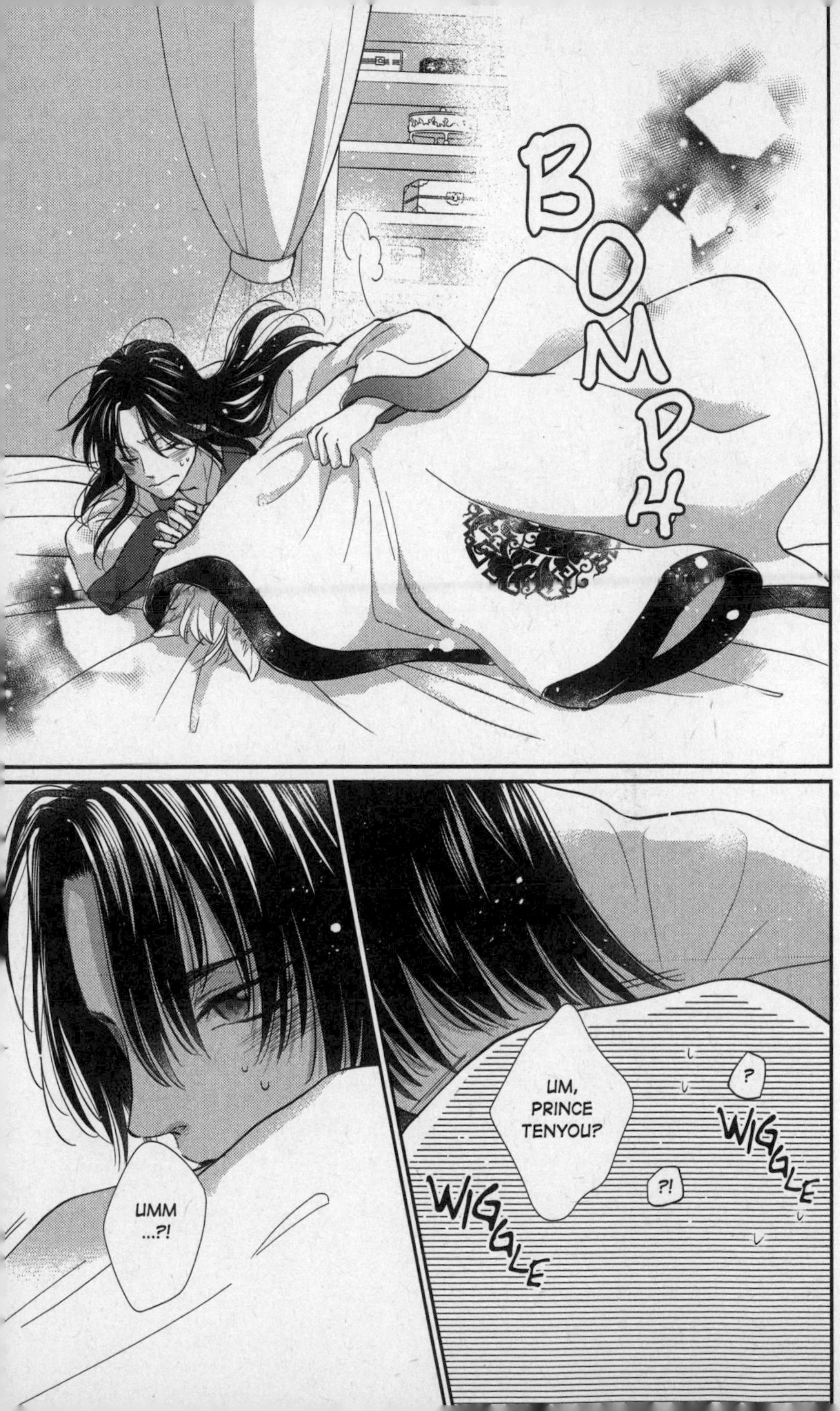
BOMPH
?
UM, PRINCE TENYOU?
WIGGLE
?!
WIGGLE
UMM ...?!

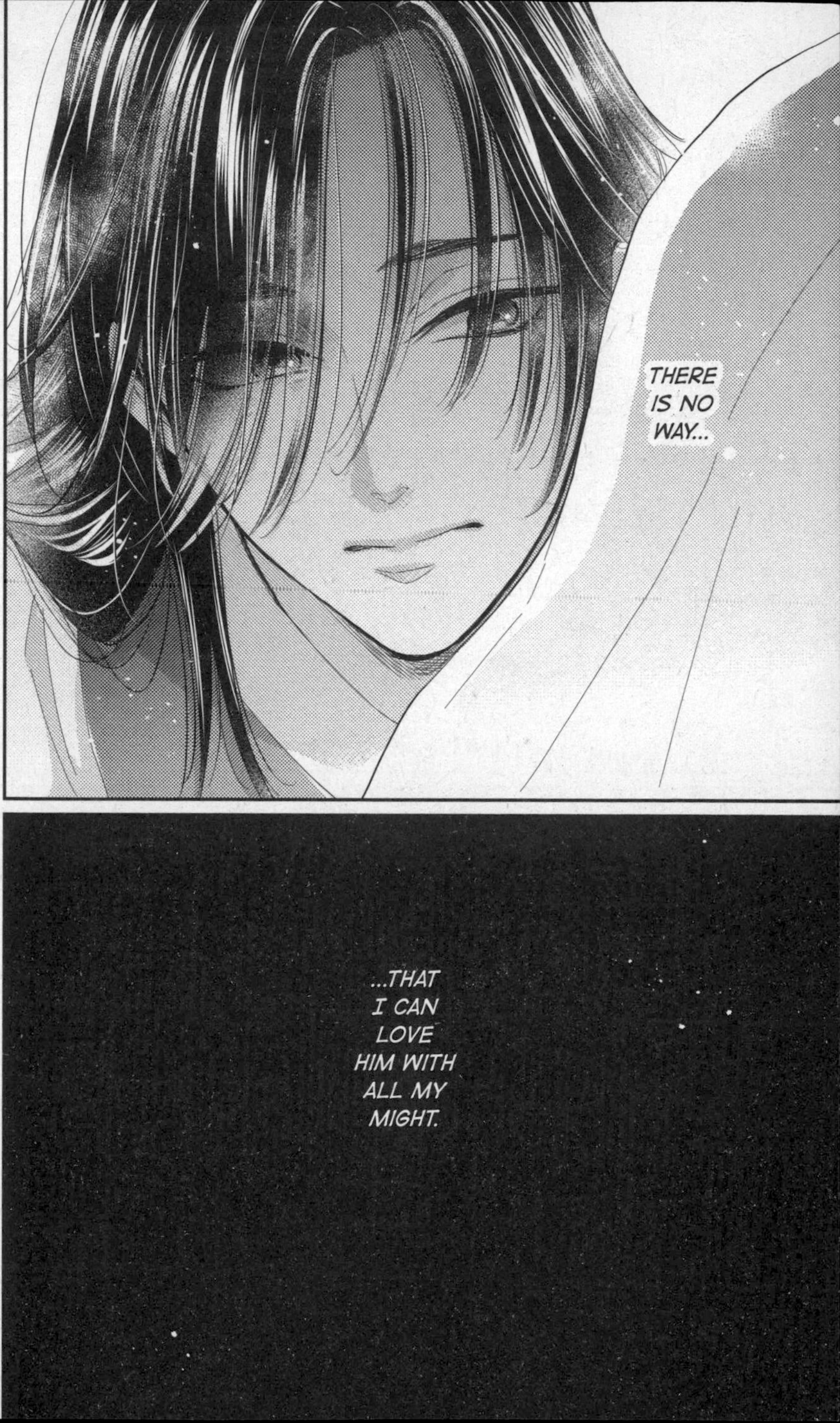
THERE IS NO WAY...
...THAT I CAN LOVE HIM WITH ALL MY MIGHT.

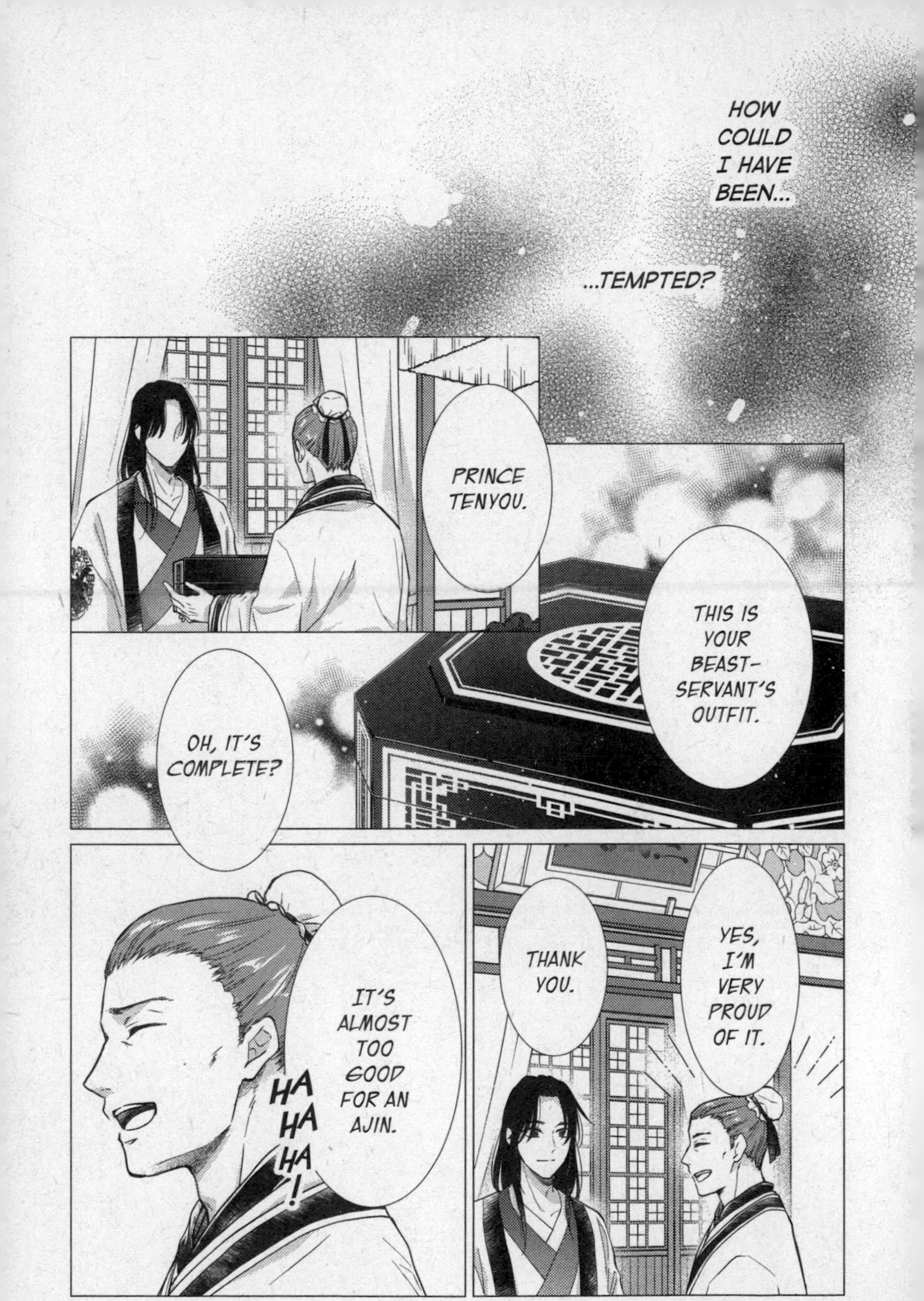
HOW COULD I HAVE BEEN...
...TEMPTED?
PRINCE TENYOU.
THIS IS YOUR BEAST-SERVANT'S OUTFIT.
OH, IT'S COMPLETE?
YES, I'M VERY PROUD OF IT.
THANK YOU.
IT'S ALMOST TOO GOOD FOR AN AJIN.
HA HA HA HA!

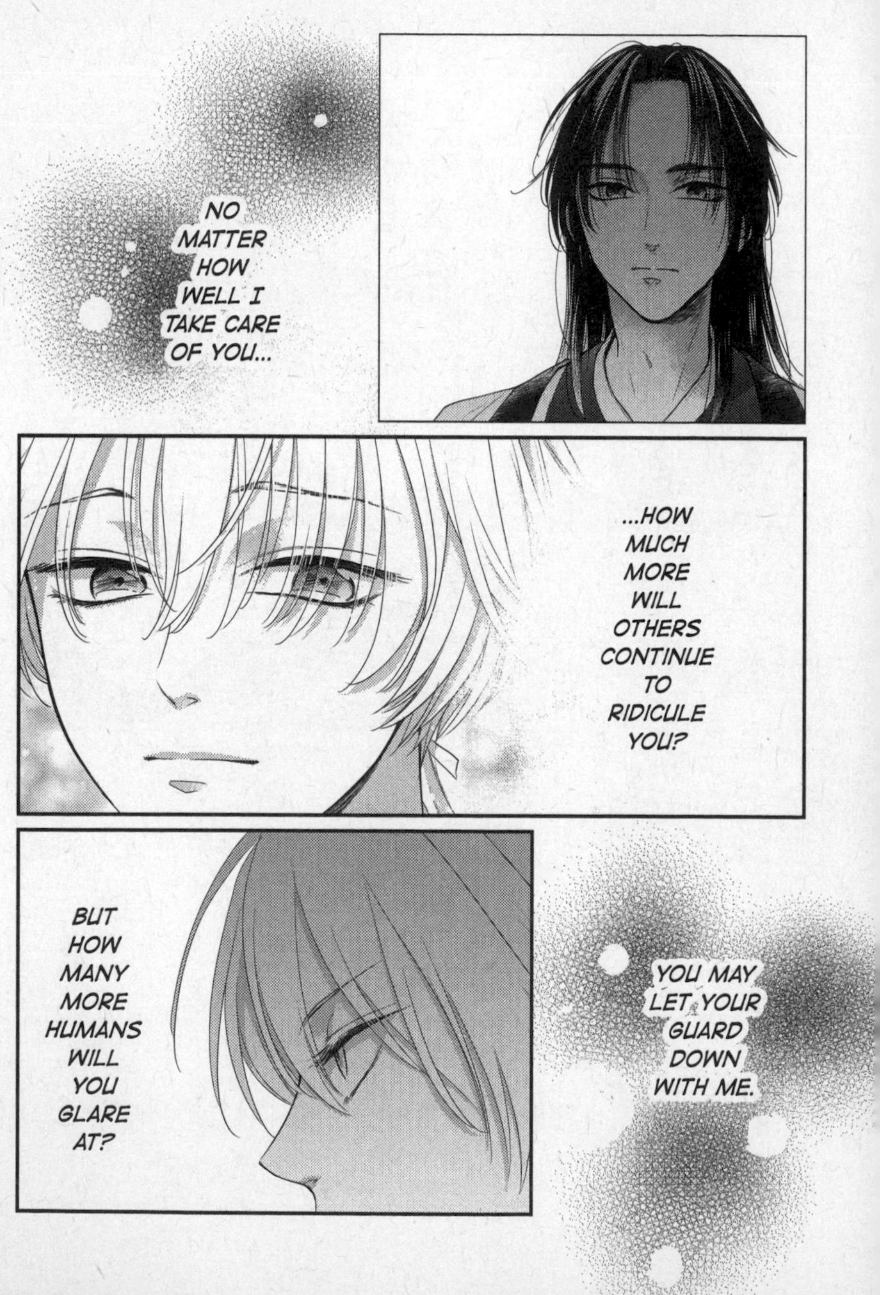
NO MATTER HOW WELL I TAKE CARE OF YOU...
...HOW MUCH MORE WILL OTHERS CONTINUE TO RIDICULE YOU?
YOU MAY LET YOUR GUARD DOWN WITH ME.
BUT HOW MANY MORE HUMANS WILL YOU GLARE AT?

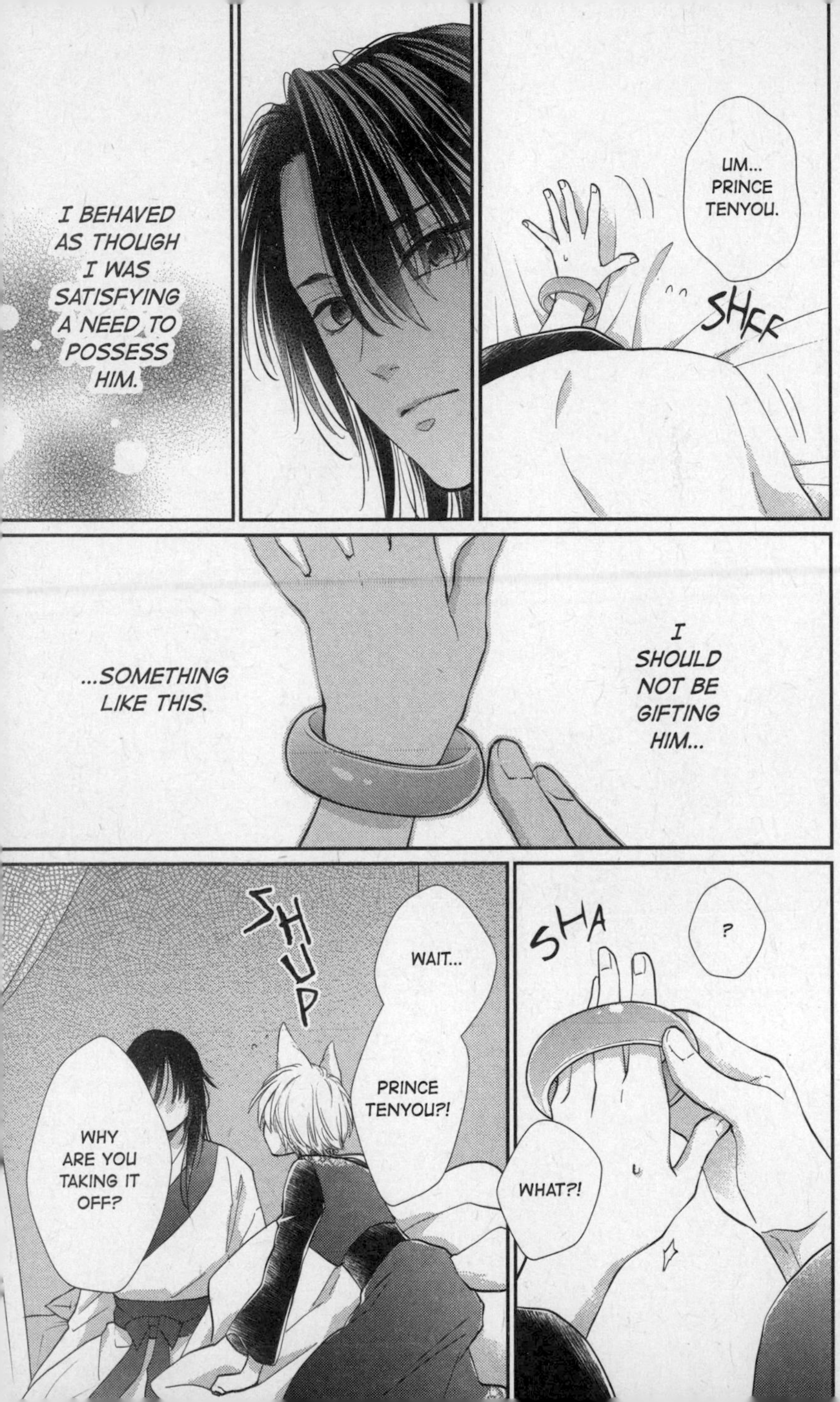
UM... PRINCE TENYOU.
SHFF
I BEHAVED AS THOUGH I WAS SATISFYING A NEED TO POSSESS HIM.
I SHOULD NOT BE GIFTING HIM...
...SOMETHING LIKE THIS.
?
SHA
WHAT?!
SHUP
WAIT...
PRINCE TENYOU?!
WHY ARE YOU TAKING IT OFF?

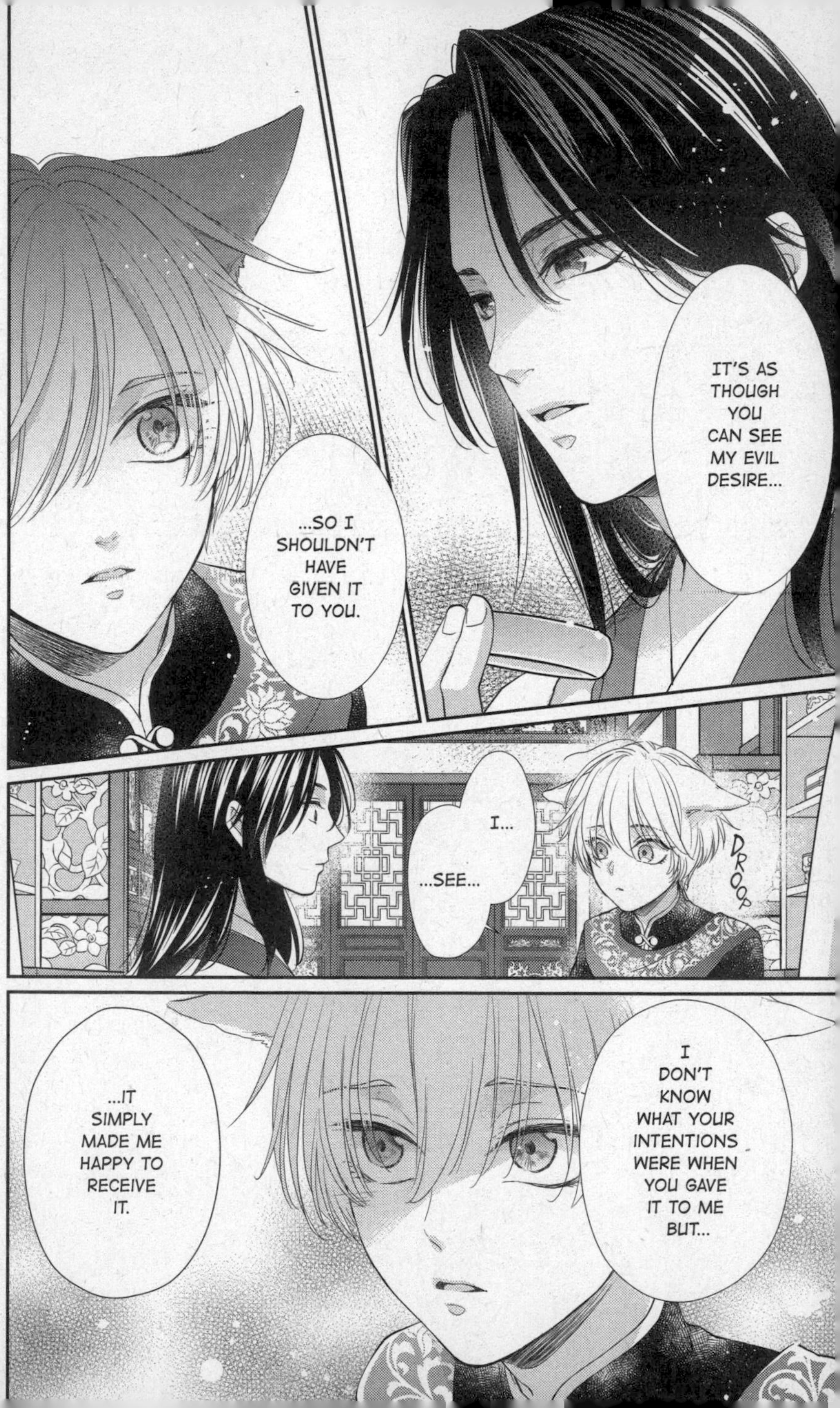
IT'S AS THOUGH YOU CAN SEE MY EVIL DESIRE...
...SO I SHOULDN'T HAVE GIVEN IT TO YOU.
DROOP
I... ...SEE...
I DON'T KNOW WHAT YOUR INTENTIONS WERE WHEN YOU GAVE IT TO ME BUT...
...IT SIMPLY MADE ME HAPPY TO RECEIVE IT.

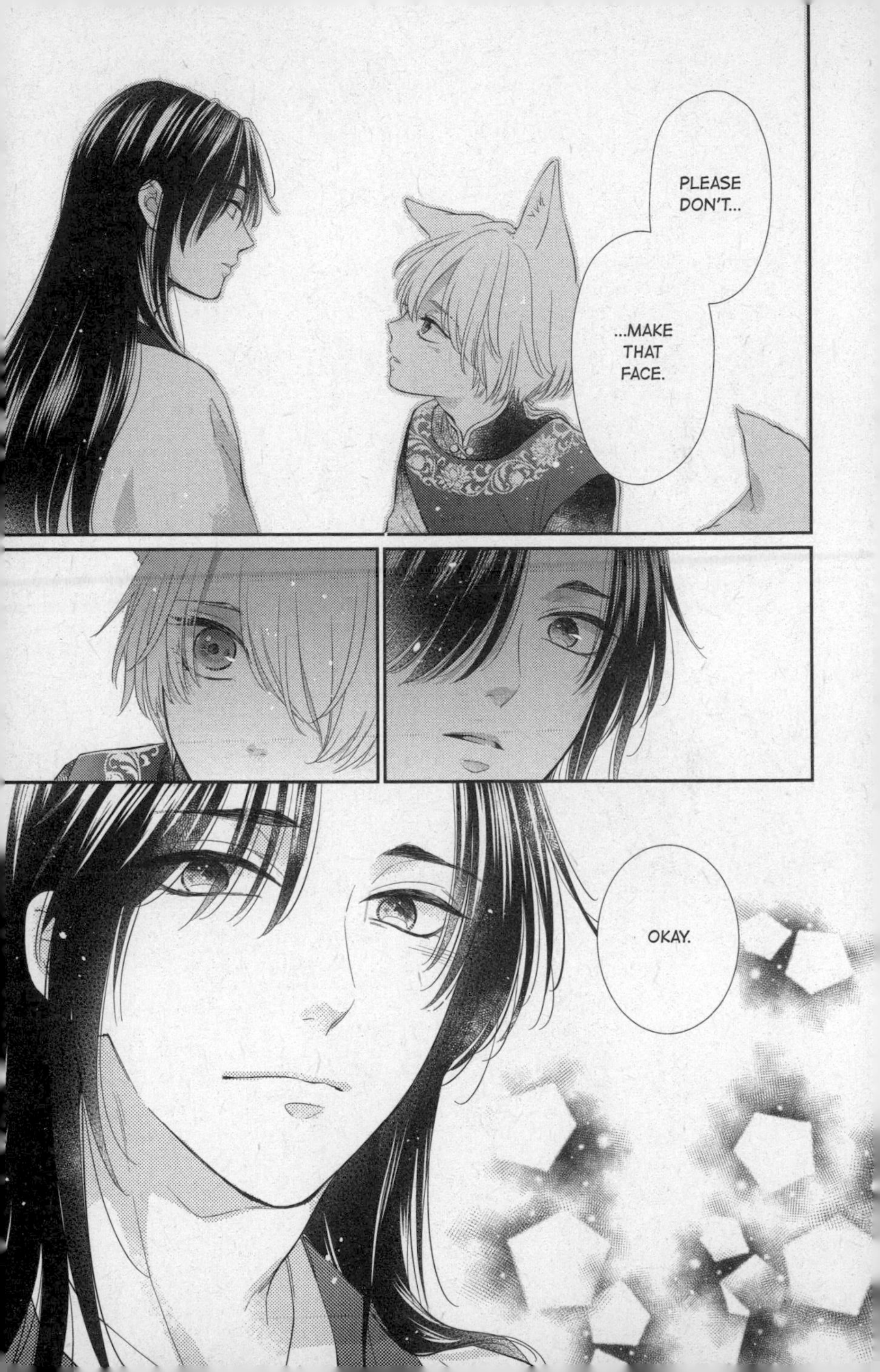
PLEASE DON'T...
...MAKE THAT FACE.
OKAY.

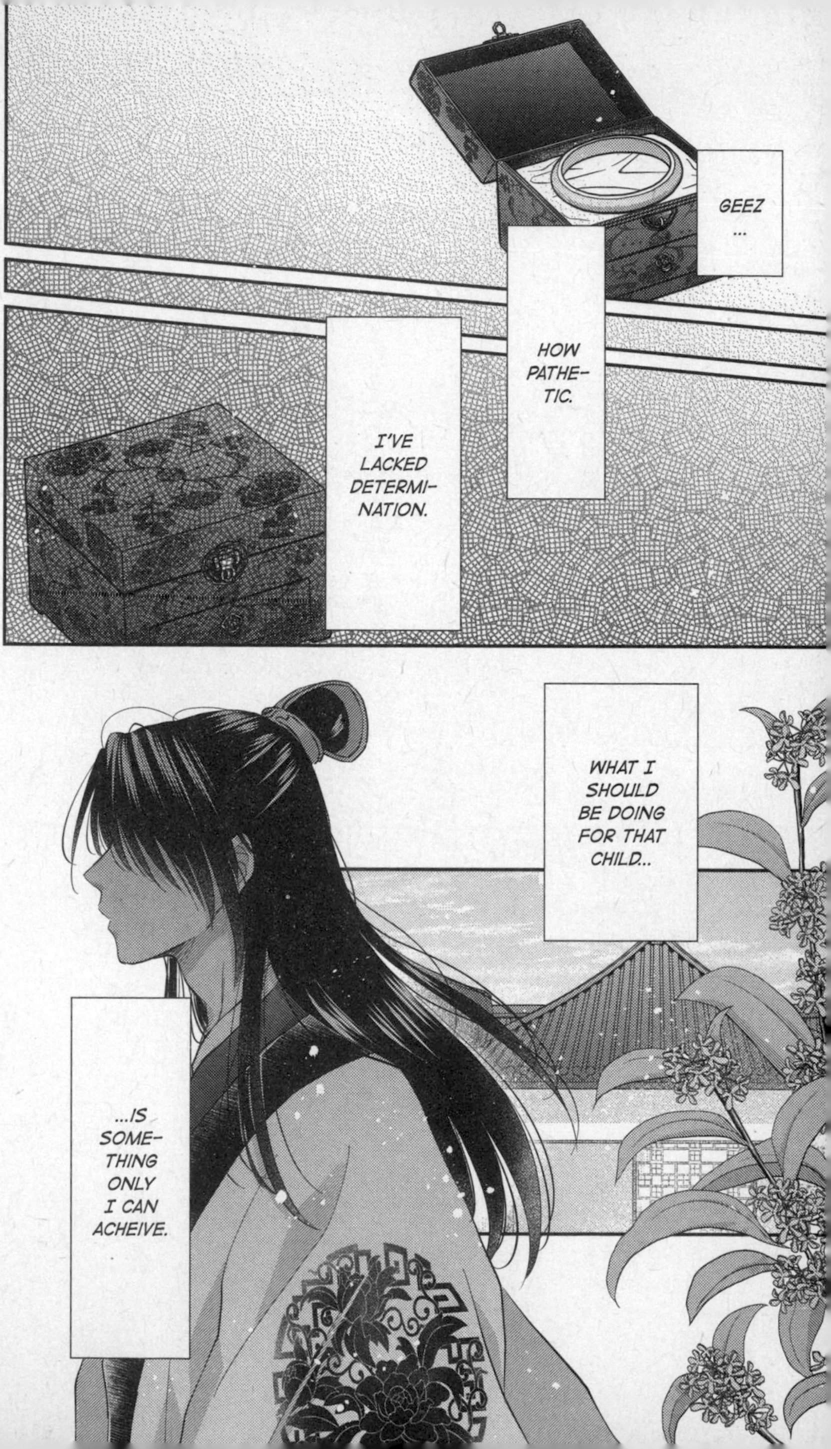
GEEZ ...
HOW PATHETIC.
I'VE LACKED DETERMINATION.
WHAT I SHOULD BE DOING FOR THAT CHILD...
...IS SOMETHING ONLY I CAN ACHEIVE.

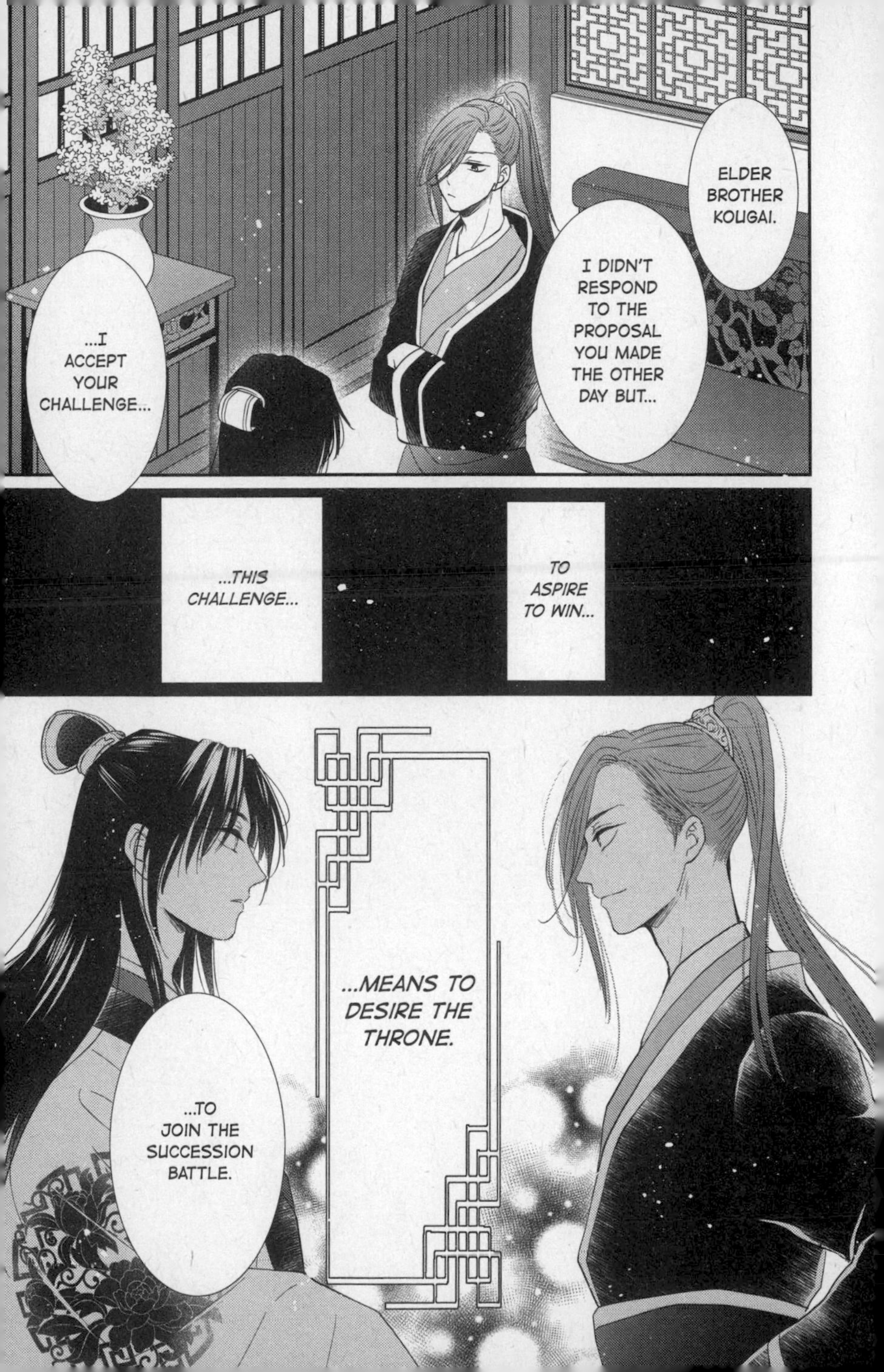
ELDER BROTHER KOUGAI.
I DIDN'T RESPOND TO THE PROPOSAL YOU MADE THE OTHER DAY BUT...
...I ACCEPT YOUR CHALLENGE...
TO ASPIRE TO WIN...
...THIS CHALLENGE...
...MEANS TO DESIRE THE THRONE.
...TO JOIN THE SUCCESSION BATTLE.

THE
KING'S
Beast

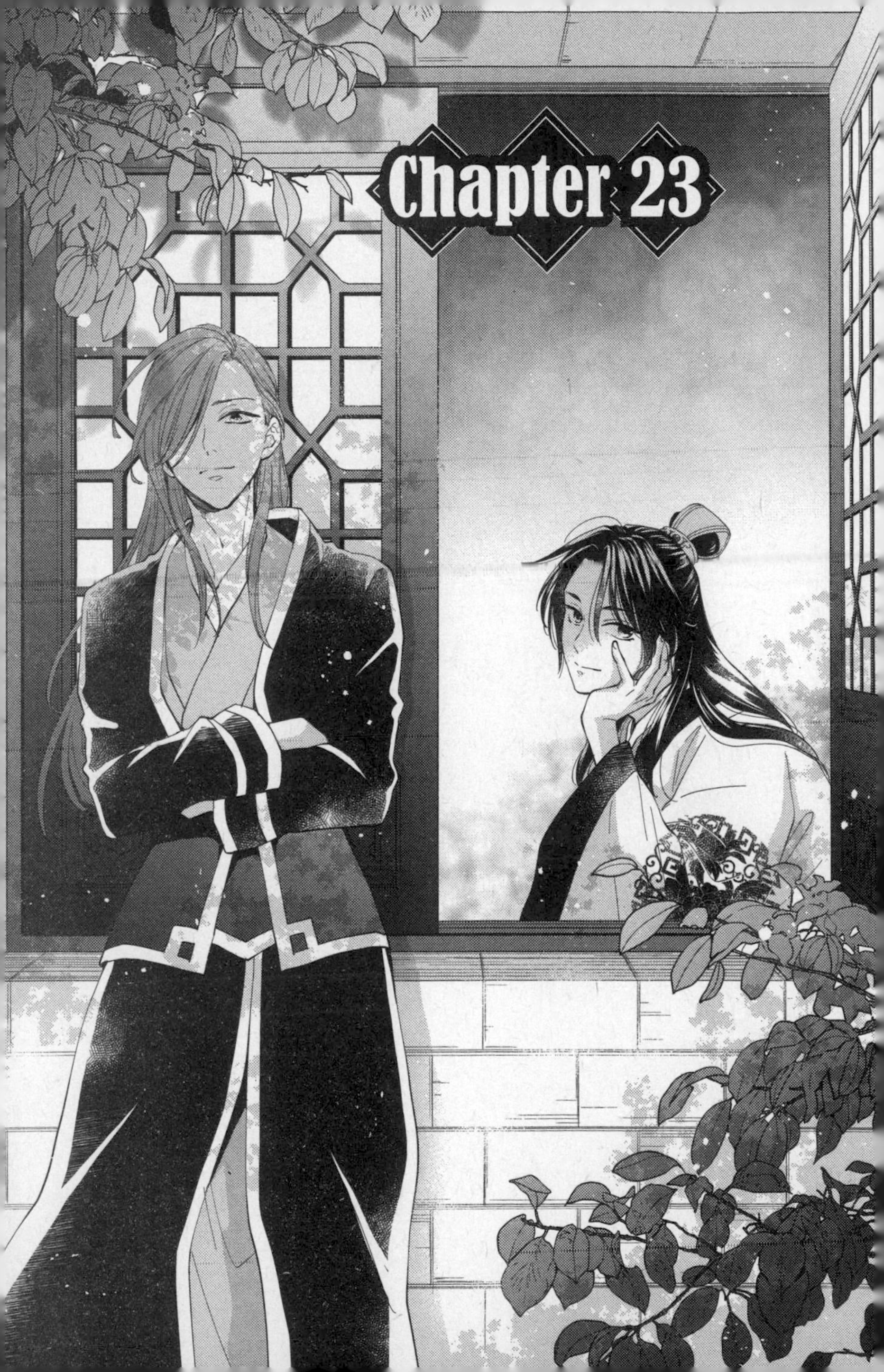
Chapter 23

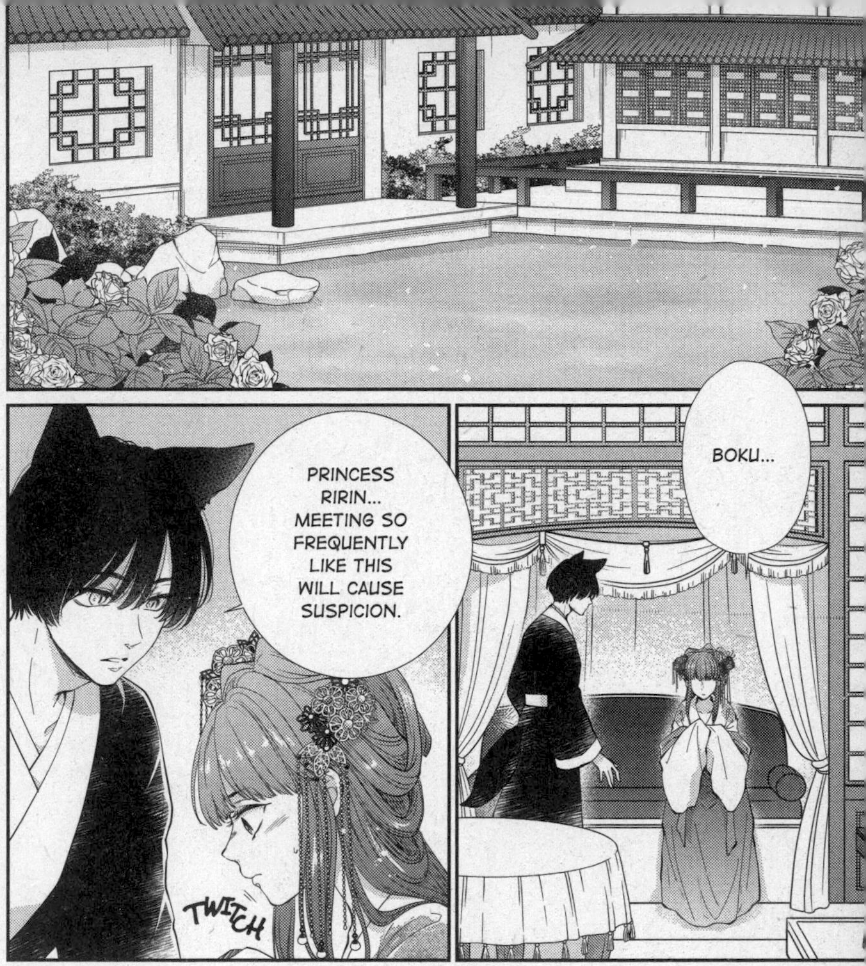
BOKU...
PRINCESS RIRIN... MEETING SO FREQUENTLY LIKE THIS WILL CAUSE SUSPICION.
TWITCH

THE KING'S Beast 麗

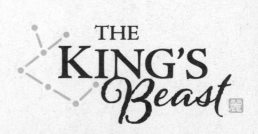

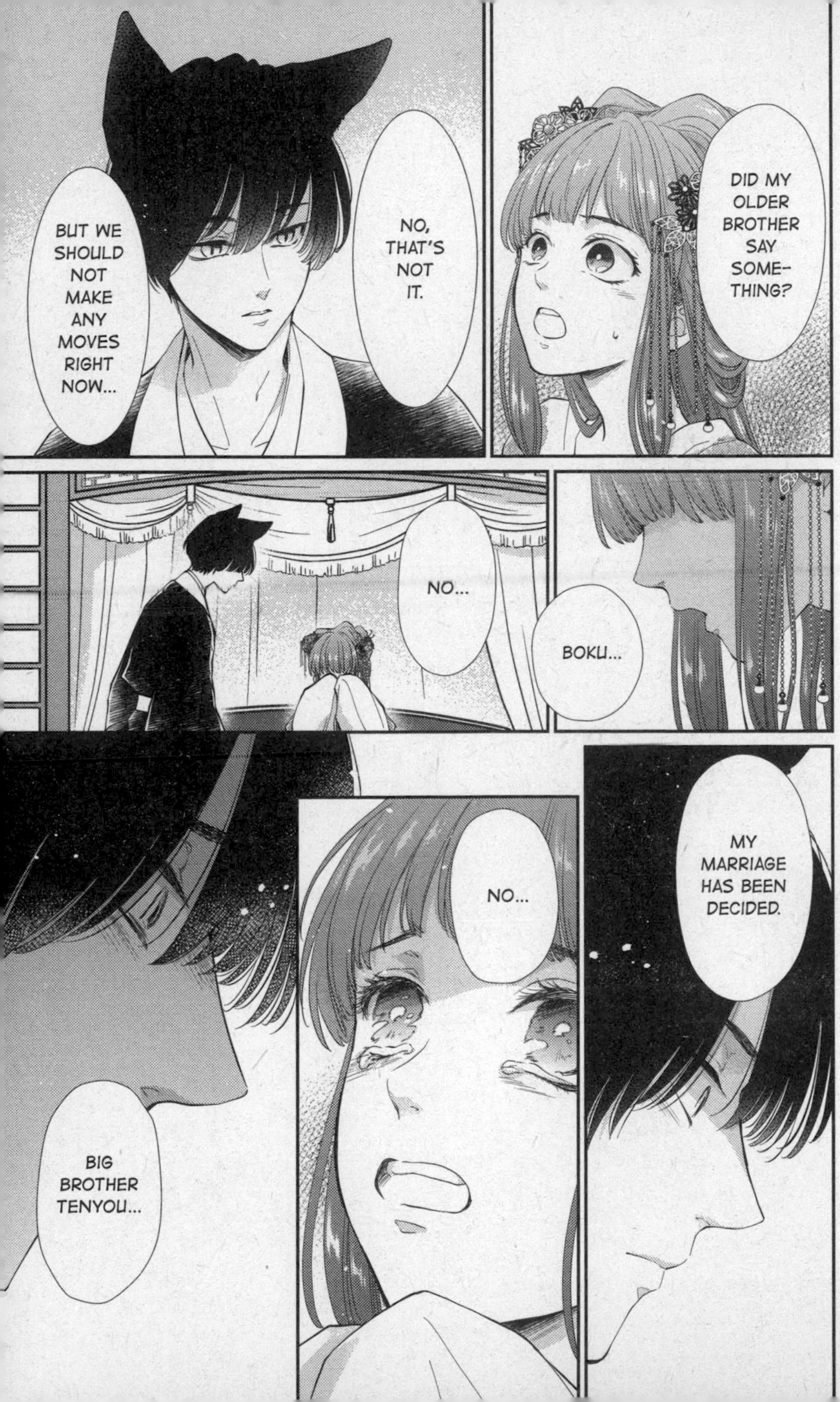
DID MY OLDER BROTHER SAY SOME-THING?
NO, THAT'S NOT IT.
BUT WE SHOULD NOT MAKE ANY MOVES RIGHT NOW...
BOKU...
NO...
MY MARRIAGE HAS BEEN DECIDED.
NO...
BIG BROTHER TENYOU...

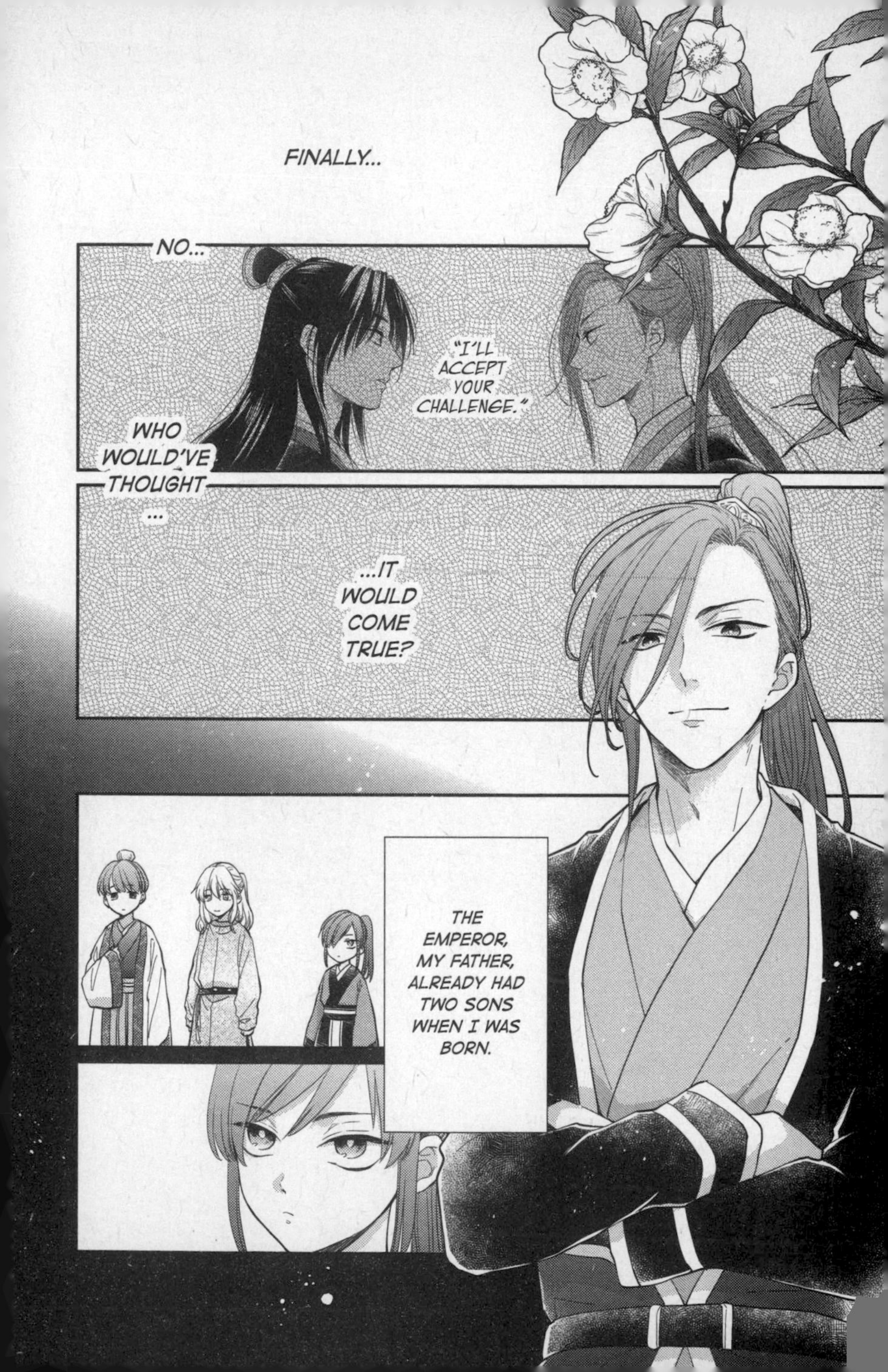
FINALLY...
NO...
"I'LL ACCEPT YOUR CHALLENGE."
WHO WOULD'VE THOUGHT...
...IT WOULD COME TRUE?
THE EMPEROR, MY FATHER, ALREADY HAD TWO SONS WHEN I WAS BORN.

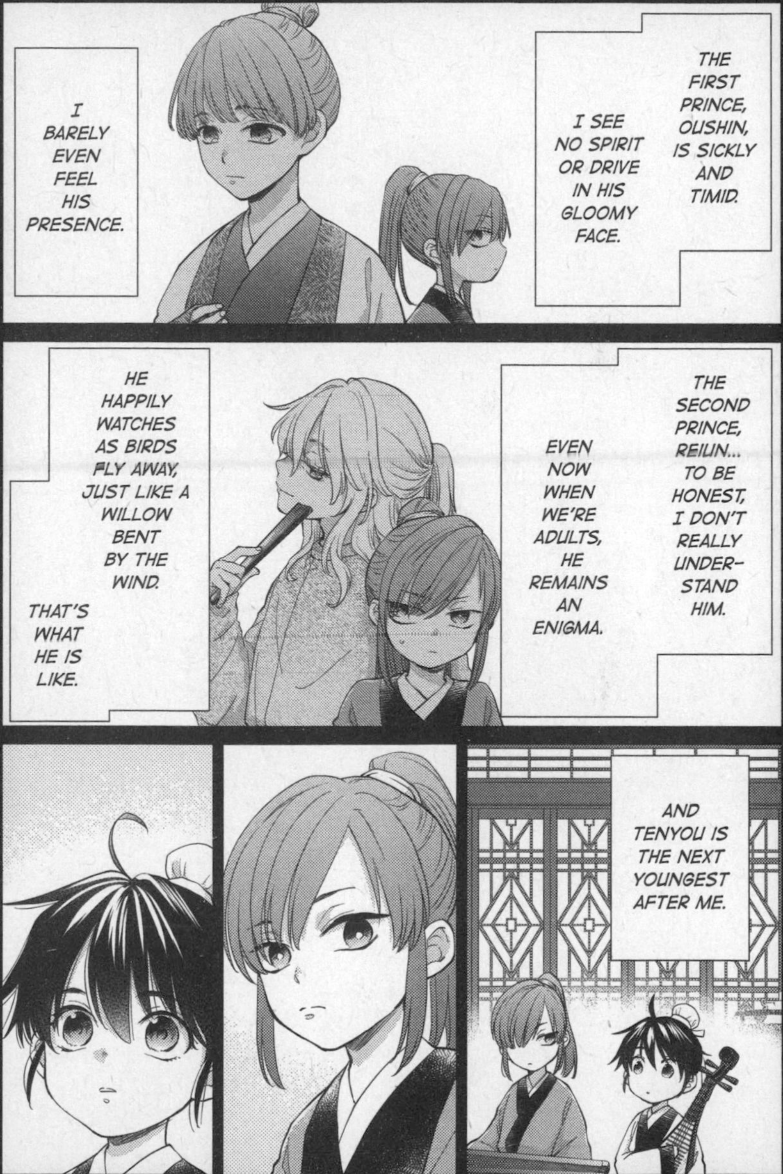
THE FIRST PRINCE, OUSHIN, IS SICKLY AND TIMID.
I SEE NO SPIRIT OR DRIVE IN HIS GLOOMY FACE.
I BARELY EVEN FEEL HIS PRESENCE.
THE SECOND PRINCE, REILIN... TO BE HONEST, I DON'T REALLY UNDER-STAND HIM.
EVEN NOW WHEN WE'RE ADULTS, HE REMAINS AN ENIGMA.
HE HAPPILY WATCHES AS BIRDS FLY AWAY, JUST LIKE A WILLOW BENT BY THE WIND.
THAT'S WHAT HE IS LIKE.
AND TENYOU IS THE NEXT YOUNGEST AFTER ME.

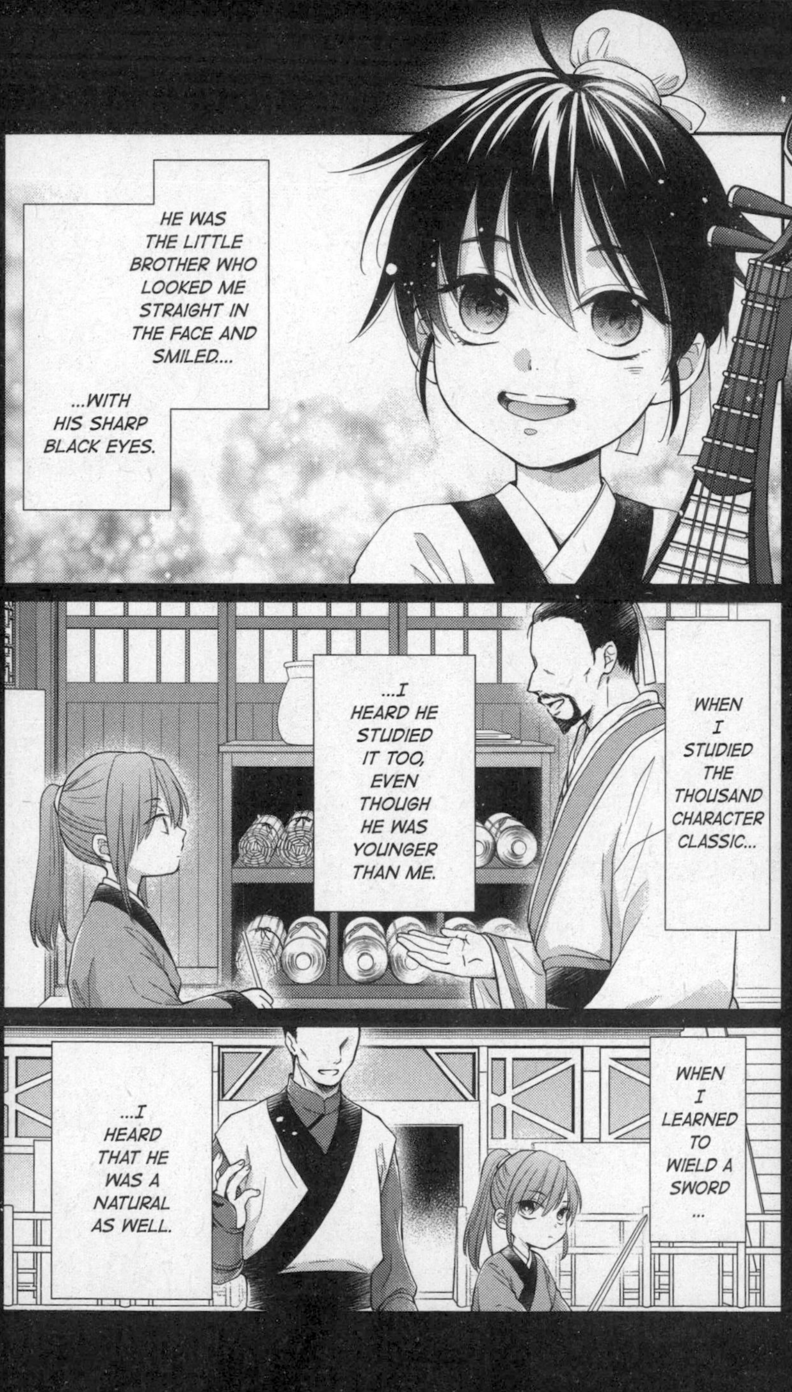
HE WAS THE LITTLE BROTHER WHO LOOKED ME STRAIGHT IN THE FACE AND SMILED....
...WITH HIS SHARP BLACK EYES.
WHEN I STUDIED THE THOUSAND CHARACTER CLASSIC...
...I HEARD HE STUDIED IT TOO, EVEN THOUGH HE WAS YOUNGER THAN ME.
WHEN I LEARNED TO WIELD A SWORD ...
...I HEARD THAT HE WAS A NATURAL AS WELL.

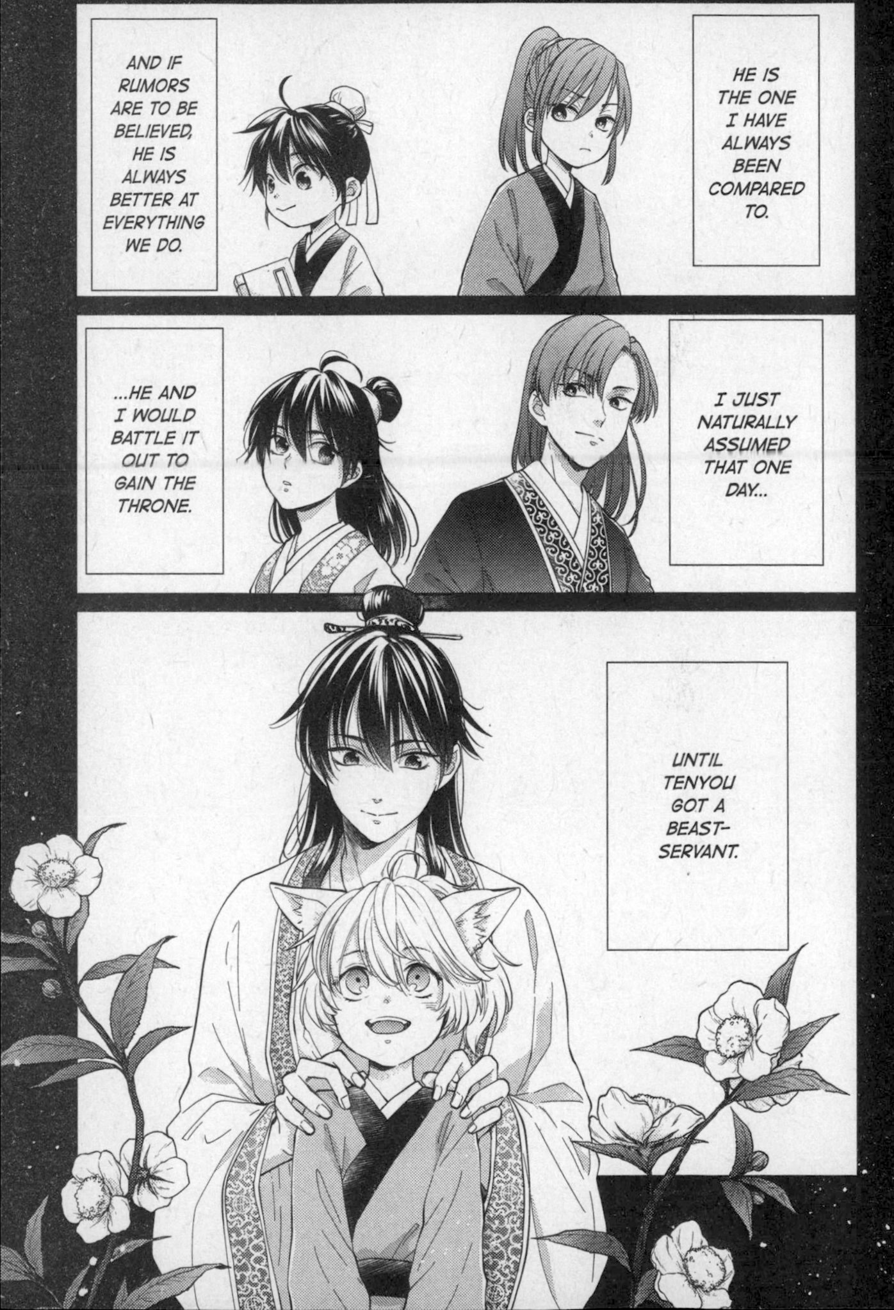
HE IS THE ONE I HAVE ALWAYS BEEN COMPARED TO.
AND IF RUMORS ARE TO BE BELIEVED, HE IS ALWAYS BETTER AT EVERYTHING WE DO.
I JUST NATURALLY ASSUMED THAT ONE DAY...
...HE AND I WOULD BATTLE IT OUT TO GAIN THE THRONE.
UNTIL TENYOU GOT A BEAST-SERVANT.

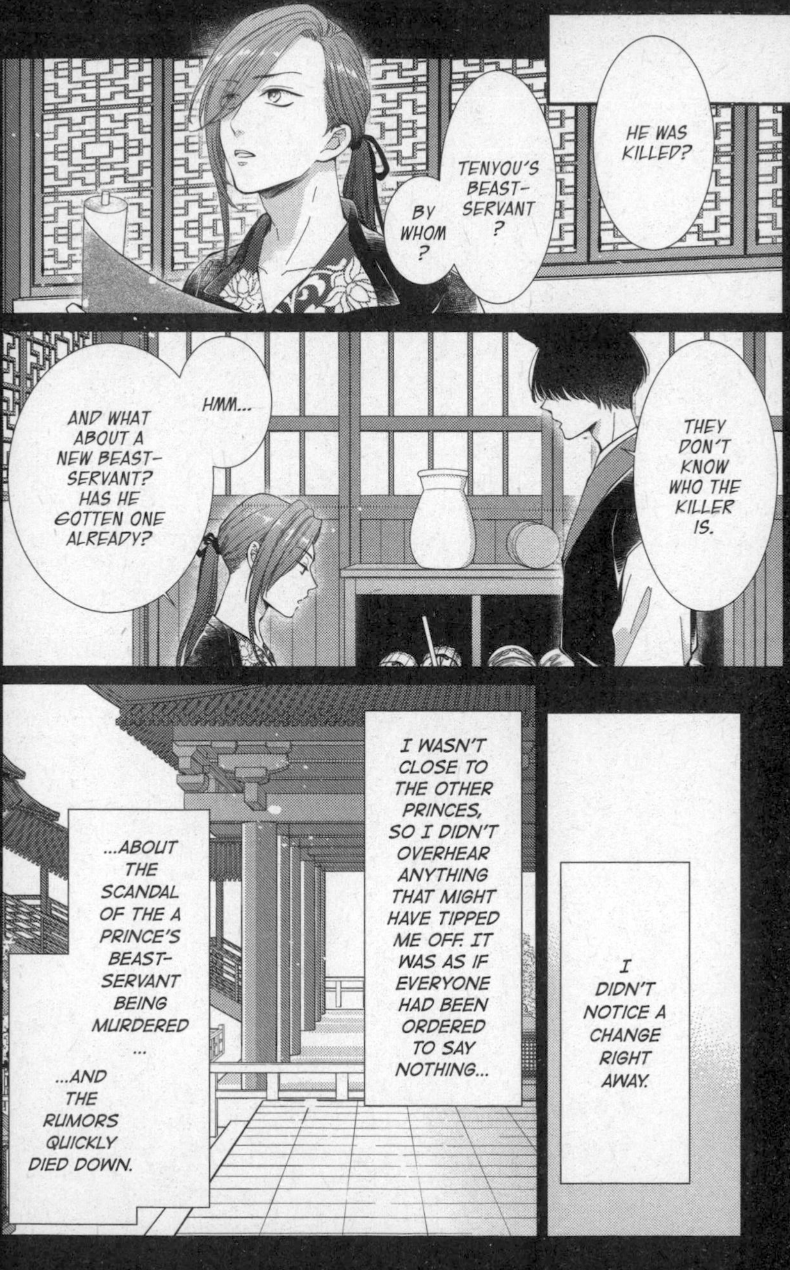
HE WAS KILLED?
TENYOU'S BEAST-SERVANT?
BY WHOM?
THEY DON'T KNOW WHO THE KILLER IS.
HMM...
AND WHAT ABOUT A NEW BEAST-SERVANT? HAS HE GOTTEN ONE ALREADY?
I DIDN'T NOTICE A CHANGE RIGHT AWAY.
I WASN'T CLOSE TO THE OTHER PRINCES, SO I DIDN'T OVERHEAR ANYTHING THAT MIGHT HAVE TIPPED ME OFF. IT WAS AS IF EVERYONE HAD BEEN ORDERED TO SAY NOTHING...
...ABOUT THE SCANDAL OF THE A PRINCE'S BEAST-SERVANT BEING MURDERED...
...AND THE RUMORS QUICKLY DIED DOWN.

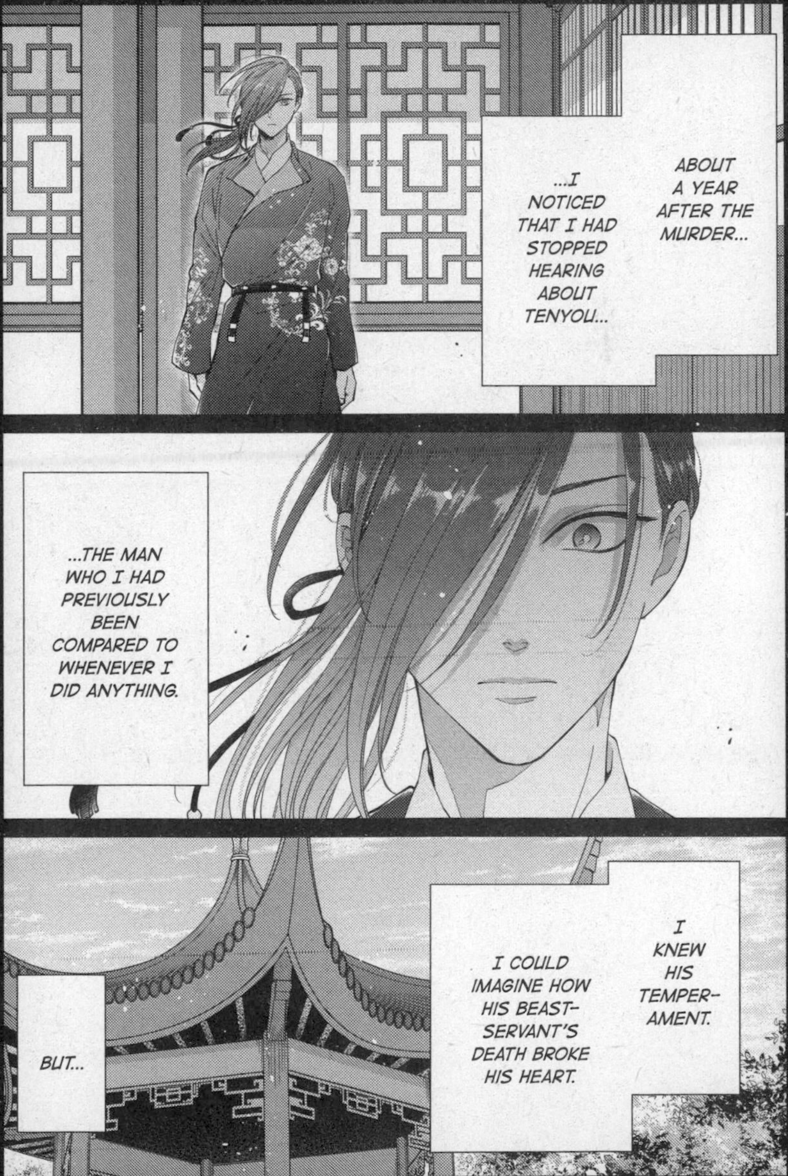
ABOUT A YEAR AFTER THE MURDER...
...I NOTICED THAT I HAD STOPPED HEARING ABOUT TENYOU...
...THE MAN WHO I HAD PREVIOUSLY BEEN COMPARED TO WHENEVER I DID ANYTHING.
I KNEW HIS TEMPER-AMENT.
I COULD IMAGINE HOW HIS BEAST-SERVANT'S DEATH BROKE HIS HEART.
BUT...

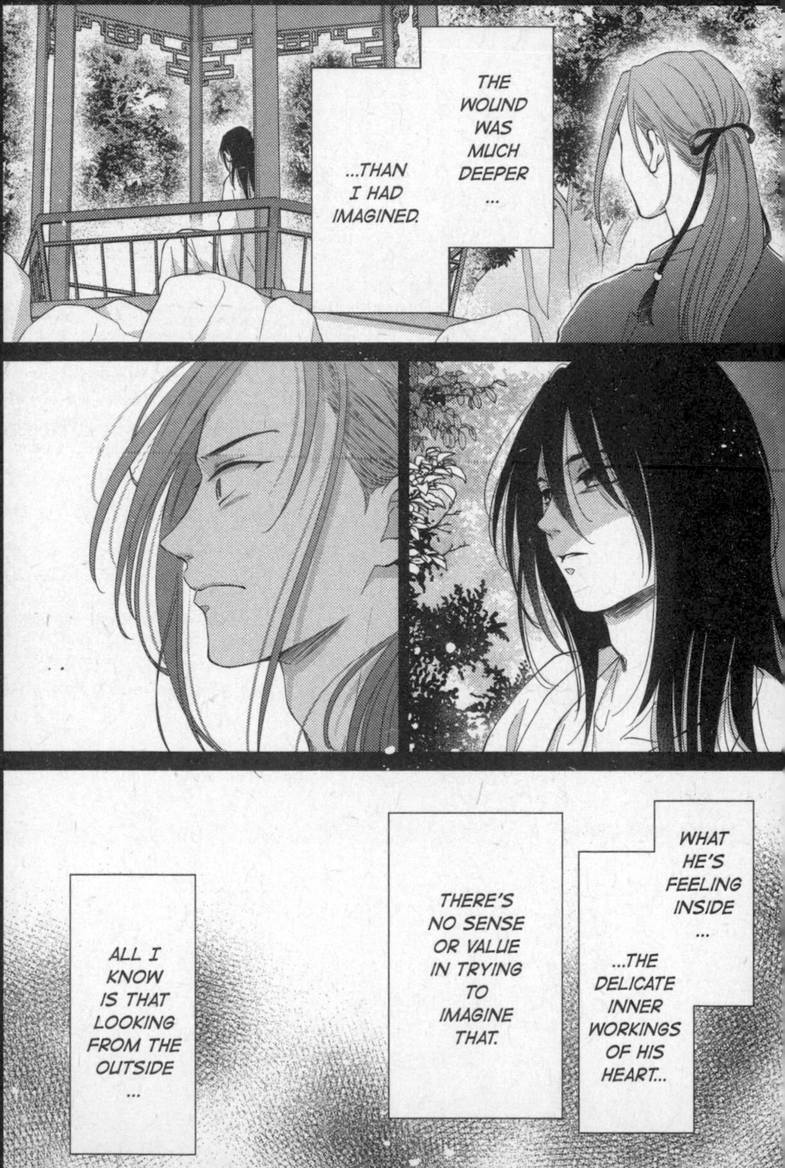
THE WOUND WAS MUCH DEEPER ...
...THAN I HAD IMAGINED.
WHAT HE'S FEELING INSIDE ...
...THE DELICATE INNER WORKINGS OF HIS HEART...
THERE'S NO SENSE OR VALUE IN TRYING TO IMAGINE THAT.
ALL I KNOW IS THAT LOOKING FROM THE OUTSIDE ...

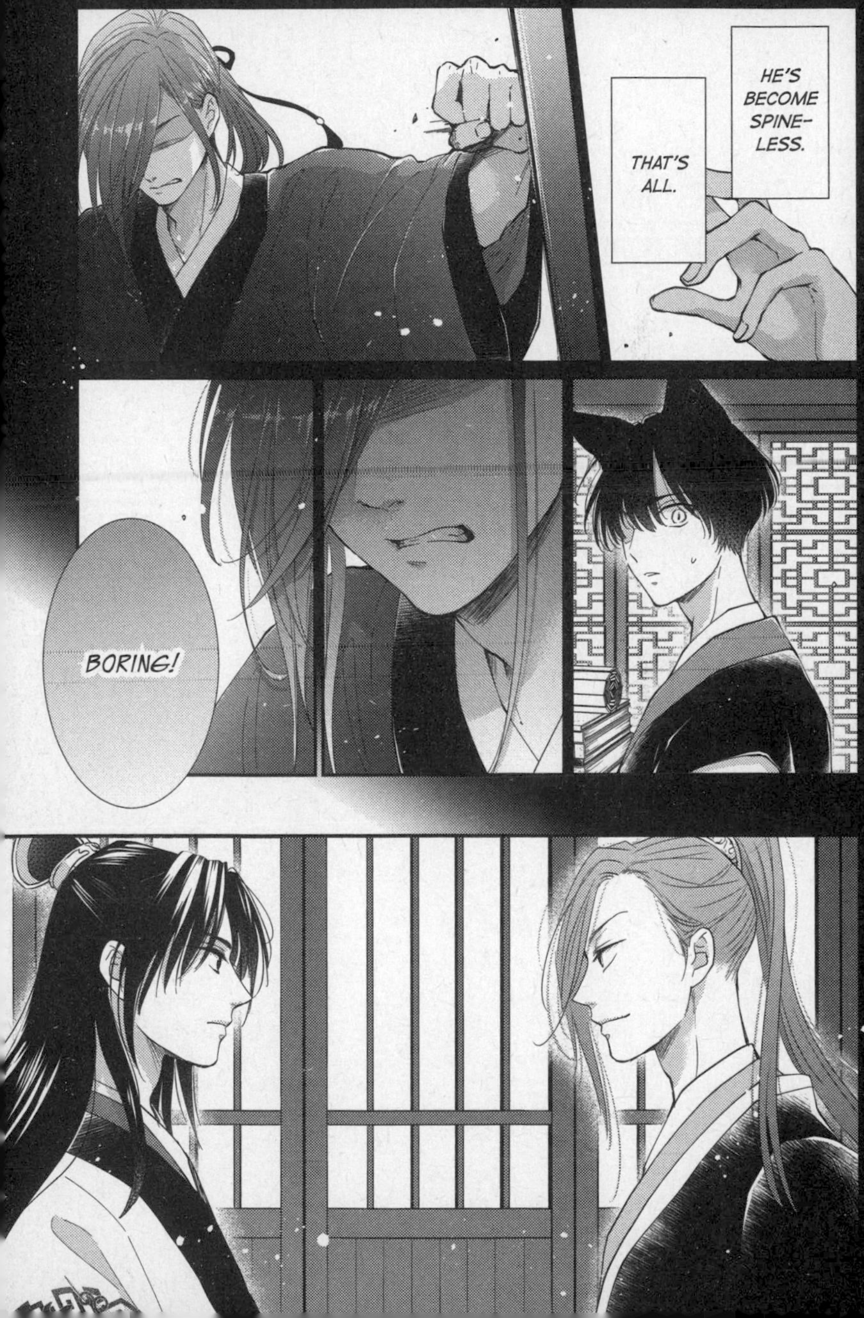
HE'S BECOME SPINE-LESS.
THAT'S ALL.
BORING!

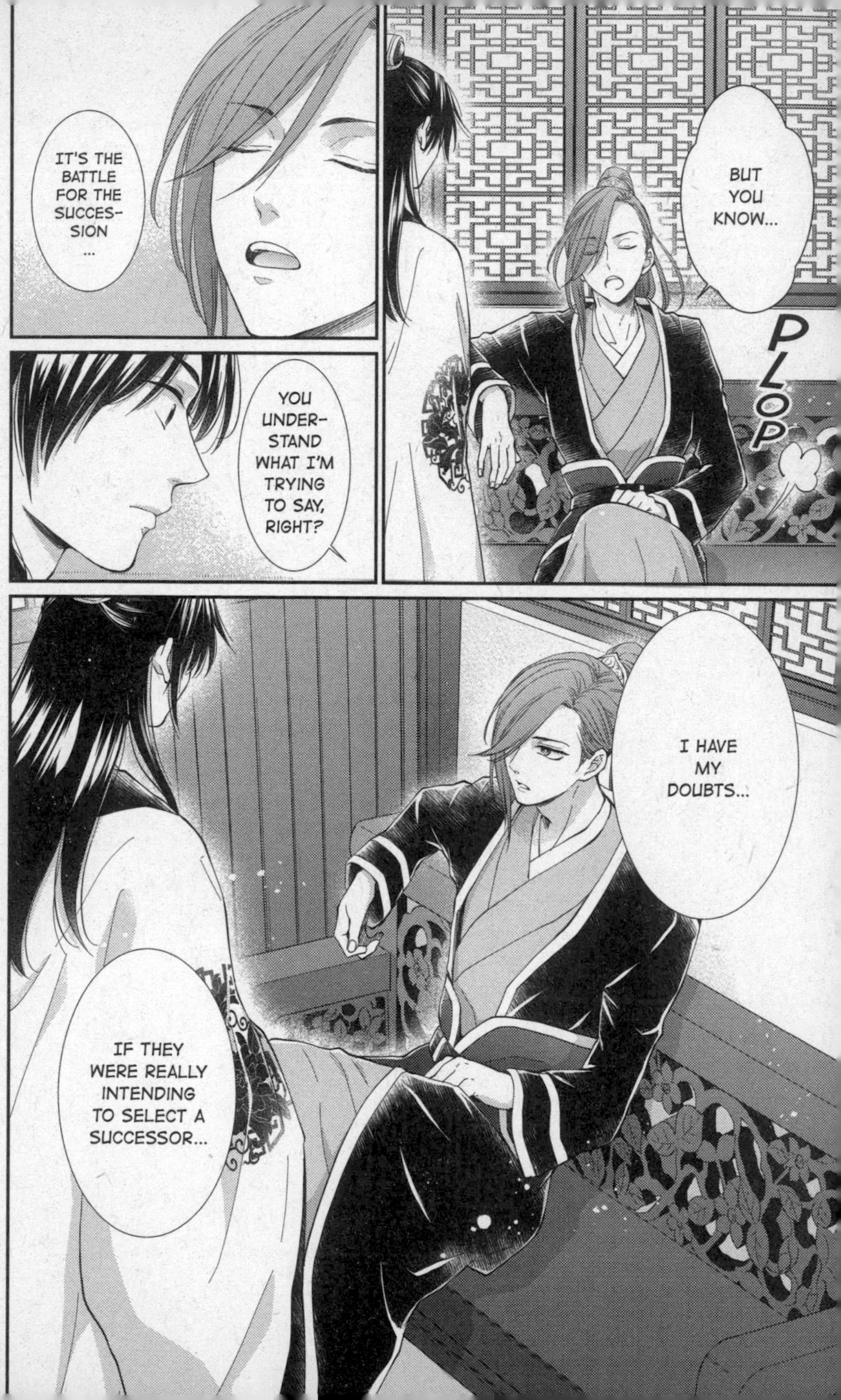
BUT YOU KNOW...
PLOP
IT'S THE BATTLE FOR THE SUCCES-SION ...
YOU UNDER-STAND WHAT I'M TRYING TO SAY, RIGHT?
I HAVE MY DOUBTS...
IF THEY WERE REALLY INTENDING TO SELECT A SUCCESSOR...

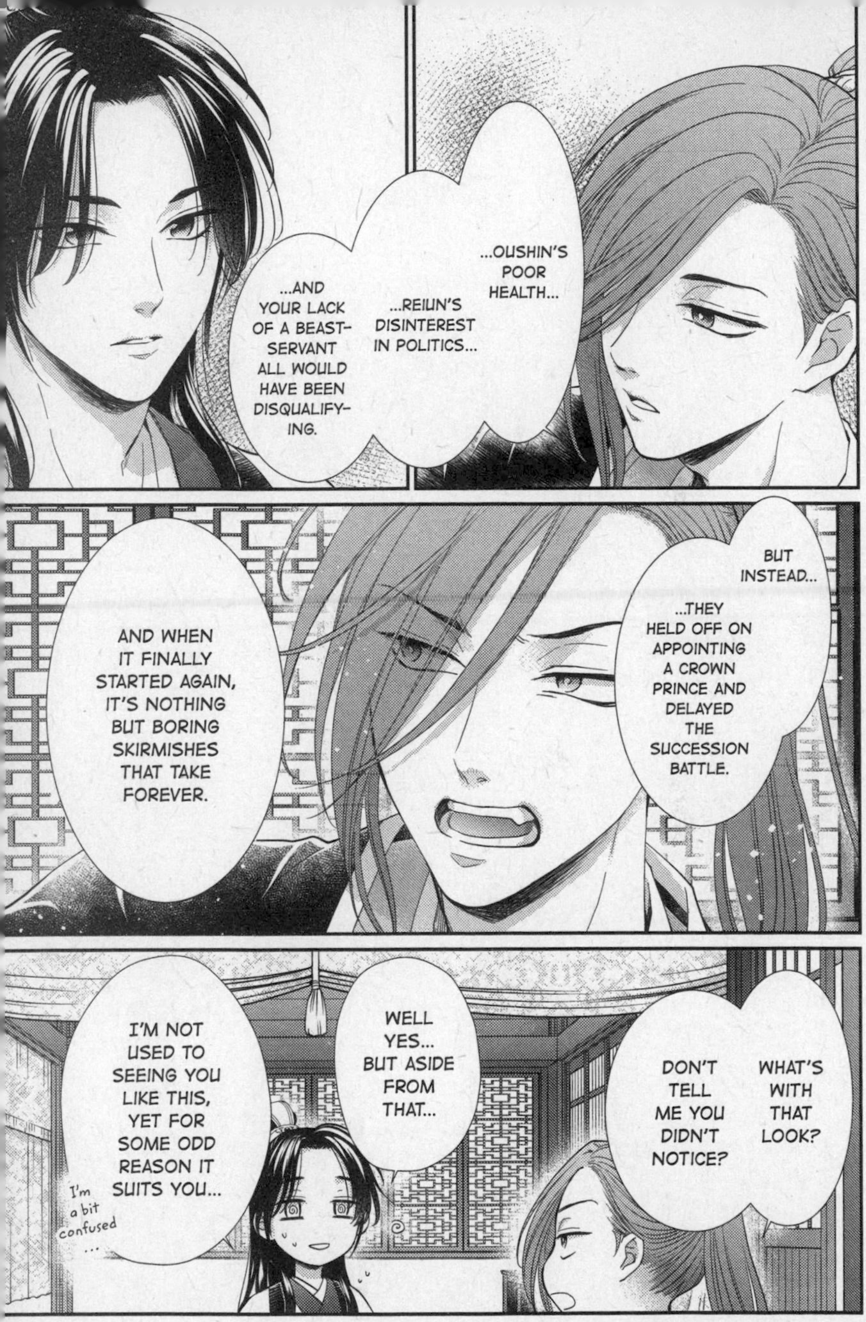
...OUSHIN'S POOR HEALTH...
...REIUN'S DISINTEREST IN POLITICS...
...AND YOUR LACK OF A BEAST-SERVANT ALL WOULD HAVE BEEN DISQUALIFYING.
BUT INSTEAD...
...THEY HELD OFF ON APPOINTING A CROWN PRINCE AND DELAYED THE SUCCESSION BATTLE.
AND WHEN IT FINALLY STARTED AGAIN, IT'S NOTHING BUT BORING SKIRMISHES THAT TAKE FOREVER.
WHAT'S WITH THAT LOOK?
DON'T TELL ME YOU DIDN'T NOTICE?
WELL YES... BUT ASIDE FROM THAT...
I'M NOT USED TO SEEING YOU LIKE THIS, YET FOR SOME ODD REASON IT SUITS YOU...
I'm a bit confused...

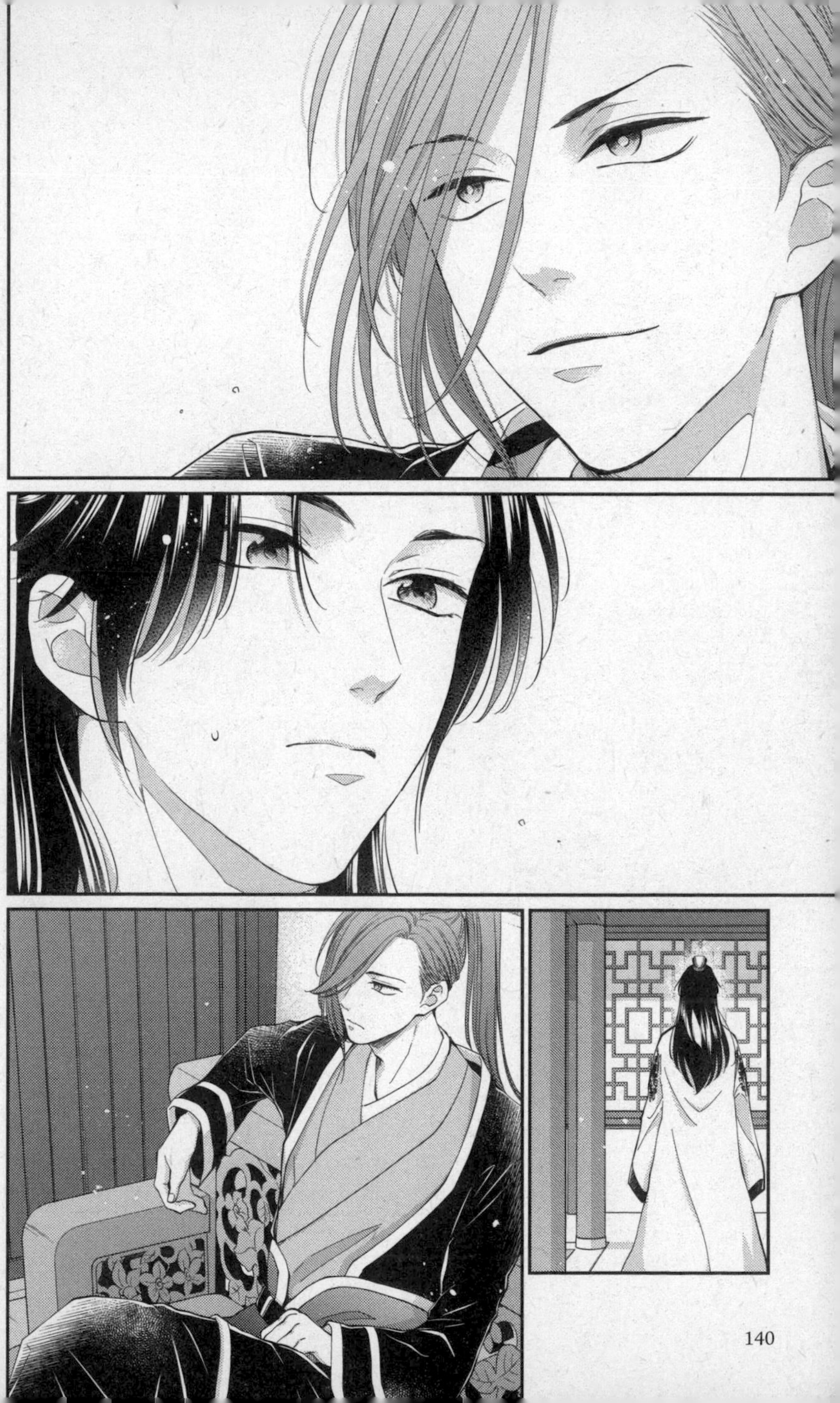

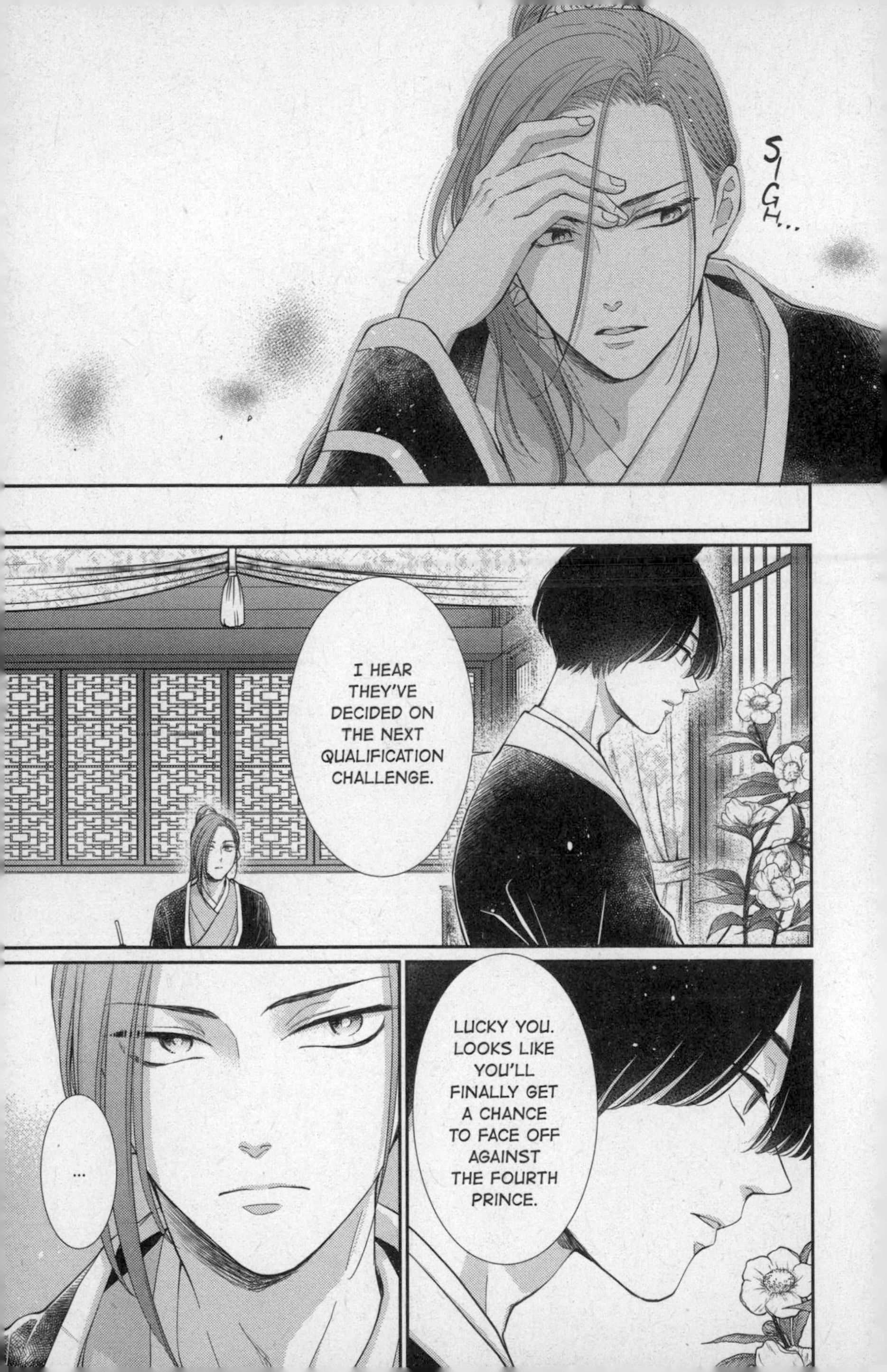
SIGH...
I HEAR THEY'VE DECIDED ON THE NEXT QUALIFICATION CHALLENGE.
LUCKY YOU. LOOKS LIKE YOU'LL FINALLY GET A CHANCE TO FACE OFF AGAINST THE FOURTH PRINCE.
...

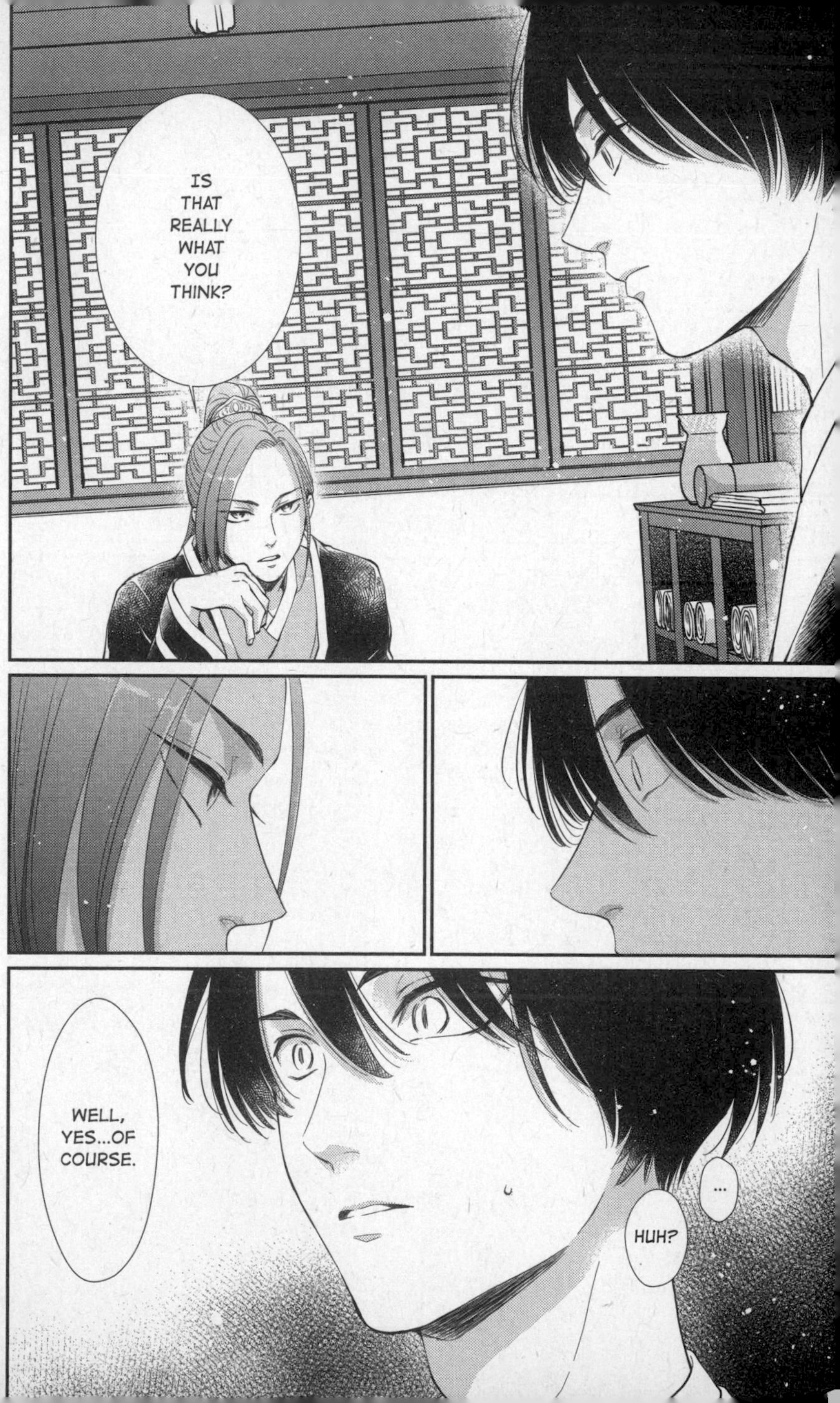
IS THAT REALLY WHAT YOU THINK?
...
HUH?
WELL, YES...OF COURSE.

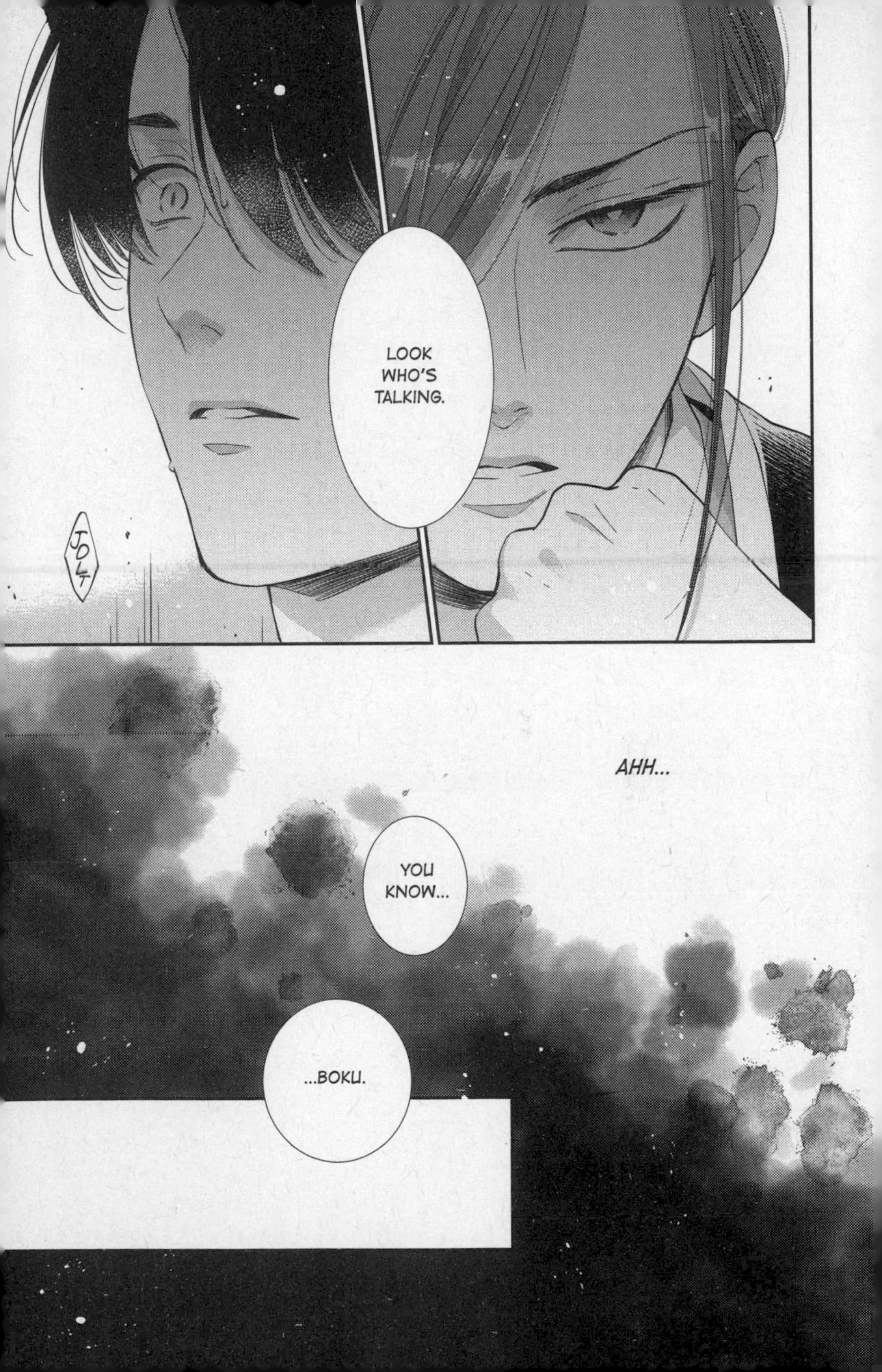
LOOK WHO'S TALKING.
JOLT
AHH...
YOU KNOW...
...BOKU.

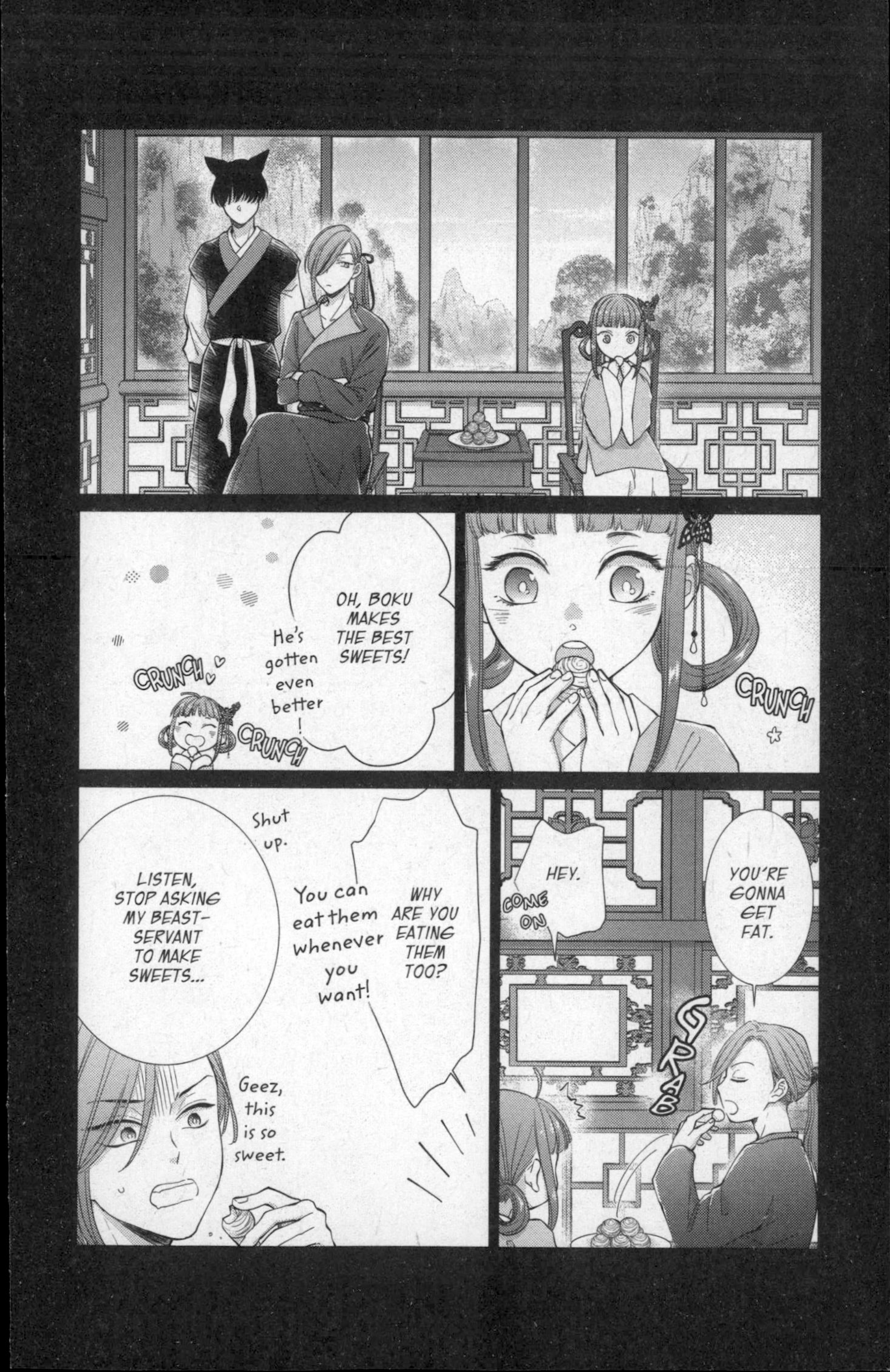
CRUNCH
OH, BOKU MAKES THE BEST SWEETS!
He's gotten even better!
CRUNCH
CRUNCH
YOU'RE GONNA GET FAT.
HEY.
COME ON
GRAB
WHY ARE YOU EATING THEM TOO?
You can eat them whenever you want!
Shut up.
LISTEN, STOP ASKING MY BEAST-SERVANT TO MAKE SWEETS...
Geez, this is so sweet.

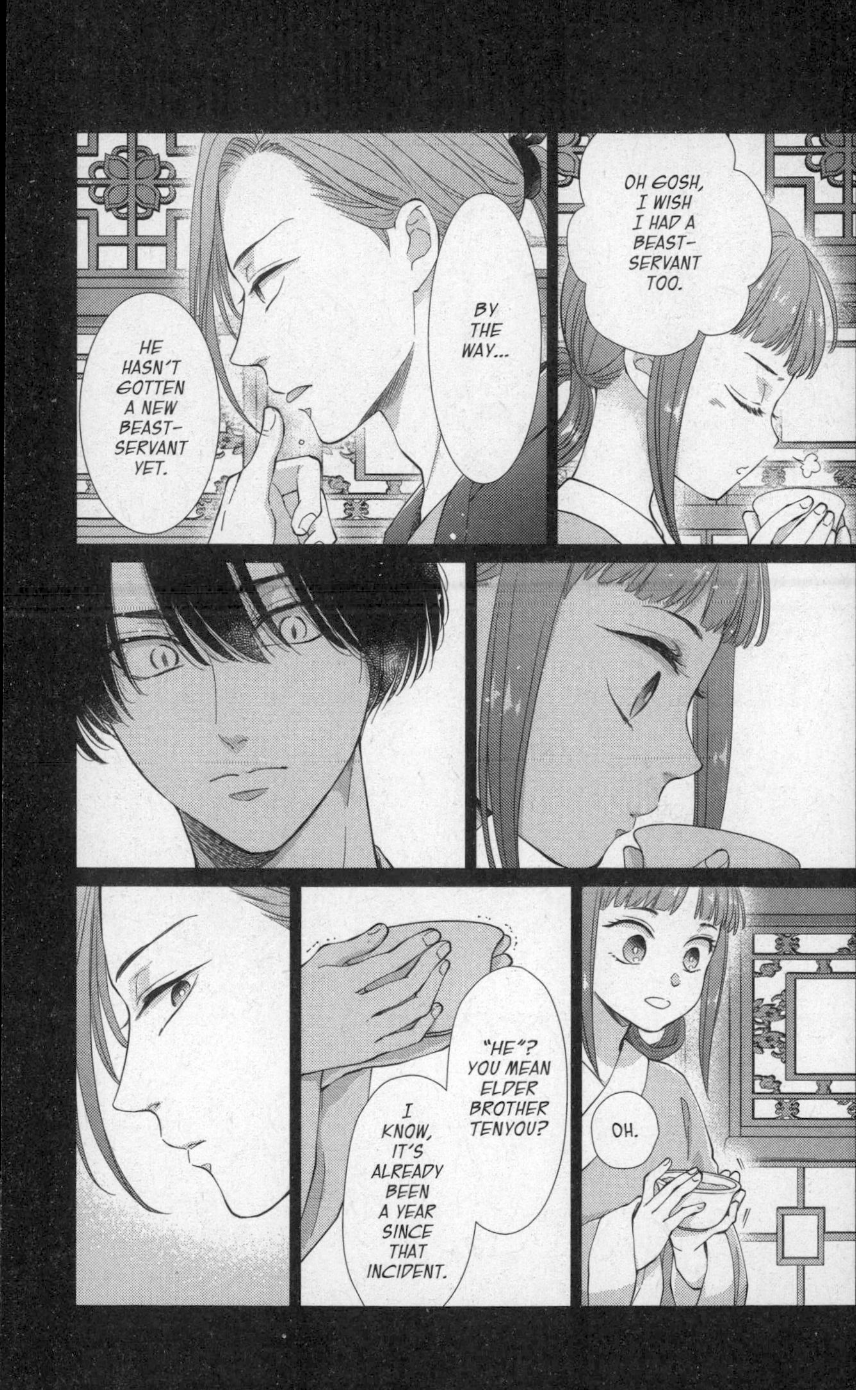
OH GOSH, I WISH I HAD A BEAST-SERVANT TOO.
BY THE WAY...
HE HASN'T GOTTEN A NEW BEAST-SERVANT YET.
OH.
"HE"? YOU MEAN ELDER BROTHER TENYOU?
I KNOW, IT'S ALREADY BEEN A YEAR SINCE THAT INCIDENT.

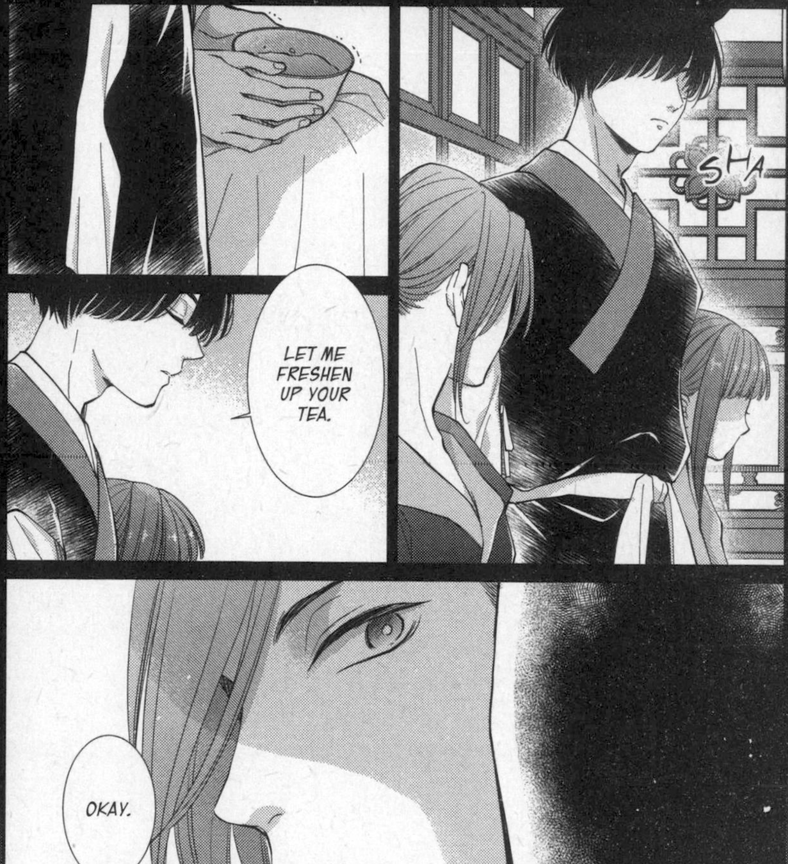
SHA
LET ME FRESHEN UP YOUR TEA.
OKAY.
YOU TWO...
...WERE THE ONES WHO KILLED TENYOU'S BEAST-SERVANT...
...AND LEFT TENYOU SPINELESS AND BROKEN-HEARTED.
I WILL NO LONGER...
...BE FORGIVEN.

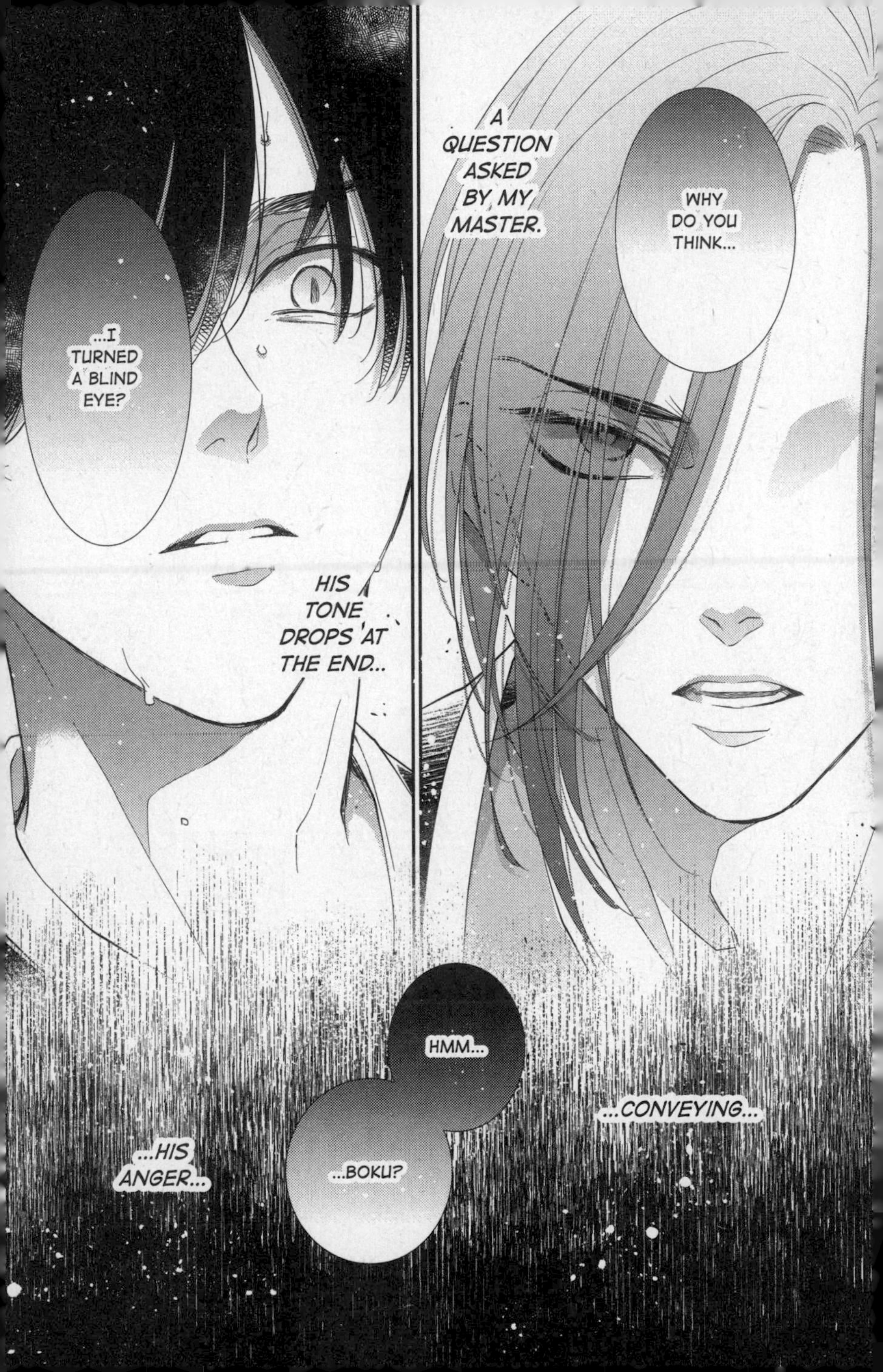
WHY DO YOU THINK...
A QUESTION ASKED BY MY MASTER.
...I TURNED A BLIND EYE?
HIS TONE DROPS AT THE END...
HMM...
...CONVEYING...
...BOKU?
...HIS ANGER...

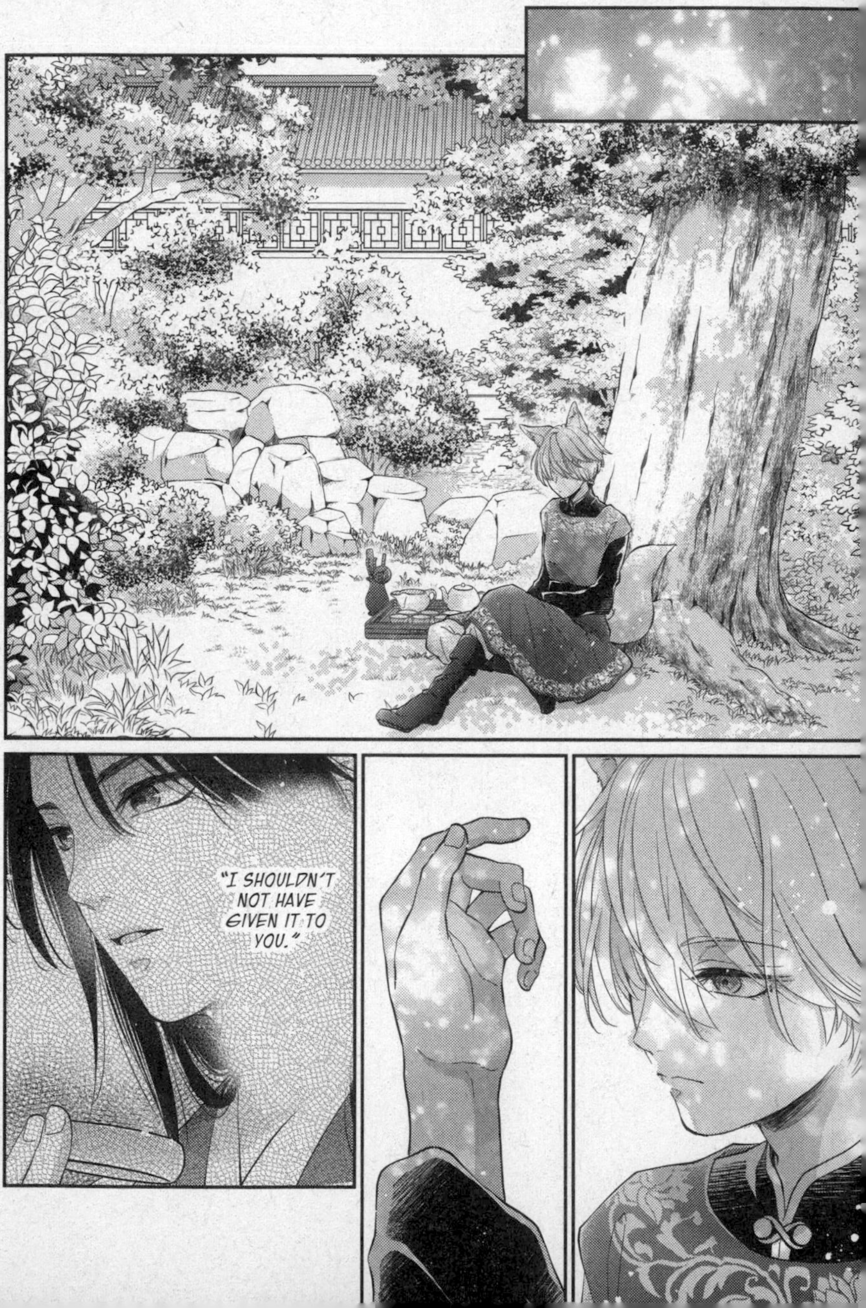
"I SHOULDN'T NOT HAVE GIVEN IT TO YOU."

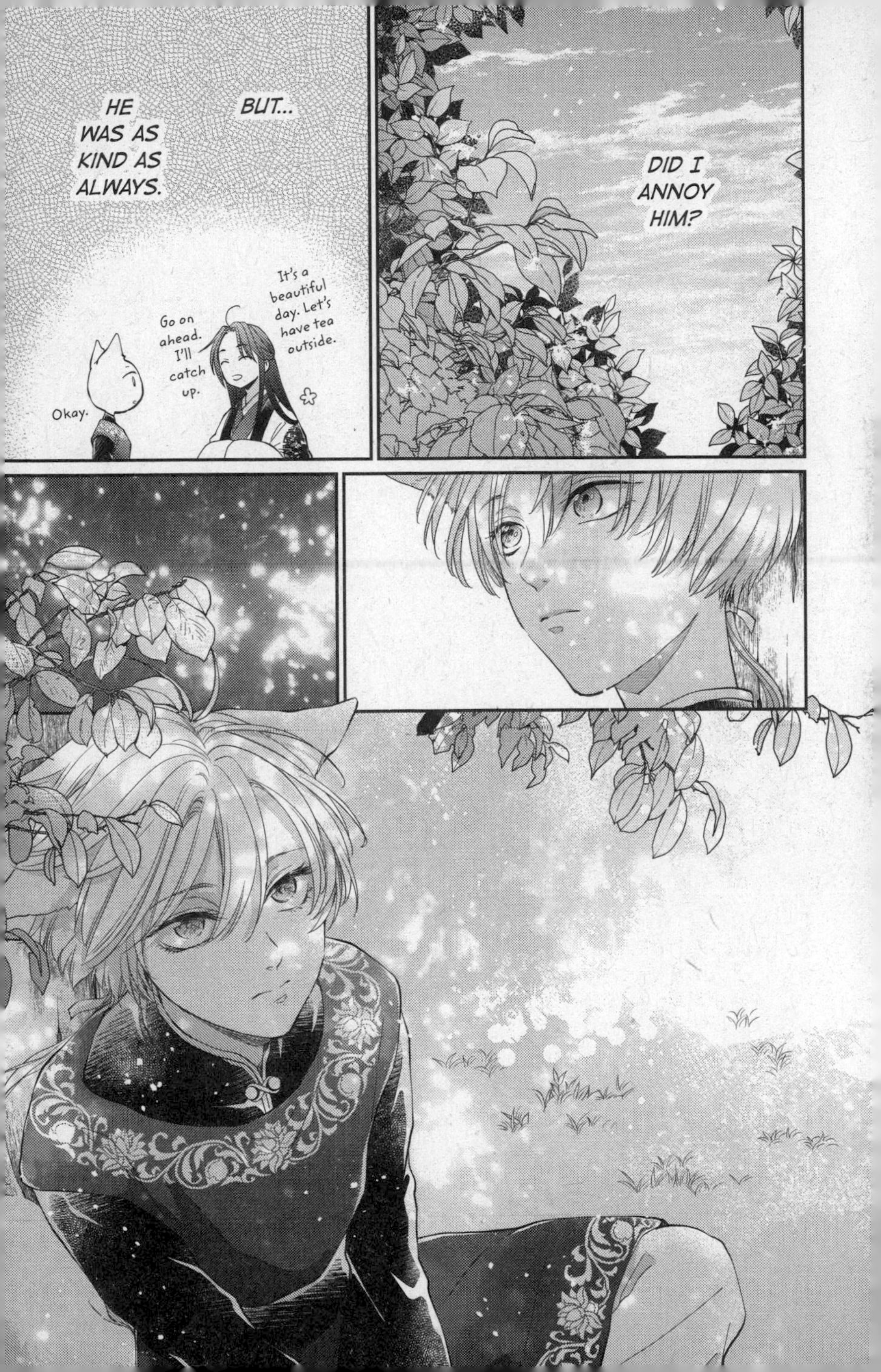
DID I ANNOY HIM?
BUT...
HE WAS AS KIND AS ALWAYS.
It's a beautiful day. Let's have tea outside.
Go on ahead. I'll catch up.
Okay.

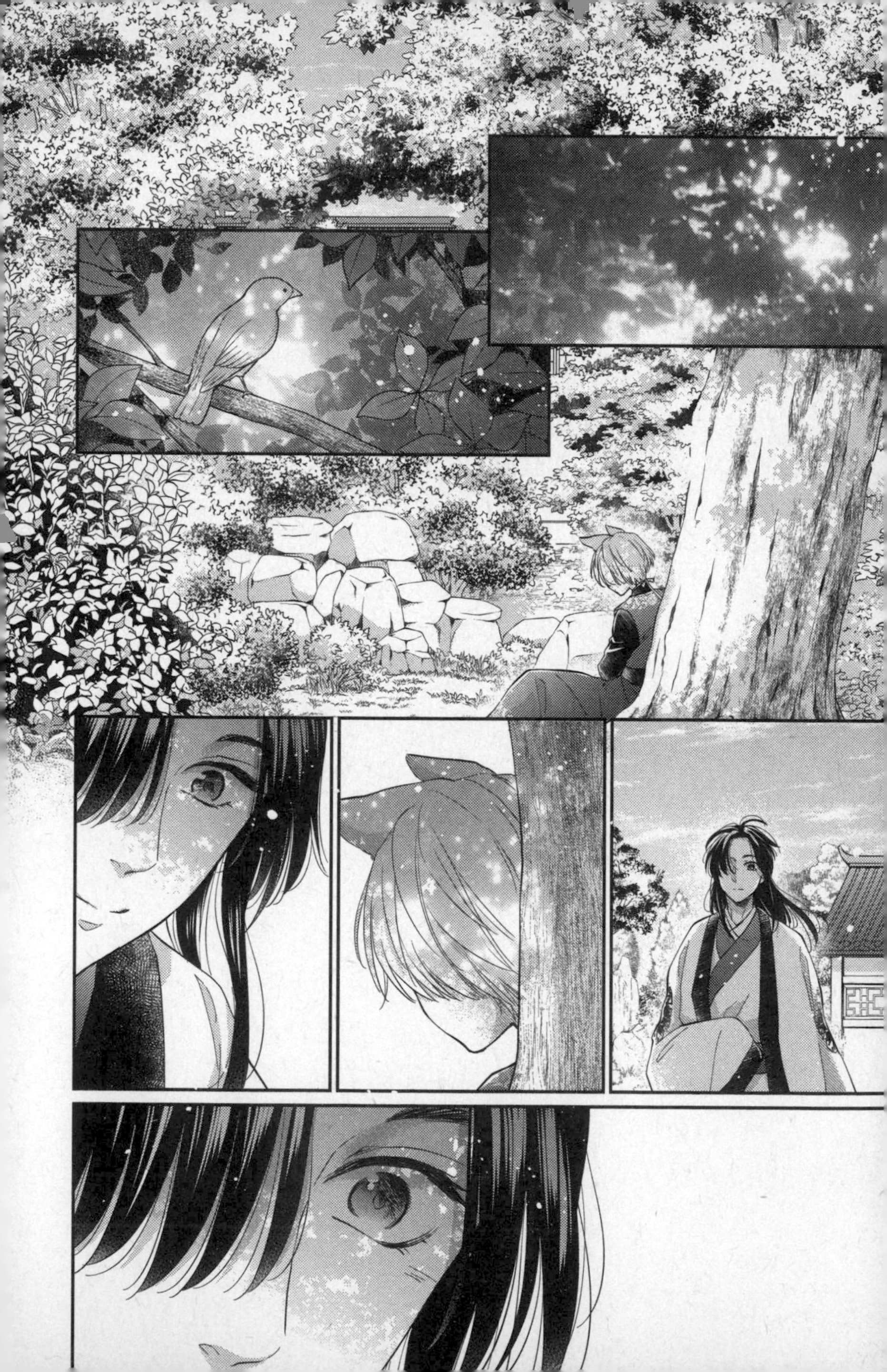

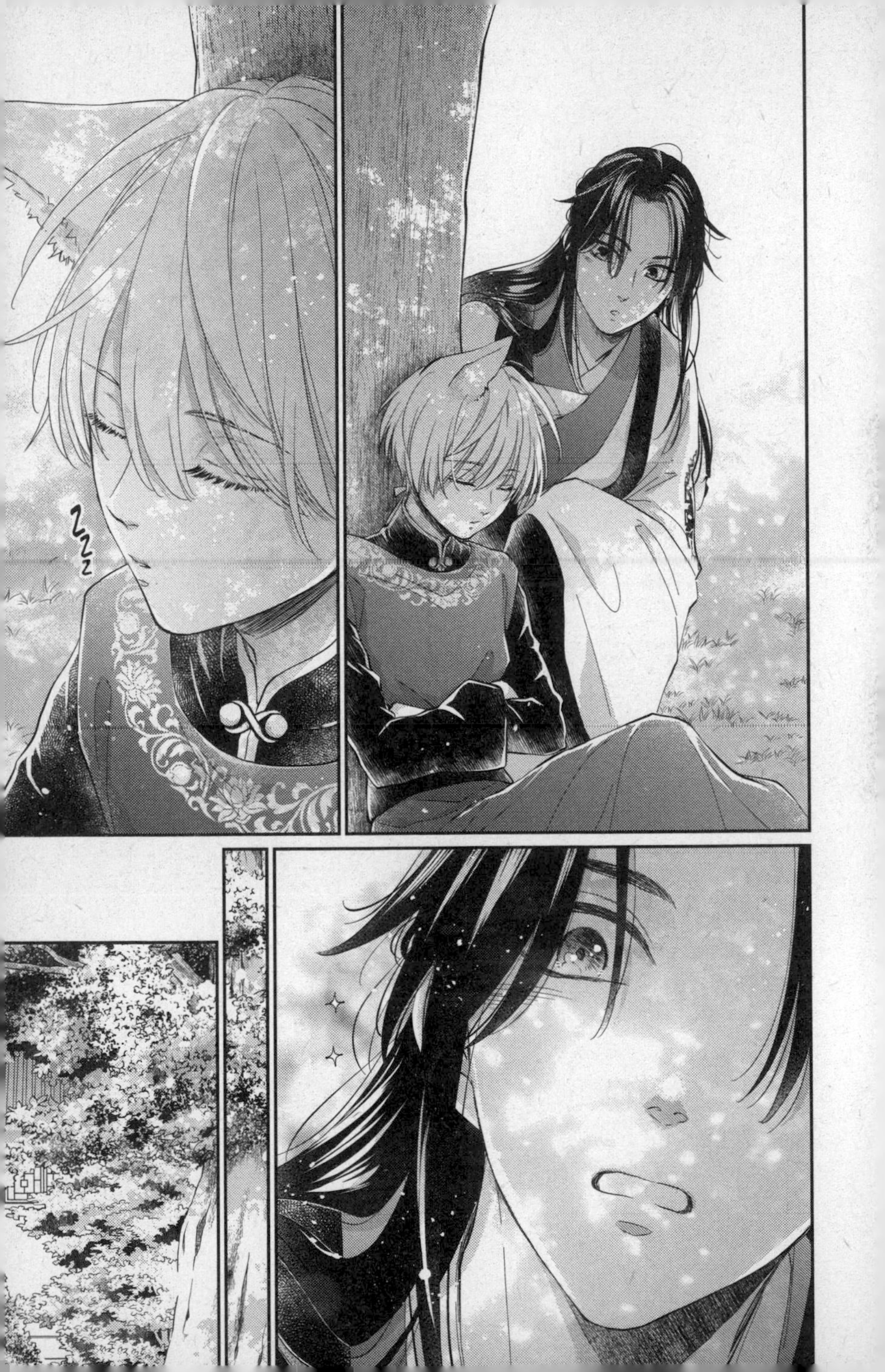

ZZZ

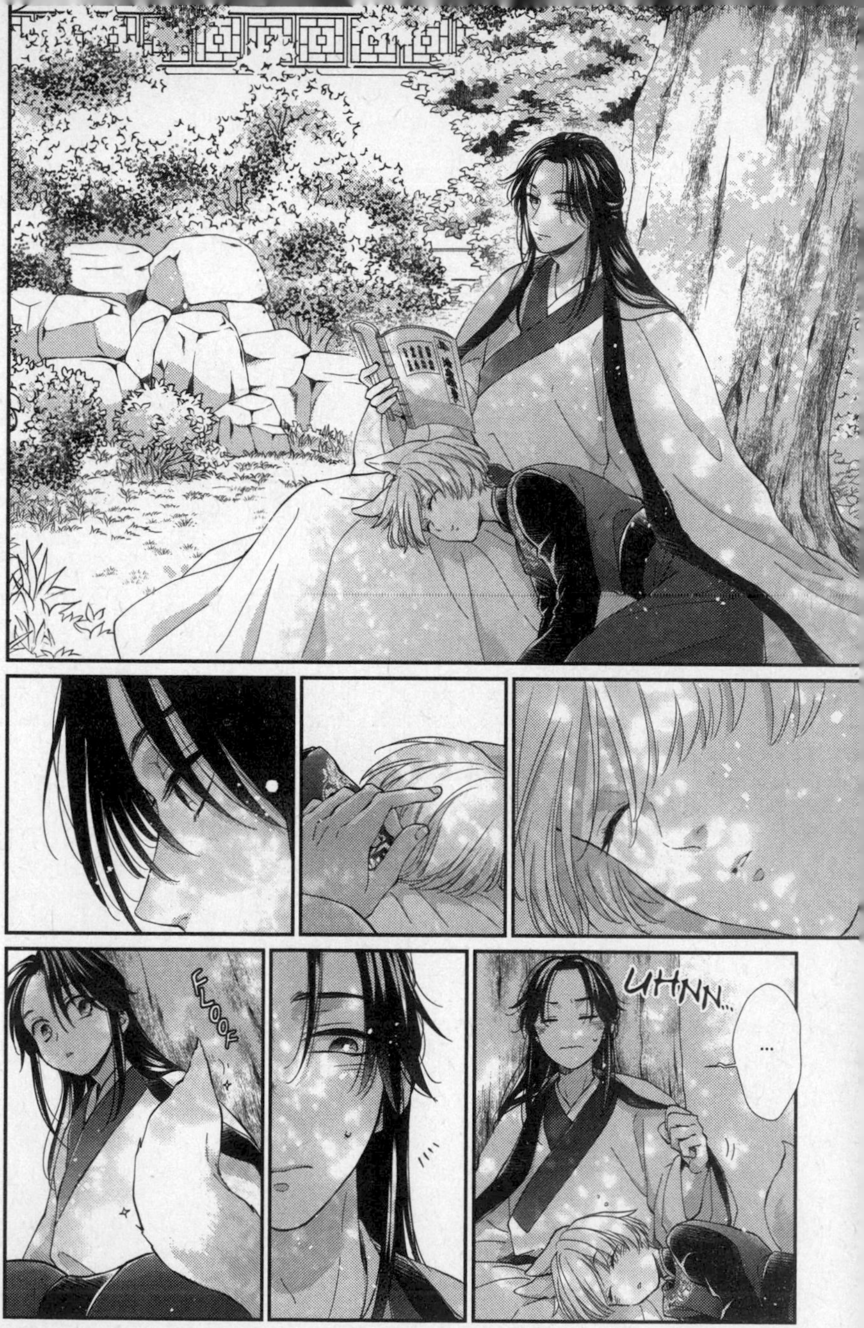
UHNN...
...
FLOOF

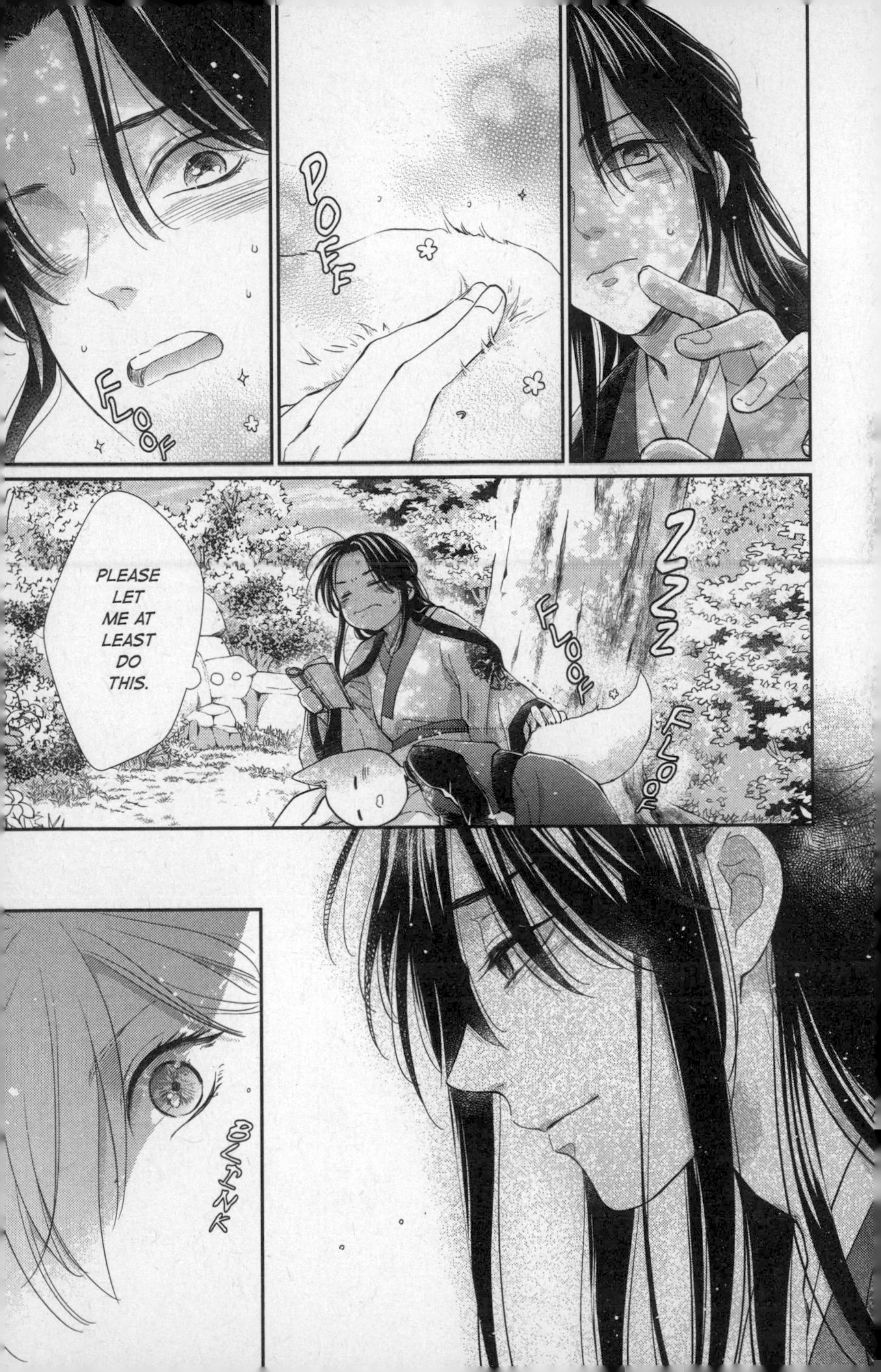
POFF
FLOOF
ZZZ
FLOOF
FLOOF
PLEASE LET ME AT LEAST DO THIS.
BLINK

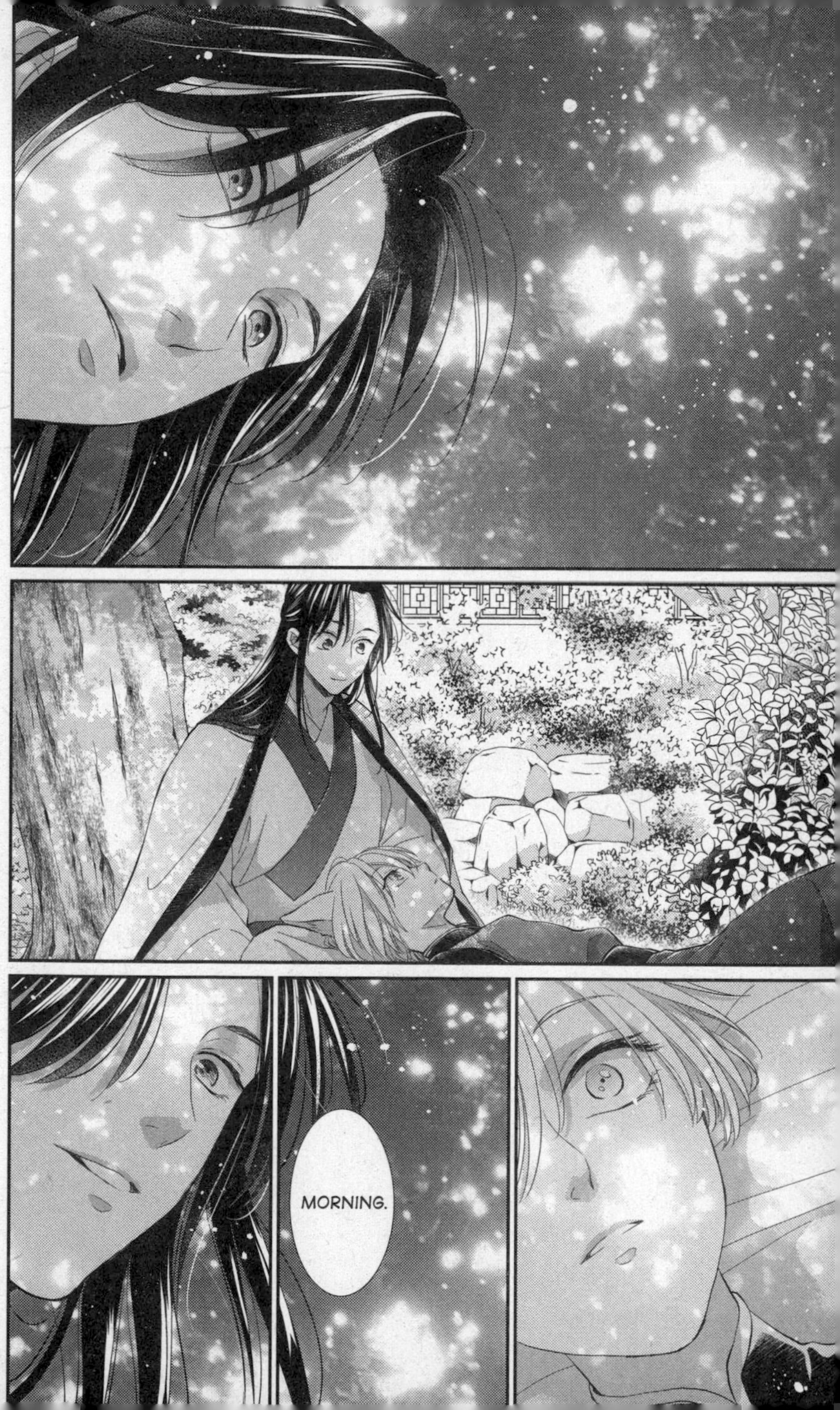
MORNING.

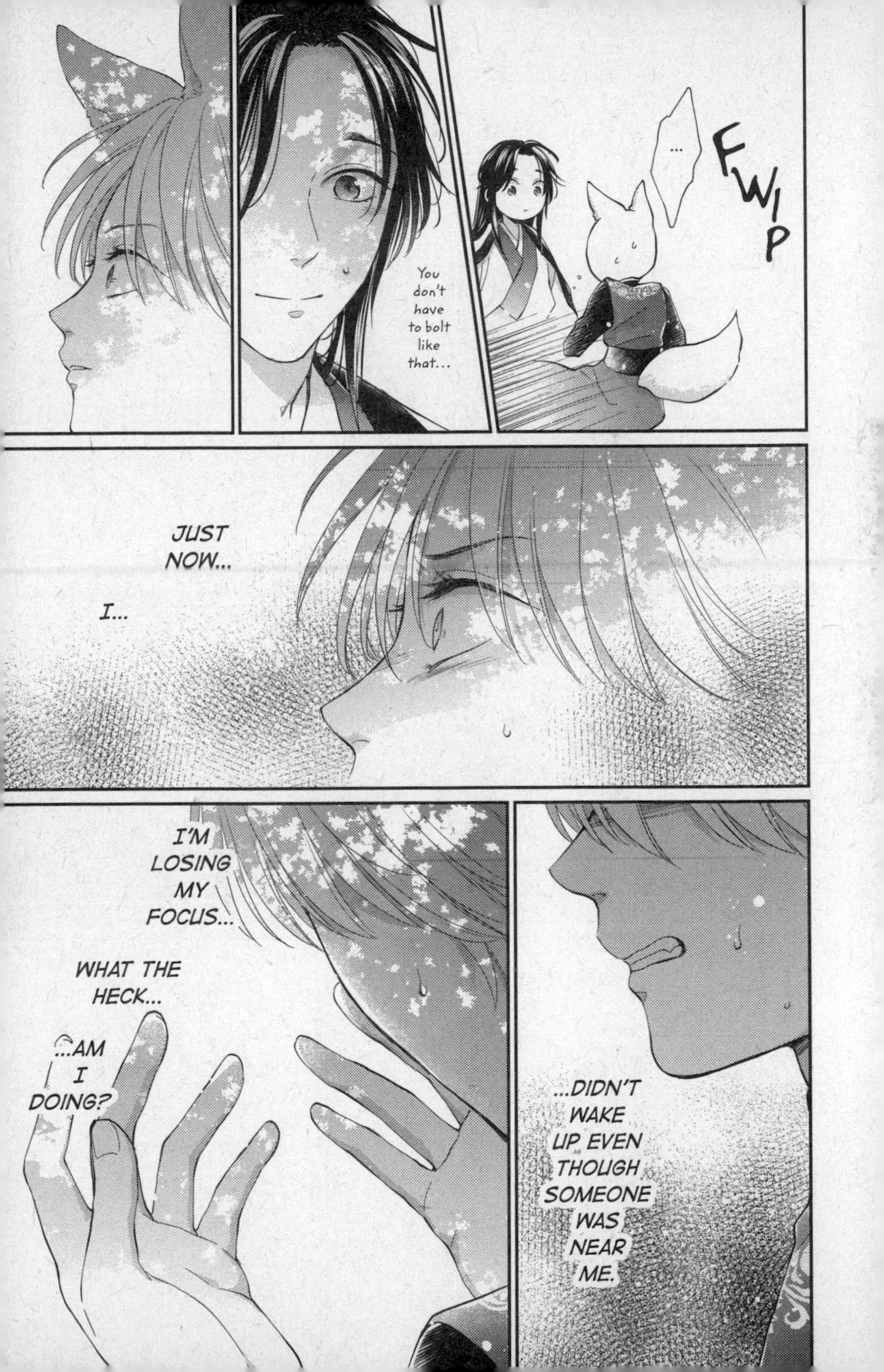
FWIP
...
You don't have to bolt like that...
JUST NOW...
I...
...DIDN'T WAKE UP EVEN THOUGH SOMEONE WAS NEAR ME.
I'M LOSING MY FOCUS...
WHAT THE HECK...
...AM I DOING?

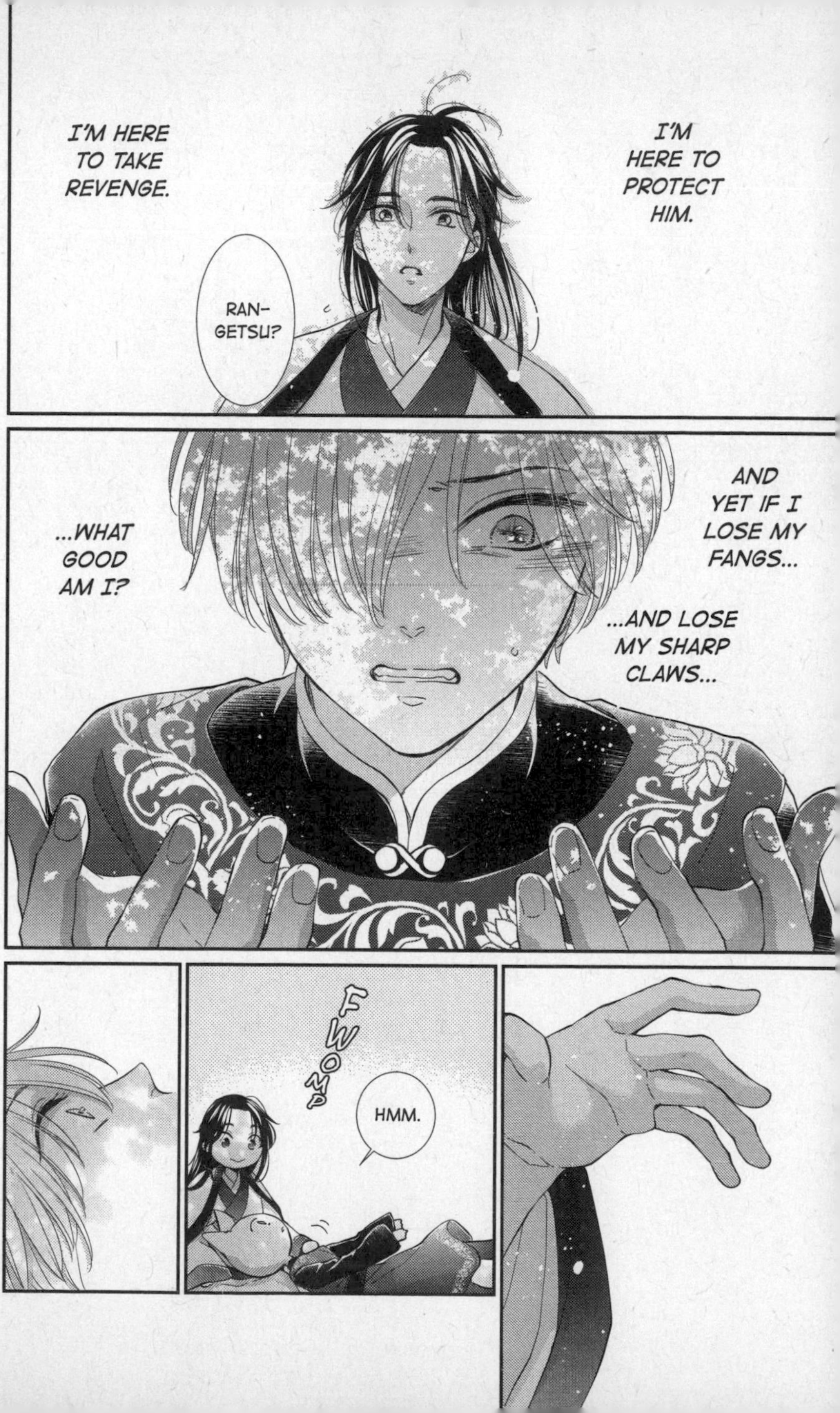
I'M HERE TO PROTECT HIM.
I'M HERE TO TAKE REVENGE.
RAN-GETSU?
AND YET IF I LOSE MY FANGS...
...AND LOSE MY SHARP CLAWS...
...WHAT GOOD AM I?
FWOMP
HMM.

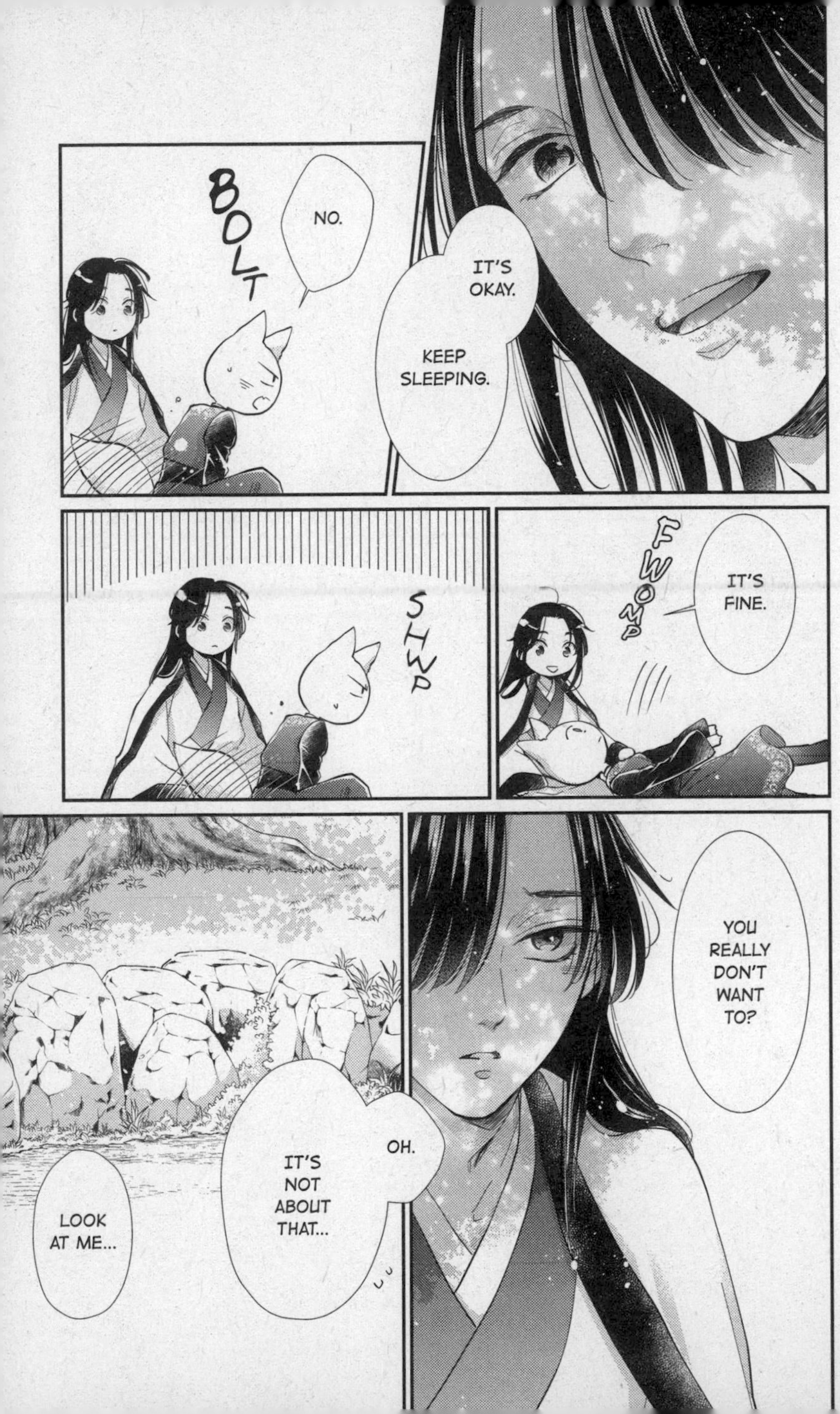
IT'S OKAY.
KEEP SLEEPING.
BOLT
NO.
FWOMP
IT'S FINE.
SHWP
YOU REALLY DON'T WANT TO?
OH.
IT'S NOT ABOUT THAT...
LOOK AT ME...

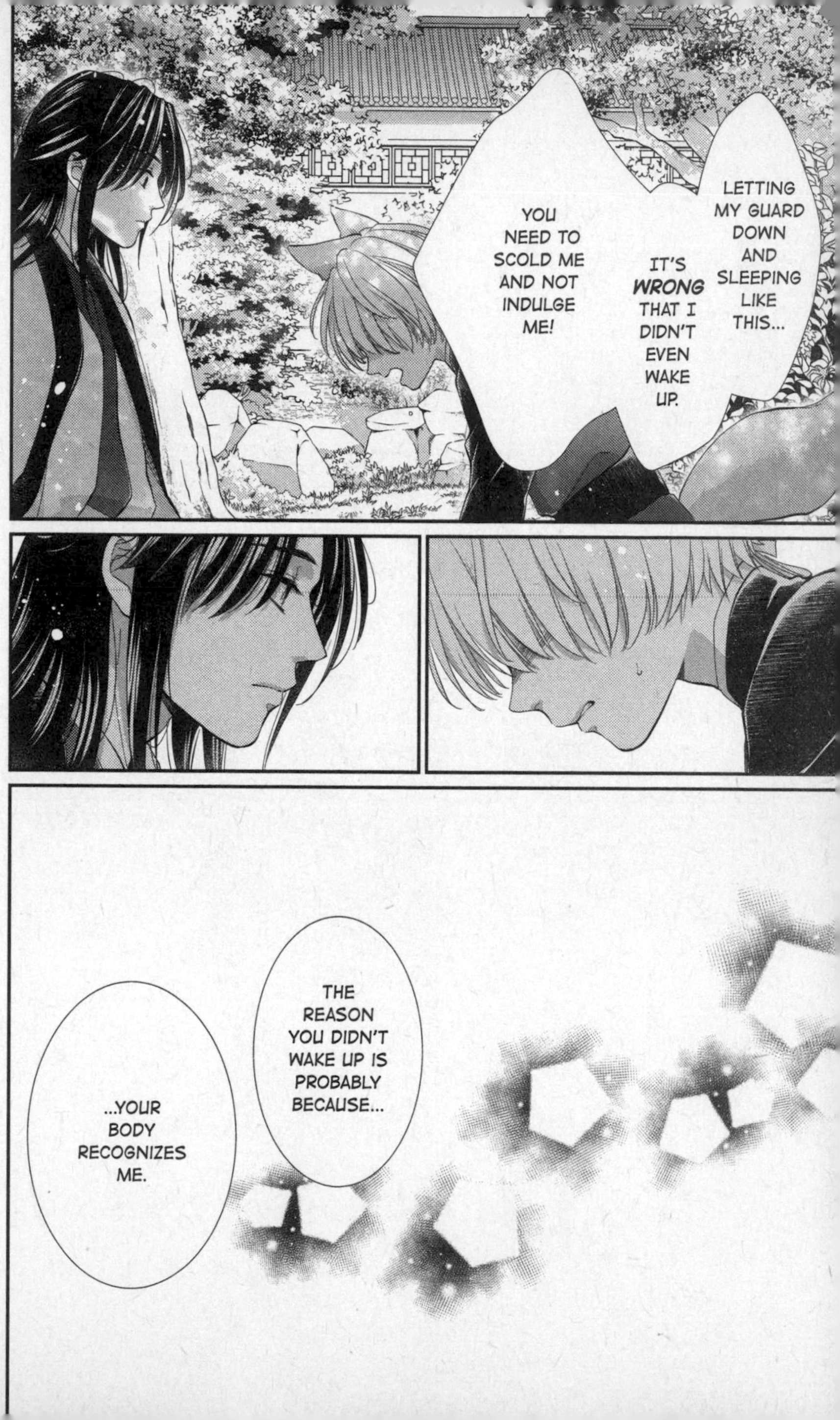
LETTING MY GUARD DOWN AND SLEEPING LIKE THIS...
IT'S ***WRONG*** THAT I DIDN'T EVEN WAKE UP.
YOU NEED TO SCOLD ME AND NOT INDULGE ME!
THE REASON YOU DIDN'T WAKE UP IS PROBABLY BECAUSE...
...YOUR BODY RECOGNIZES ME.

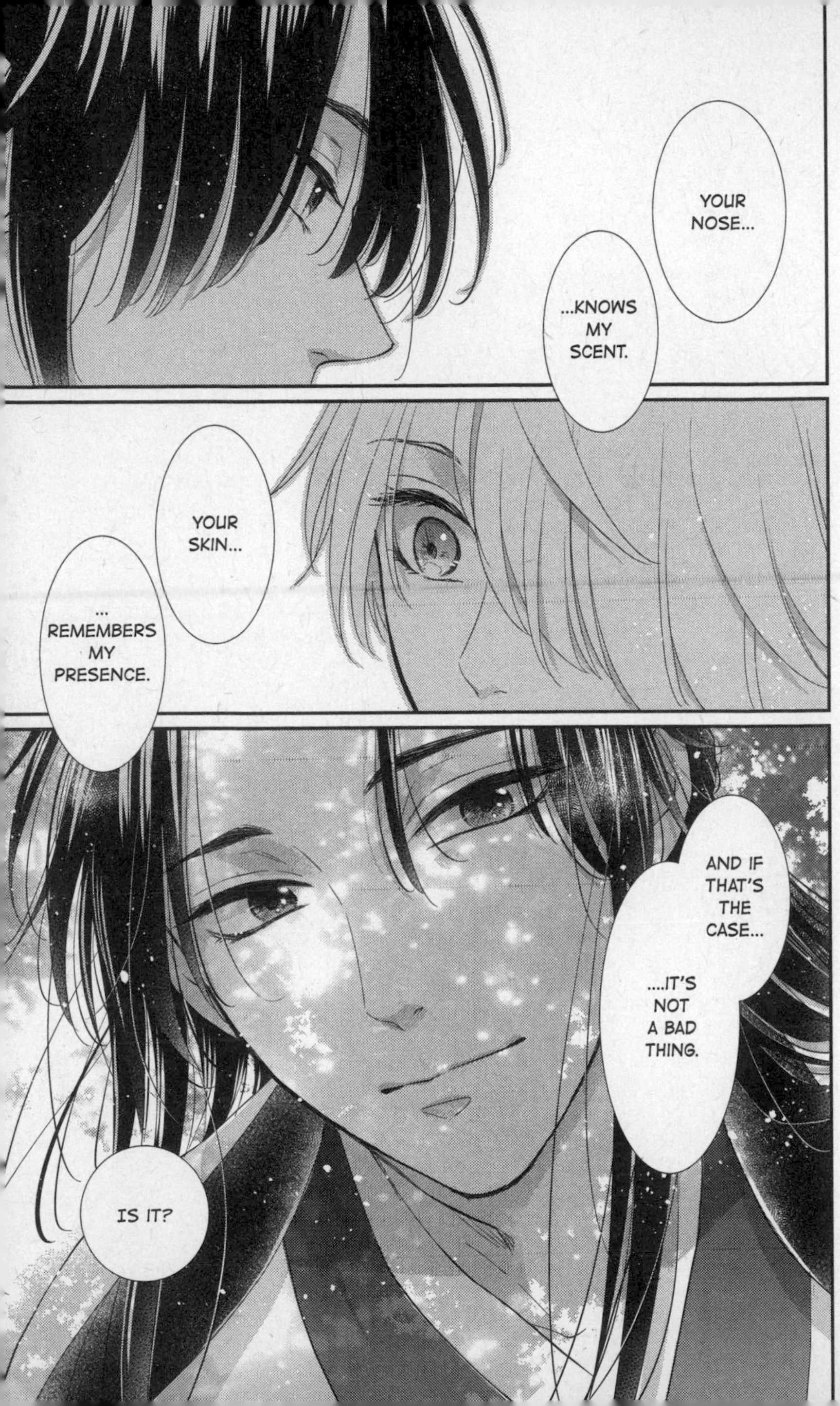
YOUR NOSE...
...KNOWS MY SCENT.
YOUR SKIN...
...REMEMBERS MY PRESENCE.
AND IF THAT'S THE CASE...
....IT'S NOT A BAD THING.
IS IT?

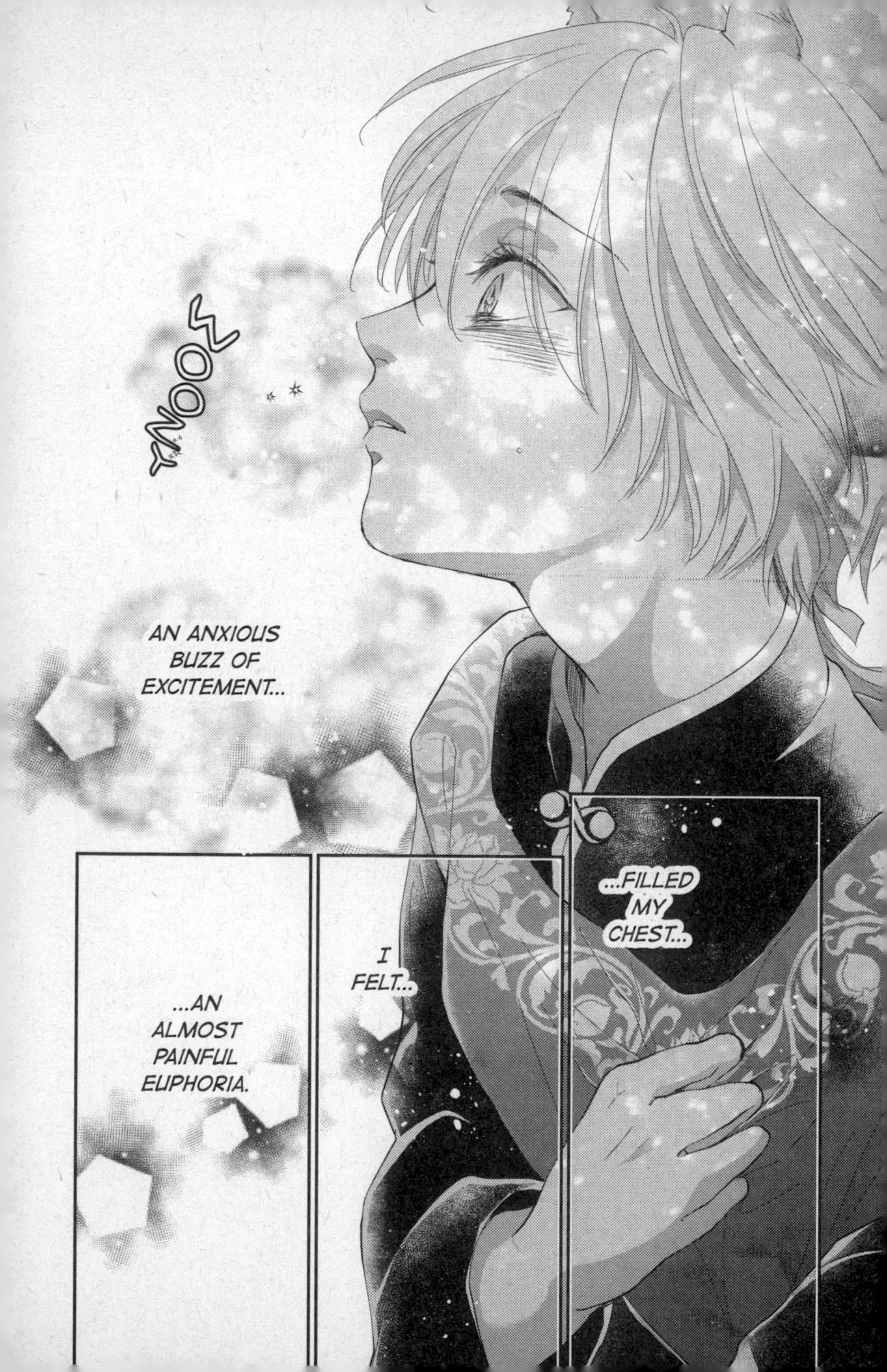
AN ANXIOUS BUZZ OF EXCITEMENT...
...FILLED MY CHEST...
I FELT...
...AN ALMOST PAINFUL EUPHORIA.

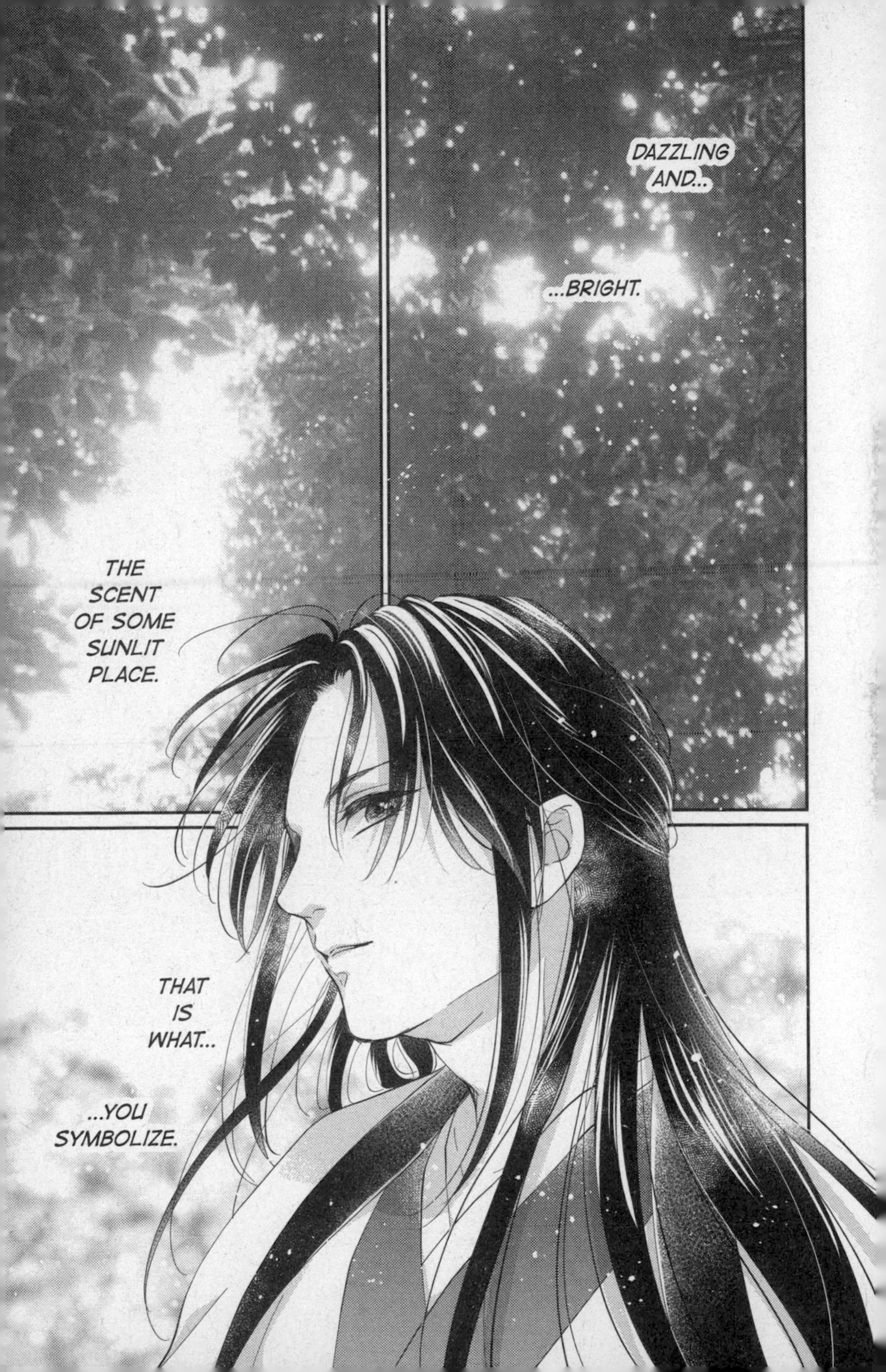
DAZZLING AND...
...BRIGHT.
THE SCENT OF SOME SUNLIT PLACE.
THAT IS WHAT...
...YOU SYMBOLIZE.

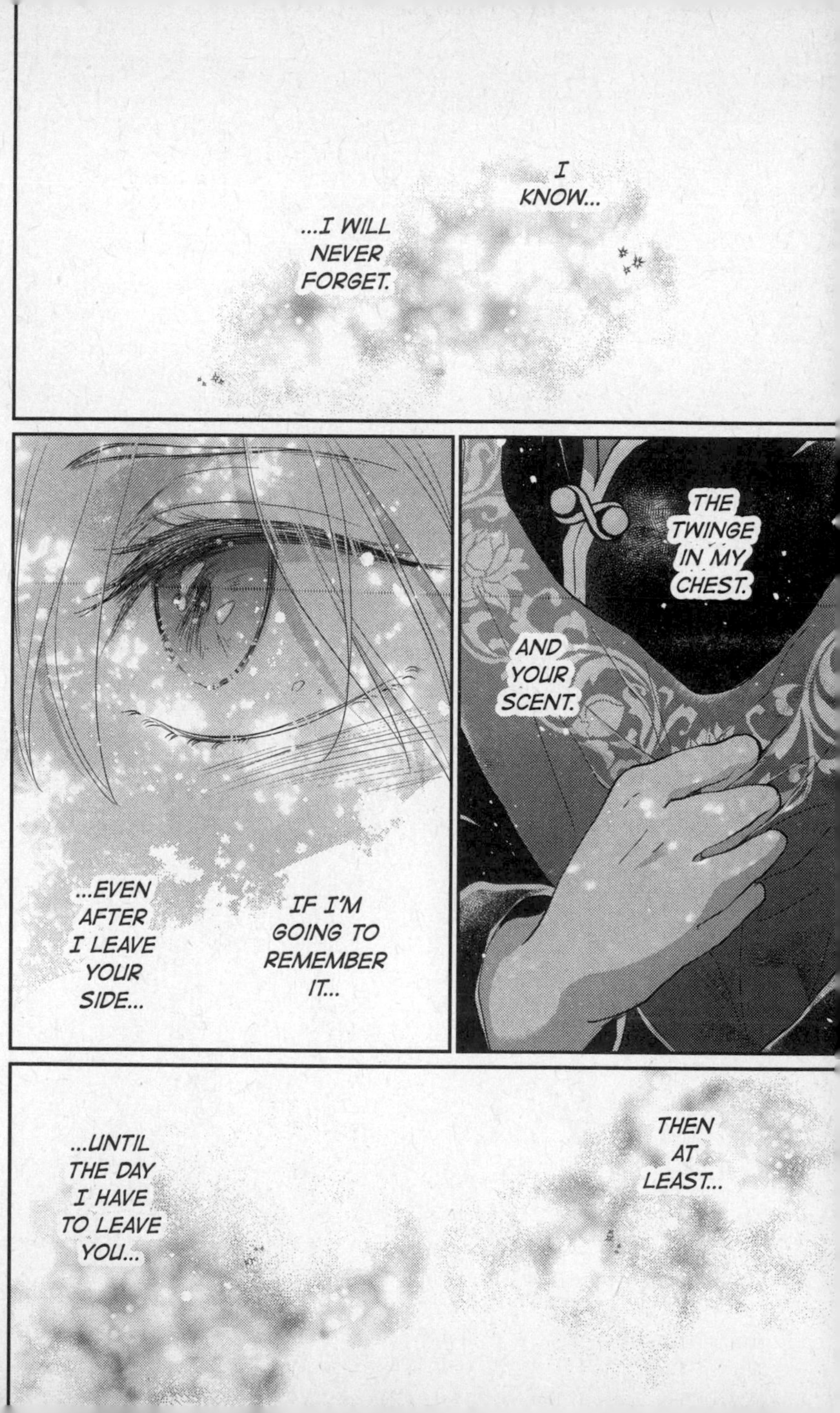
I KNOW...
...I WILL NEVER FORGET.
THE TWINGE IN MY CHEST.
AND YOUR SCENT.
IF I'M GOING TO REMEMBER IT...
...EVEN AFTER I LEAVE YOUR SIDE...
THEN AT LEAST...
...UNTIL THE DAY I HAVE TO LEAVE YOU...

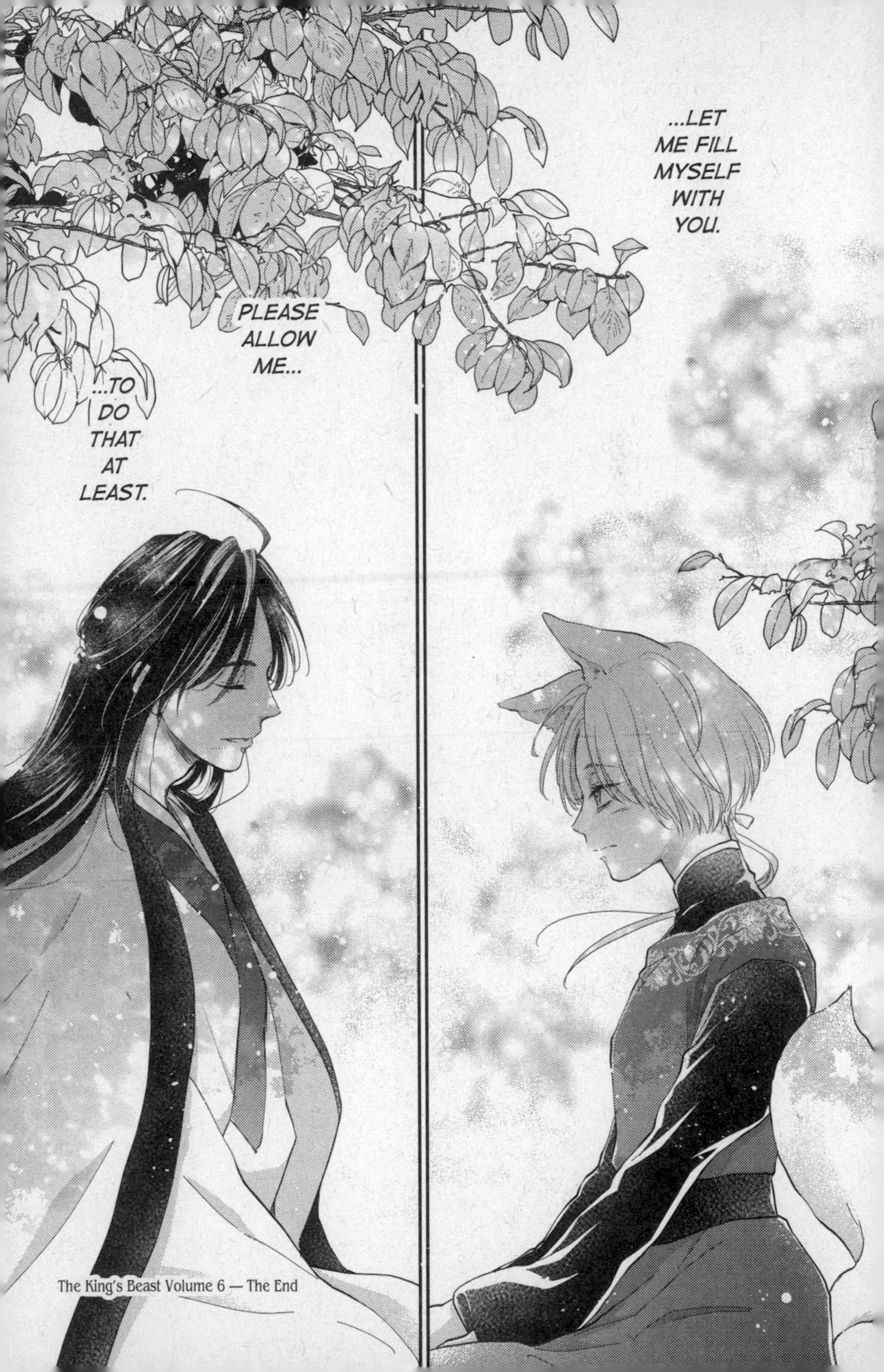
...LET ME FILL MYSELF WITH YOU.
PLEASE ALLOW ME...
...TO DO THAT AT LEAST.
The King's Beast Volume 6 — The End

I had a lot of fun drawing Kougai for the cover.

—*Rei Toma*

Rei Toma has been drawing since childhood, and she created her first complete manga for a graduation project in design school. When she drew the short story manga "Help Me, Dentist," it attracted a publisher's attention and she made her debut right away. After she found success as a manga artist, acclaim in other art fields started to follow as she did illustrations for novels and video game character designs. She is also the creator of *Dawn of the Arcana* and *The Water Dragon's Bride*, both available in English from VIZ Media.

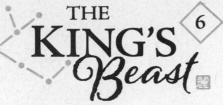

THE KING'S Beast 6

SHOJO BEAT EDITION

STORY AND ART BY **Rei Toma**

ENGLISH TRANSLATION & ADAPTATION **JN Productions**
TOUCH-UP ART & LETTERING **Monaliza De Asis**
DESIGN **Joy Zhang**
EDITOR **Pancha Diaz**

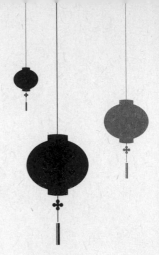

OU NO KEMONO Vol. 6
by Rei TOMA

Original Japanese edition published by SHOGAKUKAN.
English translation rights in the United States of America, Canada, the United Kingdom, Ireland, Australia and New Zealand arranged with SHOGAKUKAN.

Original Cover Design: Hibiki CHIKADA (fireworks. vc)

Fox Mask Design Inspired by W. Mushoku (WALTZ)
Kitsune Kuchi Men Ajisai Komendou
https://www.komendou.com/SHOP/Kom-Kt-03.html

Printed in the U.S.A.

Published by VIZ Media, LLC
P.O. Box 77010
San Francisco, CA 94107

10 9 8 7 6 5 4 3 2 1
First printing, May 2022

RATED T TEEN ratings.viz.com

PARENTAL ADVISORY
THE KING'S BEAST is rated T for Teen and is recommended for ages 13 and up. This volume contains death, violence, nonconsensual sexual situations, and systemic oppression.

VIZ MEDIA
viz.com

Shojo Beat
shojobeat.com

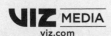

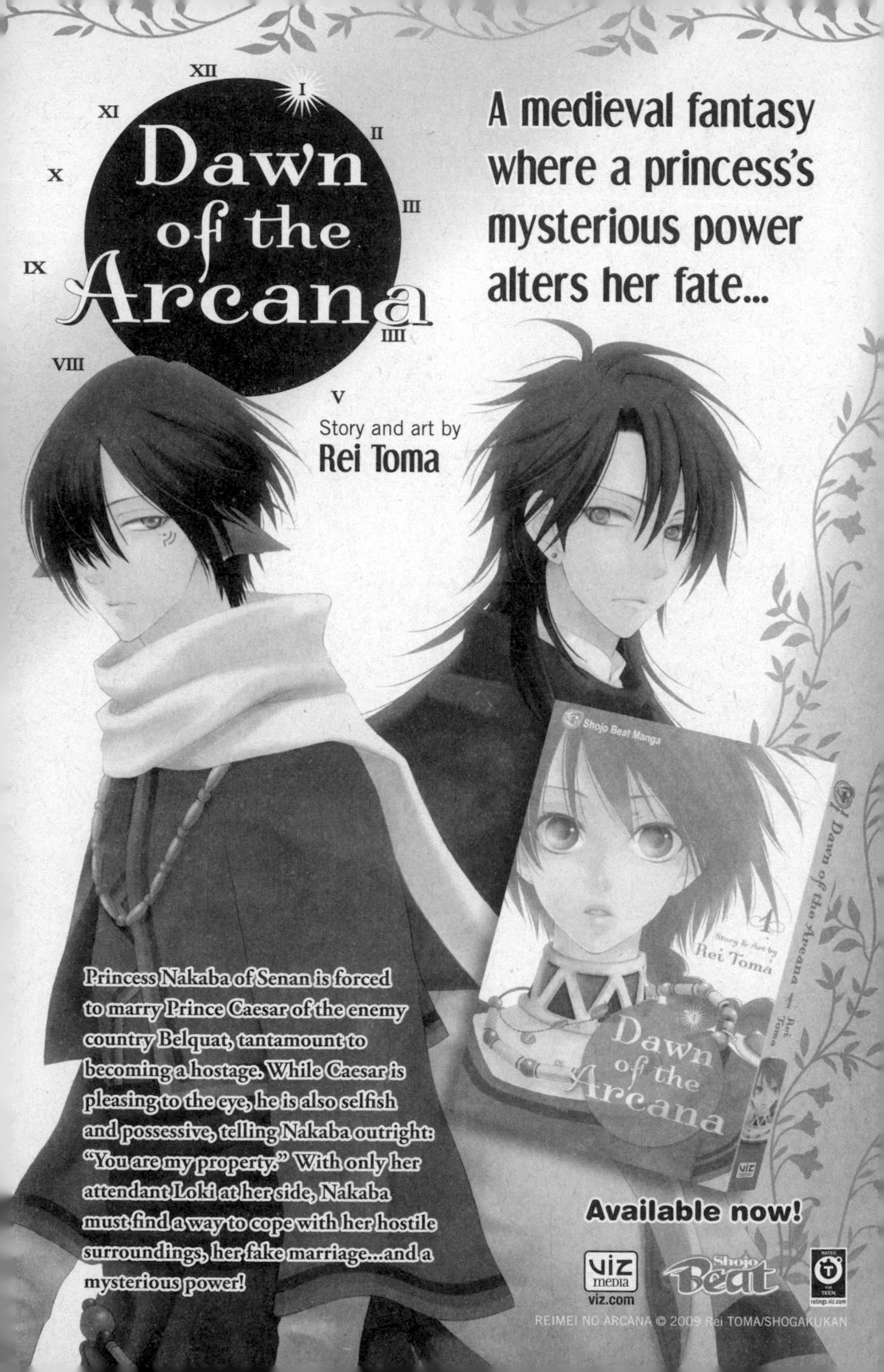
Dawn of the Arcana
A medieval fantasy where a princess's mysterious power alters her fate...
Story and art by
Rei Toma
Shojo Beat Manga
Dawn of the Arcana 1
Story & Art by Rei Toma
Princess Nakaba of Senan is forced to marry Prince Caesar of the enemy country Belquat, tantamount to becoming a hostage. While Caesar is pleasing to the eye, he is also selfish and possessive, telling Nakaba outright: "You are my property." With only her attendant Loki at her side, Nakaba must find a way to cope with her hostile surroundings, her fake marriage...and a mysterious power!
Available now!
VIZ media
viz.com
Shojo Beat
RATED T FOR TEEN
ratings.viz.com
REIMEI NO ARCANA © 2009 Rei TOMA/SHOGAKUKAN

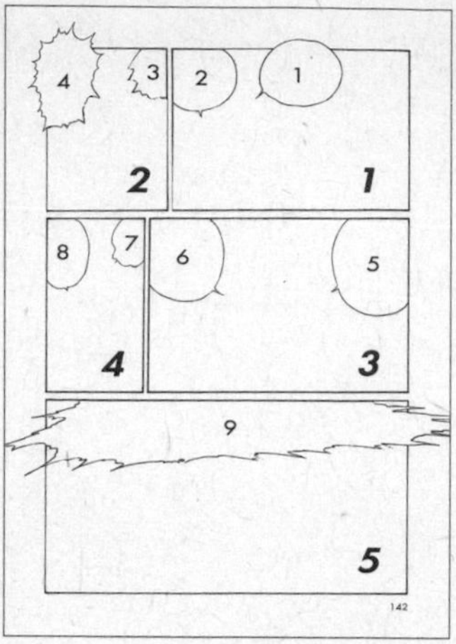
1
2
3
4
5
6
7
8
9
142

THIS IS THE LAST PAGE.

THE KING'S BEAST has been printed in the original Japanese format to preserve the orientation of the artwork.

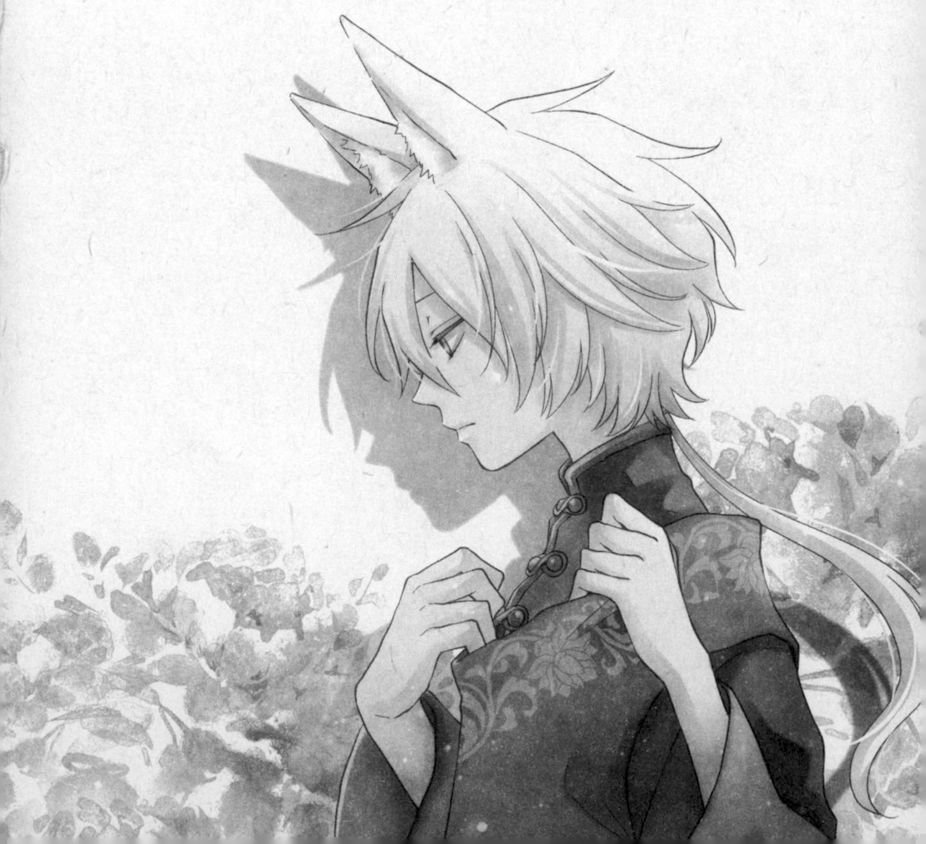